Alfred Ernest Knight

Victoria, her Life and Reign

An Illustrated Biography of the Queen, from the Year 1819 to the Present Time

Alfred Ernest Knight

Victoria, her Life and Reign
An Illustrated Biography of the Queen, from the Year 1819 to the Present Time

ISBN/EAN: 9783337025182

Printed in Europe, USA, Canada, Australia, Japan

Cover: Foto ©ninafisch / pixelio.de

More available books at **www.hansebooks.com**

From photo. by]   [Messrs. W. & D. Downey.

VICTORIA

HER LIFE AND REIGN

An Illustrated Biography

OF

THE QUEEN

FROM THE YEAR 1819 TO THE PRESENT TIME.

BY

ALFRED E. KNIGHT

AUTHOR OF "TOBIAH JALF," "UNCLE PEPPERDEW; OR, THE MAMMON OF UNRIGHTEOUSNESS," ETC.

LONDON
S. W. PARTRIDGE & CO.
8 & 9 PATERNOSTER ROW, E.C.
1896

PREFACE.

UMBERLESS books have been written about the Queen, but comparatively few biographies. My aim, as the Author of the present work, has been to write a biography. Whether — and to what extent—I have produced a readable biography is another matter, which must be left to readers of the book to determine.

There is not much to be said by way of preface. Whatever labour of research appeared to me to be necessary has been honestly faced; and, so far as I am aware, no important source of information has been overlooked. I have plodded carefully through the Queen's *Leaves* and *More Leaves*, and have given —not merely a few long quotations, chosen haphazard and thrown in to make up "copy," but—what is practically an epitome of both volumes. This has involved a good deal of tedious labour; but if the biography has gained in completeness and interest by the process (the only end contemplated), there is no need to regret the course pursued.

I have also had Sir Theodore Martin's voluminous *Life of the Prince Consort* continually before me, and do not think that any passage in it, which bears in a special way on the Queen's own life, has been overlooked. I thankfully acknowledge my obligations to that full and able work, which, indeed, has been my chief source of information for the eventful period between the years 1840 and 1862. The *Memoirs of Baron Stockmar* have also been frequently consulted; and Greville's *Journal* (particularly the first five volumes) has proved a veritable storehouse of entertaining matter. Nor have the more chatty *Reminiscences* of Lady Bloomfield, Lady Lyttleton, and Lord Ronald Gower been overlooked, though they have yielded less than I had anticipated. Among the other works which have been kept at hand for reference, and which have been found more or less useful, may be enumerated Ward's *Reign of Victoria*, M'Carthy's *History of Our Own Time*, Grey's *Early Years of the Prince Consort*, the memorial volume entitled *Princess Alice*, Mr. Pope Humphrey's *Queen at Balmoral*, Tytler's *Life of the Queen*, and a valuable collection of magazine and newspaper articles ranging in date from the year 1819 to 1896.

It only remains to be said that the biography has been brought down to the present time; and that the later years of the Queen's reign have been treated with the same fulness as the earlier, and her childhood with the same particularity as both.

A. E. K.

CONTENTS.

CHAPTER I.
DOLL-DAYS, ... 9

CHAPTER II.
IN THE DAYS OF WILLIAM THE FOURTH, . . . 35

CHAPTER III.
THE KING IS DEAD!—LONG LIVE THE QUEEN! . 50

CHAPTER IV.
THE MAIDEN QUEEN, . . . 74

CHAPTER V.
WOOED, WON, AND WEDDED, ... 88

CHAPTER VI.
THE HOME IN THE PALACE (1840–1848), . 105

CHAPTER VII.
THE QUEEN AS GUEST AND GUEST-RECEIVER (1840–1848), . 136

CONTENTS.

CHAPTER VIII.

BALMORAL DAYS AND OTHER MATTERS (1848–1860), . . 164

CHAPTER IX.

THE QUEEN AMONG HER OWN PEOPLE (1848–1860), . . 190

CHAPTER X.

ROYALTY ABROAD, AND AN EMPEROR'S VISITS (1848–1860), . 209

CHAPTER XI.

THE YEAR OF THE GREAT SORROW (1861), . . . 229

CHAPTER XII.

SHADE AND SHINE TO THE JUBILEE (1861–1887), . . 250

CHAPTER XIII.

THE JUBILEE AND AFTERWARDS (1887–1896), . . . 298

VICTORIA:

HER LIFE AND REIGN.

CHAPTER I.

DOLL-DAYS.

THE old Court suburb of Kensington, so rich in Royal memories, is distinguished by no event of greater interest—and certainly by none of greater moment, when viewed in the light of subsequent events—than that which occurred on the genial May morning in the year 1819, when the Duchess of Kent, daughter-in-law of George III., gave birth to the Princess Victoria. On the evening preceding that event, any one sauntering in the vicinity of the lonely old Palace to which the suburb gives its name, might have seen carriage after carriage, adorned with mitres and coronets, driving up to the Royal mansion, or have watched their titled occupants alighting at the great entrance under the clock-tower, and passing silently through into the square red-flagged inner courtyard. Among the rest might have been recognised the Duke of Sussex, Prince of Great Britain and sixth son of George III.; the Duke of Wellington; the Archbishop of Canterbury (Dr. Manners Sutton); and George Canning, the eminent statesman and orator; for the Crown Ministers and Privy Councillors (to one or both of which classes these exalted personages belonged) were assembling at the Palace in view of the birth of a possible heir to the throne.

At 4 A.M. on the 24th of May the little Princess was born. The room in which she first opened her eyes remains to this day much as it was on that memorable morning, though the bedstead has been temporarily removed. It is not a large room, as palaces go, being only thirty feet by twenty-four, and about twelve feet high; but the gilt-framed chairs and couches, with their handsome crimson and gold silk furniture, give it a right Royal look. The walls are distempered a pretty, pale duck-egg green, and have a plain oak dado running round them surrounded by a simple gilt moulding, which serves as a support to several large mirrors. On one of the walls is a brass plate bearing the following brief inscription:—

> In this Room
> **Queen Victoria**
> was born,
> **May 24th, 1819.**

The room is provided with three windows on one side, which look out upon the private pleasure grounds of the Palace; and here, at the particular day and hour of which we write, the chirrupings of blackbirds and thrushes—too sleepy as yet to break into full song—would doubtless have been heard; for the Kensington of seventy or eighty years ago was quite a rural suburb, surrounded by vegetable gardens, nurseries, and orchards (those favourite feeding grounds of birds), and on that account was much frequented by the feathered tribe. It is said that nightingales sang in Holland Lane.

The little Princess was very fortunate in her parents. Her father it is true, died within a few months of her birth, but she inherited many of his finer qualities, and particularly his firmness of character and love of order. The Duke was the fourth son of George III., and the best. He was born in November, 1767, and was thus in his fifty-second year when Victoria was born. His education up to his seventeenth year was watched over by Dr. Fisher, Bishop of Salisbury; and he was afterwards sent abroad to study military tactics under the care of General Budé, a Swiss officer high in the estimation of George III. The young Prince, indeed, was intended for a military life, and while in Germany he was subjected to all the strictness of the Prussian discipline. Of the severity of that discipline, as well as of his own conformity to military rules, he was wont to relate an anecdote, which we will give in his own words. "Being placed as a cadet at Hanover, the regiment on duty was discharged in the usual form; but the general commanding happened to forget to dismiss me, which was always accompanied with a distinct and peculiar ceremony. On this I continued in a very uneasy position, and was actually forgotten for four hours, when at length the commanding officer rode up, and apologised. I should have remained, but for this, at my post, until I had fainted with fatigue."

GEORGE III.

This rigid tuition had a somewhat injurious effect upon the Prince, who became in consequence so severe a disciplinarian himself, that when he obtained the command over British soldiers, his conduct made him enemies, and produced mutiny oftener than once. From Hanover he was removed to Geneva, where he completed his education, remaining there till the month of January, 1790, when he returned to England without parental permission, and in consequence was sent off to Gibraltar. Four years later we find him at the West Indies with Sir Charles Grey, under whom he displayed great gallantry in the attack on St. Lucie and also in the capture of Guadaloupe and Martinique. In April, 1799, he again returned to England, and having now attained his thirty-second year, was created Duke of Kent, with an annual allowance of £12,000.

In May, 1802, the Duke went to Gibraltar as governor of the fortress, but the appointment was not a wise one, and His Royal Highness was recalled, never more to be re-instated in actual service. The cause and circumstances of his failure have been left on record by one of his warmest friends and admirers, and as they are interesting in themselves, and illustrate in a striking manner some of the strongest features of his character, we make no apology for quoting the passage. The friend writes : " Being now possessed of the supreme command, the Duke determined to introduce all the rigour of the German tactics. A striking example of military obedience in his own person, he required the most complete subordination from all around him. Rising before the sun—abhorring the excesses of the table—punctual in the discharge of all his duties, however numerous—he exacted nothing from others but what he himself was ready to comply with. Yet it was found utterly impossible for any body of men, particularly of soldiers, to imitate the abstemiousness, the regularity, and the austere habits of the new governor On the Continent he had imbibed a taste for the most correct uniformity in the dress, accoutrements and equipments; and, while the hair was to be cut according to a certain precise standard, the garrison rather felt disgusted by additional parades and daily reviews. But, on the other hand, it should be recollected that the inhabitants of the Rock had been loud in their complaints of military licence; that the troops were slovenly and insubordinate, and that, as the means of intoxication were so easy, its effects became everywhere visible. To correct this evil His Royal Highness, notwithstanding the loss accruing to himself, determined to shut up many of the wine-houses, to restrain the soldiers within the barracks, and to adopt such a system of inspection as should preclude inebriety and insubordination. These regulations, however necessary, were not attended with the salutary effects that might have been expected. At the end of the year, a mutinous conspiracy, which had the assassination of the governor for its object, was formed; but providentially a timely discovery took place, and order was restored. Such a spirit, however, had been raised in the garrison that it was deemed prudent to recall the Duke, who returned in May, 1803; and though he continued to hold the office till his death, he never again visited the Rock." *

THE DUKE OF KENT.
After a portrait by G. E. DAWE.

Granting that the Duke had erred, it is evident that he had erred only through excess of zeal. His motives were pure and above suspicion; and the desire so clearly manifested for needed and wholesome reform, was highly creditable to His Royal Highness. Of the genuineness of his zeal in the public service we have, indeed, evidence from various sources, yet, if we may believe the almost unanimous testimony of the newspapers of the day,

* *Life and Times of William the Fourth*, 498, 499.

the Royal Duke was treated by successive administrations with singular neglect and even cruelty. Why he alone should have been kept from the peerage beyond the accustomed age cannot easily be accounted for, any more than his long and apparently penal absence from his native land. It is certain that his income at all times was extremely confined; and for this reason he was reduced to many painful embarrassments—became, in fact, heavily involved in debt, though without being chargeable with profligacy. His embarrassments increasing, he at last made over his income to a committee, honourably determined from henceforth to circumscribe his expenditure within very narrow limits.

In pursuance of this plan of economy, he left England in 1816 and settled at Brussels; where he lived in great privacy and at a small expense. From thence he made excursions into Germany to visit his royal relatives; and it was during one of these that he saw and admired the Princess Victoria-Maria-Louisa, youngest daughter of the Duke of Saxe-Coburg and sister of Prince Leopold, who became King of the Belgians. She was born in 1786, and, in her sixteenth year, became the consort of the hereditary Prince of Leiningen—a man old enough to be her father, to whom she bare a son, Charles Emich, and a daughter, Feodora. The Prince did not live long, and at his death appointed his widow regent of the principality during the minority of his son and heir. The death of the Princess Charlotte—only child of George IV. and wife of the Prince Leopold above alluded to—made it necessary for the Duke of Kent to think seriously of marriage, and he had not long to seek an object worthy of his hand. With the entire approbation of both families, His Royal Highness and the Princess of Leiningen were united at Coburg, on the 29th of May, 1818;* and the union was a union of hearts. The Princess is described as being, about this time, a woman of fine figure, with "good features, brown hair and eyes, a pretty pink colour, winning manners, and graceful accomplishments—particularly music."

After being re-united according to the Anglican form a month or two later—a condition required by the Royal Marriage Act—

* *Life and Times of William the Fourth*, 524.

the happy couple returned to the Continent, and settled at Amorbach, which Her Royal Highness, as guardian of her son, had occupied during her widowhood. But when there appeared the promise that this union would give an heir to the British throne, the Duke, respecting the attachment of the people to native-born princes, resolved to bring over his Royal Consort to Kensington, that the child which she bore might draw its first

THE DUCHESS OF KENT.

breath in England. The happy issue of this patriotic resolution we have already seen, and it only remains for us to take up the thread of the narrative at the Princess's birth, and to return to the palace-home at Kensington.

Exactly a month later the baptism of the Royal child took place in the grand saloon of the Palace. The event was solemnised with splendid ceremony; the Archbishop of Canterbury and the Bishop of London officiating, while the Prince Regent (present in person), and the Emperor Alexander of Russia (represented by the Duke of York), were godfathers to the babe. Her godmothers were the Queen Dowager of Würtemberg, represented by the Princess Augusta, and the Duchess-Dowager of Coburg, represented by the Duchess of Gloucester. Prince Leopold—whose wife, had she lived, would have been queen in place of Victoria—nobly put aside his own feelings on this occasion to be present at the christening, though we know from one of his own letters what an effort it cost him. At that time, and for many years after, the Queen had no truer friend than "Uncle Leopold." To give additional splendour to the ceremony, the gold font was removed from the Tower to Kensington, and fitted up in the Royal saloon, with crimson coverings from the Chapel Royal. It is stated* that the Duke of Kent wished to name his child Elizabeth, that being a popular name with the English people; but at the baptism the Prince Regent gave only the name of Alexandrina. On her father requesting that another name might be added, the Prince answered: "Give her her mother's also, then; but it cannot precede that of the Emperor." So the Princess came to be called Alexandrina Victoria. Greville, to whose deeply interesting *Journal* we shall have frequent occasions to refer, tells us that the name Georgiana had been also proposed, but the idea was dropped because the Prince Regent, who had originated the proposal, would not suffer his name to stand second on the list. On the evening of the christening, the Duke of Kent gave a grand dinner, at which nearly all the members of the Royal Family were present.

Of life in the Palace during the babyhood of the Princess we have but few glimpses. Everything, however, seems to have gone on with the regularity of clockwork. The Duke, like his father, was an early riser; and, to insure punctuality, he kept a servant, whose business it was, in the winter, to light the fire at a precise hour, for which purpose he was not allowed to go to bed till he had discharged that office. Precisely at six o'clock

* By the Hon. Amelia Murray in her *Recollections*.

a cup of coffee was brought to the Duke by one attendant, and the tray removed by another. In the course of the morning, all the chief servants made their appearance in turn; and a bill of the expenses of the preceding day was produced by the house steward, whose statement included the minutest articles, and all of them distinctly classed. A Welsh judge named Hardinge, who was a frequent visitor at the palace, tells us that the Duke had his bells enumerated to ensure regularity of attendance, and that a hair-dresser was kept on the premises for all the livery servants, so great was His Royal Highness's fondness for smartness of appearance.

Of the Princess herself we hear but little. That she was an extremely pretty baby we may well believe, and of this Sir Thomas Lawrence's charming drawing, made five months after the christening, is confirmatory enough. We can imagine her in those days of helplessness and innocence, lying in her cradle at Kensington, watched over with jealous care by the fondest of mothers and the most faithful of nurses. The nurse's name was Mrs. Brock, and the little Princess used to call her her "dear, dear Boppy." We can picture the child lying there, with blue, wide-open eyes, wondering, perhaps, at the sounds which ever and anon break in upon the silence; for the palace in the Duke's time abounded with musical clocks, two of which chimed every quarter of an hour, and the Queen has herself told us of "a large watch in a tortoise-shell case" belonging to her father, which she "always used to hear at night." We can imagine, too, the gleam of joy, not unmingled with pride, which would have lighted up the Duke's face on one interesting occasion, when, if chroniclers speak truly, he lifted his little daughter in his arms to show her to some friends, and uttered the prophecy: "Look at her well, for she will yet be Queen of England!"

In regard to these words of her father, it should be pointed out that the probabilities of the Princess succeeding to the throne were at that time very remote. The dissolute Prince Regent (afterwards George IV.) was already seeking a divorce from the unhappy Caroline of Brunswick, and if his efforts were successful he might marry again and have heirs. Then, too, the Duchess of Clarence—who, in March, 1819, had given birth to a daughter that had only survived a few hours—might yet be the joyful mother of living children; and these would all take precedence of their cousin Victoria, the Duke of Clarence being an elder brother of the Duke of Kent. Lastly, the baby princess might herself be the predecessor of a prince or princess of the Kent branch.

The last-mentioned possibility was unexpectedly removed by the untimely death of the Duke of Kent in the January of the following year. The Duchess has herself spoken very pathetically of the event: "A few months after the birth of my child, my infant and myself were awfully deprived of father and husband. We stood alone, almost friendless and unknown in this country. I could not even speak the language of it."

The circumstances of this great sorrow are soon told. Shortly after the birth of the Princess, the child's health as well as that of her mother rendered a change of scene and climate advisable, and the family repaired to Sidmouth, a picturesque little town on the south coast of Devonshire. The effects were such as had been anticipated: the Duchess recovered rapidly, and the child grew rosy, healthy, and strong. The Duke was delighted with the country, and still more by the beneficial changes produced upon his wife and little one. The Devon climate and the fresh sea breezes worked wonders, and no better place could have been chosen for their autumn flitting. It was here the Duke died.

A month or two before his death, the Princess herself had a narrow escape. A boy who was sparrow shooting in the vicinity of Woolbrook Cottage discharged his gun so close to one of the nursery windows, that some panes of glass were broken and several of the shot passed within an inch or two of the precious baby head. The future Queen and Empress was reposing in the arms of Mrs. Brock at the time, and we may be sure the faithful "Boppy" was mightily alarmed. It was only an accident, however, and the reckless young sportsman shed copious tears of contrition when brought before the Duke, who lectured him and let him go.

Little did the Duke think how near his own end was! On the evening of the 13th of January, 1820, he came back from a long walk in the snow, heated, tired, and with his boots wet through to the feet. His equerry and great friend, Captain Conroy, advised him to make a change without delay, but the sight of his little daughter took off his attention from himself, and he sat for a considerable time amusing her on his lap. The delay proved fatal. He was taken with a chill, and inflammation of the lungs ensued. The next morning he was reported to be in imminent danger, and though there was an apparent improvement in his condition during the day, the alarming

WOOLBROOK COTTAGE.

symptoms returned with increased violence as night drew on, and within a week he was dead.

"The Duchess," says a contemporary chronicler, "performed all the offices of his sick-bed with the most tender and affectionate anxiety. She did not even take off her clothes for five successive nights, and all the medicines were administered by her own hands. She yet struggled to prevent his seeing the agony of her apprehensions, and never left his bedside but to give vent to her sorrow."

For some days the body lay in state at Woolbrook Cottage, and was then removed to Cumberland Lodge, the solemn journey thither lasting nearly a week. At Cumberland Lodge the body remained in state another day, and then was removed by night to its last resting-place at Windsor. The procession, by torchlight, must have been a weird and impressive spectacle under that January night sky, when, amid the glittering of the flambeaux and the sound of martial music, the Duke's body, under pall and canopy, and followed by princes of the blood and field-marshals, by pursuivants and heralds, by knights and pages, passed down the Long Walk at Windsor on its way to the Royal tomb.

Leopold was present as one of the pall-bearers, and when the funeral was over he hurried down to Sidmouth to impart what comfort he could to the lonely and disconsolate widow. The Prince had lost a wife, and was well fitted to sympathise with one who had lost a husband. Though he had been present at the christening, it was only now that "he had the courage to look upon the blooming face of his infant niece; but from this moment he assumed her father's place, and discharged its duties with conscientious devotion."* In his company the Duchess and her orphan child returned to Kensington.

A few days later, and before the first month of her widowhood was well by, the Duchess "received Viscount Morpeth and Viscount Clive, the deputation bearing to her the address of condolence from the House of Commons. She met them with the infant Princess in her arms. The child was not only the sign that she fully acknowledged and appreciated the nature of the tie which united her to the country, it was the intimation of the close, inseparable union with her daughter which continued through all the years of the Queen's childhood and youth, till the office of sovereign forced its holder into a separate existence—till she found another fitting protector, when the generous, ungrudging mother gave way to the worthy husband, who became the dutiful son of the Duchess's declining years."†

Sad must have been the recollections of the Duchess, and slowly must have dragged the days, after her return to Kensing-

---

* *Life of the Prince Consort*, vol. i. 3.
† Tytler's *Life of the Queen*, vol. i. 18.

ton. She had left the palace in the company of her husband, a happy wife and mother; she had come back to it a widow— her child an orphan. Yet she never seems to have sunk under her sorrow. The consolations of Christianity were her support; the Friend of the widow and the fatherless was no stranger to the bereaved lady; and she still had her little one to live for. About this time she was visited, at her own request, by the noble-hearted William Wilberforce, who afterwards narrated the circumstances of his visit in a letter to Hannah More. "She received me," he wrote, "with her fine animated child on the floor by her side, with its playthings, of which I soon became one. She was very civil, but as she did not sit down I did not like to stop above a quarter of an hour; and there being but a female attendant and a footman present, I could not well get up any topic so as to carry on a continual discourse. She apologised for not speaking English well enough to talk it; intimated a hope that she might talk it better and longer with me at some future time. She spoke of her situation, and her manner was quite delightful."*

Those early days at Kensington after the death of her father were probably not unhappy days to the orphan Princess. Her half-sister, the Princess Feodora, who was some years her senior, came to stay at the palace, and was a welcome playmate and companion to the child. She used to pull the infant Victoria about the palace grounds in a child's phaeton, and doubtless they had fine fun together. We can picture the fair-headed occupant of the little carriage on these occasions in her snow-white dress and her broad blue sash, her large blue eyes, beautiful bloom, and fair complexion making her a model of infantine beauty. Gentlemen who saw the sisters together would raise their hats to the younger of the two, and the child, baby though she was, seemed to like the notice taken of her, and had an answer for all who addressed her. "She would say 'lady' and 'good-morning,' and when told, would hold out her soft dimpled hand to be kissed, with an arch expression on her face." "Why do all the gentlemen take off their hats to me and not to

* *Life and Letters of Wilberforce*, vol. v. 71, 72.

my sister Feodora?" she is said to have asked on one occasion, for at that time (as, indeed, for years after) she was ignorant of her high destiny.

Between mother and child the closest union subsisted. They were never apart for long together, night or day; and the devoted parent nursed her baby, would see it dressed by the maid, or even dress it herself if the maid was away on a holiday. During the Princess's infancy the Duchess was her chief instructress, being ably seconded by the Baroness Lehzen, daughter of a Hanoverian clergyman, and the Queen's friend through life. Her Majesty, we are told, became familiar with three languages at an age "when other children have scarcely acquired the rudiments of their native tongue. And in the use of them the Queen soon made a discovery which did credit to her heart and her intelligence. If she had a favour to ask, or a request to prefer, she readily perceived that it was most agreeable to the maternal ear when lisped in the Teutonic accents of the Duchess's beloved fatherland, whereupon many caressing phrases were addressed by the little Princess to the Royal mother in German. But the vernacular language of the Princess was English, and though the love she bore her mother stimulated her to speak German occasionally, yet she spoke it with effort, and lapsed into English with an alacrity and ease that showed that English was truly her native tongue."* The Duchess appears to have had the Duke's love of routine and method, and also—what the Duke never had—a taste for simplicity such as one is not wont to associate with Royal ladies. At eight o'clock the Duchess and her family, having paid their morning tribute of prayer and thanksgiving, partook together of their first social meal, Victoria having her bread-and-milk and fruit put on a little table by her mother's side. After breakfast the little Princess went for an hour's walk or drive with her half-sister, Feodora; then came lessons, from ten to twelve; and after that they might amuse themselves with their toys (Feodora had not quite grown out of dolls at that time) or romp about through the suite of rooms which extended round two sides of the Palace. Two o'clock was the Duchess's

* *Windsor Magazine*, Feb., 1895.

luncheon time, and the children's dinner hour; and our chronicler is careful to inform us that the latter meal was always extremely plain. After dinner there were more lessons, and then another drive, or perhaps a visit; and later still, if the evening were fine, the whole party would sit out on the lawn under the trees. Then, while her mother dined, the Princess Victoria would take her supper, which, like the rest of her meals, was always laid beside the Duchess, and consisted of the simplest fare; and then, after a romp with "Boppy," she would join the party at dessert, when she would probably be made much of by the guests. At nine o'clock she would retire to her bed, "a beautiful little French bed," which was placed beside her mother's; and there we may picture her as she lies listening to the musical clocks or to the big watch in the tortoise-shell case till the heavy eyelids droop in sleep, and the dream-world opens to her view.

When she was three years old the Princess met with a narrow escape by being thrown out of a pony carriage. The carriage overturned, and must have crushed her had not a soldier caught her by the dress in time and swung her into a place of safety.

GEORGE IV.

Her saviour was an Irishman named John Maloney. The Duchess took down the man's name and the name of his regiment, and promised to use her influence in his behalf. She afterwards sent him five pounds.

On her fourth birthday the Princess received a magnificent present from her uncle, George the Fourth, who also gave a State dinner to the Duchess and her daughter. The birthday token was a miniature of himself, set in diamonds. Even at that early age the Queen is said to have taken the greatest delight in music, her sense of harmony being very true, and probably inherited from her mother. There was at that time before the public a little musical prodigy known as "Lyra"—a child performer on the harp, whose praises were in everybody's mouth. The Duchess consented to have the infant harpist introduced into her apartment to amuse the Princess, and the sequel was very interesting. The Princess was greatly delighted with Lyra, towards whom she behaved in the most engaging manner. "While the infant musician was playing one of her most fascinating solos, the Duchess, perceiving how deeply her daughter's attention was engrossed by the music, ventured to leave the room for a few minutes. On her return she found the harp deserted, the juvenile minstrel having been beguiled from the instrument by the display of some of the little Princess's costly toys. Both were seated side by side on the hearthrug in a high state of enjoyment, surrounded by the Princess's playthings, from which she was making the most liberal selection for the acceptance of poor little Lyra. This surprising musical prodigy was supposed to be then about five years old, and she died a few years later."*

Speaking of Royal playthings, there is still to be seen, we believe, in the Swiss Cottage at Osborne, a quaint little doll's house, with its different rooms, which the infant Victoria loved to arrange. "The small frying-pans and plates still hang above the kitchen dresser, the cook stands unwearied by the range, the chairs are placed round the tables, the tiny tea-service, which tiny fingers delighted to handle, is set out ready for company. But the owner has long done with make-believes, has worked in earnest, discharged great tasks, and borne the burden and heat of the day in ruling over a great empire."† It should be added, however, that the Princess's playthings were not playthings *merely*, like those of other children; they served an important educational purpose as well. In fact, the worthy Baroness Lehzen, her governess, had the gift of diplomacy, and originated the happy idea of instructing her pupil in the forms and ceremonies of the Court by means of the dolls which the Princess loved so well. A long board full of pegs, which fitted into

* *Windsor Magazine*, Feb., 1895.
† Tytler's *Life of the Queen*, vol. i. 12; and *Woman at Home*, Feb., 1894.

holes in the feet of the little manikins, served as the stage upon which the mimic ceremonials took place; and the dolls were put into Court costume, with plumes and lappets for the occasion. "In this way the future Queen and Empress, while holding her make-believe drawing-rooms and levees, with all their attendant *dramatis personæ* of state, learned unconsciously to perform her part in the functions of her high position with that ease and grace which have since characterised her every act."*

And now another tutor appears upon the scene. In the Princess's fifth year, the services of Dr. Davys, who had graduated as tenth wrangler at Cambridge in 1803, were called in, and the child's education went on in a more regular and systematic manner. The engagement of Dr. Davys arose out of a request from the Duchess to read English with her for an hour every morning,—a request which was at once acceded to; and when a month had gone by, Her Royal Highness said to him: "You teach me so well, I think you shall teach my little daughter;" and so it was settled. From time to time other teachers were engaged—that is, for special subjects—but Dr. Davys remained to the end the director of the "solid department" of the Princess's studies. Her chief instructor in music was John Bernard Sale, son of the composer, and her singing master the famous vocalist, Luigi Lablache; but it was not till several years later, viz., in 1836, that the latter was engaged. Professor Lablache had no indifferent pupil to train, for the Princess was fond of singing, and her voice—a mezzo-soprano—was greatly admired for its flexibility and richness of tone. Her drawing-master was Mr. Westall, the Academician, who detected much promise in her early work, and affirmed that she would have made the first woman-artist of the day could she have given her undivided attention to painting. But this was probably courtier's language.

Her Majesty was certainly an apt scholar, and at times gave evidence of a good deal of natural wit. She was reading Roman history with her tutor one day, and came to the passage where Cornelia, the mother of the Gracchi, introduced her sons

* *Windsor Magazine*, Feb., 1895.

to the first of Roman ladies with the words, "These are my jewels." Lifting her eyes from her book, the Princess looked archly at her tutor, and remarked, "She should have said 'my *Cornelians.*'" During a pianoforte lesson, on another occasion, when the scales and exercises had proved rather too much for the patience of the little pupil, Mr. Sale happened to remark that there was no Royal road to music—that princesses must practise like other children. Whereupon the little autocrat quietly locked the piano, and slipping the key into her pocket, answered sedately, "There, you see! There is no *must* in the matter."

An interesting anecdote belonging to this period was related to the eloquent Bishop Wilberforce by Dr. Davys. "The Queen," said the doctor, "always had from my first knowing her a most striking regard to truth. I remember when I had been teaching her one day, she was very impatient for the lesson to be over—once or twice rather refractory. The Duchess of Kent came in, and asked how she had behaved. Lehzen said, 'Oh, once she was rather troublesome.' The Princess touched her and said, 'No, Lehzen, twice; don't you remember?'" The worthy doctor, who was afterwards made Dean of Chester and, on the Queen's accession, promoted to the bishopric of Peterborough, used to preach every Sunday morning in the private chapel of the palace, and on one of these occasions was complimented in the following manner by the Duchess: "I like your sermons so much, Mr. Dean"—the Dean bowed low—"because they are so short," said the Duchess, completing the sentence.

Every year, in the summer months, there were excursions to the sea—welcome changes, we may be sure, to the active-minded child; for even life in a palace may become monotonous at last. We have already seen her at Sidmouth. In her second year she was at Brighton, lodging in that extraordinary edifice the Pavilion; and afterwards she was several times at Ramsgate, which became a favourite spot, both to the Princess and her mother. The Royal child has been sketched for us during one of these Ramsgate visits, and the picture is attractive enough. A simply-dressed child, full of gaiety and cheerfulness, with "as pretty a pair of shoes on as pretty a pair of feet" as one would wish to see. She is on the sands, and near her stands her mother in conversation with William Wilberforce. The good man laughs—a kind, genial laugh—when an unexpected wave ripples over those tiny feet, causing the child to start back in the prettiest alarm. This was in her fifth year.

About the same time she was taken to Claremont, where her Uncle Leopold was staying, and here was spent one of the happiest of her early holidays. Writing to her uncle from the

THE PAVILION, BRIGHTON.

same spot many years after, she said: "This place has a peculiar charm for us both, and to me it brings back recollections of the happiest days of my otherwise dull childhood, when I experienced such kindness from you, dearest uncle, kindness which has ever since continued. . . . Victoria [the Princess Royal] plays with my old bricks, and I see her running and jumping in the flower-garden, as *old*—though I feel still *little*—Victoria of former days used to do."* At Claremont, the Queen saw her maternal grandmother, the Dowager-Duchess of Coburg, for the first time, the genial old lady being then on a visit to this country.

* *Life of the Prince Consort*, vol. i. 24.

Another guest at Claremont during the Princess's stay was Captain Parry, the Arctic explorer, who describes her as a dear and lovable child, full of innocent playfulness and simplicity. "She and her mother sat down quietly to the piano after breakfast, and sang with remarkable sweetness and taste some beautiful German duets and some Tyrolese airs," which the gallant officer had not heard before.

Anon we meet with the little Princess at Tunbridge Wells, then, as now, a favourite resort of wealth and fashion. Harriet Martineau was staying there at the time; and we are indebted to that gifted lady for an anecdote of the child which might never otherwise have come down to us. "It became known at Tunbridge Wells that the Princess had been unable to buy a box at the bazaar because she had spent her money. At the bazaar she had bought presents for almost all her relations, and had laid out her last shilling, when she remembered one cousin more, and saw a box priced half-a-crown which would suit him. The shop people, of course, placed the box with the other purchases; but the little lady's governess admonished them by saying, 'No; you see the Princess has not got the money; therefore, of course, she cannot buy the box.' This being perceived, the next offer was to lay by the box till it could be purchased; and the answer was, 'Oh, well, if you will be so good as to do that.' On quarter day, before seven in the morning, the Princess appeared on her donkey to claim her purchase." We have in this anecdote another instance of the careful training of the future Queen of England, and anecdotes of a similar character might be multiplied. While making a hay-cock on one occasion, some other object took her fancy, whereupon, with child-like impulsiveness, she threw down her rake, and was running off, when the Baroness Lehzen called her back. "No, no, Princess; you must always complete what you have commenced," she said; and the eager little lady had to finish the hay-cock before she was permitted to gratify the new desire.

Another interesting episode of her early childhood is the Princess's visit to the keeper of a certain lighthouse on the

Kentish coast—a lonely and childless widow. The widow was a Christian, in deed as in name; poor, but a hearty giver in the cause of missions. One source of her living was the gratuities received from visitors to the lighthouse, and it was her habit to set apart for mission purposes whatever money she received in this way *on Monday mornings*. Now, it happened on one of these missionary days that a gentleman, going over the lighthouse before noon, gave the poor woman a piece of gold—a sovereign. Here was an unexpected windfall! what should she do with the money? She thought of her many pressing needs, and had a mind to keep it. She thought of her weekly custom and the claims of the heathen, and then, with trembling fingers, dropped the whole amount into the missionary collecting-box. Later in the same day, a lady and her daughter, with several attendants, asked to be shown over the lighthouse, and on leaving gave the widow a handsome donation. The matter did not end there. The lady—a widow herself—had become interested in the lonely woman, and a day or two after the visit a messenger called at the lighthouse, and requested her acceptance of thirty pounds. Twenty-five pounds were a present from the lady, and the remainder of the sum was sent in the name of her little daughter. Is it necessary to add that the generous givers were the Duchess of Kent and the Princess Victoria?

These early seaside holidays, when the restraints of the palace were temporarily thrown aside, brought the Princess into contact with many in the humbler walks of life, and doubtless were the beginning of that interest in, and kindly feeling towards, her sailor-subjects which the Queen has so often shown. Many years later, an old sailor, who was watching Her Majesty's yacht cruising in the Solent, was heard remarking to a friend: " I mind how that brave lady, ever from her childish days, has had a kind heart for poor Jack Tar. Why, in her walk about the coast years agone, with the Duchess of Kent, many's the time she's listened to a poor sailor's yarns about his shipwrecks, his troubles, ay, and his joys, for there's fair weather as well as rough. My old comrade, Timber Tough, as we call him, now in Greenwich Hospital, told me that once upon a time, when the Princess Victoria was at Dover, and used to walk about the cliffs, he and his son, Jim, the fisherman, were mending their nets in a sheltered cove, when all of a sudden a grand lady, and a bright-looking little missy, and another lady, and two men-servants at a distance, came round the point of the cliff right afore them. A camp-stool was brought for the lady with the grand look, and Timber Tough, who knew a bit of manners, made a sign for his son to gather up the nets, and meant to go away; but the lady said very sweetly, 'Don't let us disturb you,' and the little missy added, 'You need not go away;' and somehow they got to asking about nets and fishing, and then about the sea, and p'r'aps the young lady had been reading about the perils of the great deep, for she asked, 'Have you ever been shipwrecked?' 'Yes, miss, that I have,' says Timber Tough, 'upon a desolate island, too.' 'Indeed!' says the little miss, 'where?'" And the old sailor went on to relate how Timber Tough had told the story of his shipwreck to the wondering child, only discovering on the following day that his little auditor and questioner was the Princess Victoria.

In these stories of the Queen's childhood we may see the bright promise of her future years, and how pleasant is the picture!

> "Whether in seaside happiness, and air
>   Rosing the fair cheek,—sand, and spade, and shell,—
>   Or raced with sister-feet, that flashed and fell
>   Printing the beach, while the gay comrade-wind
>   Played in the soft light hair;—
>   Or if with sunbeam smile and kind
>   Small hand at cottage-door
>   Her ample alms she tendered to the poor:
> Love's healthy, happy heart in all her steps was seen,
> And God, in life's fresh springtime, bless'd our Queen."*

About this time an event happened which had an important bearing upon the future of the Royal child. On the 5th of January, 1827, the Duke of York, an elder brother of the Duke

---

* Palgrave's *Visions of England*, 181.

of Kent, and for many years Commander-in-Chief of the Army, was removed by death, and the Duke of Clarence became heir-presumptive to the Crown. The Princess Victoria was thus brought one step nearer the Throne; but the fact was wisely concealed from her. The accompanying table will help to explain how matters stood at this time:—

GEORGE THE THIRD (DIED 1820).

GEORGE THE FOURTH.	DUKE OF YORK	DUKE OF CLARENCE	DUKE OF KENT
Only issue—Princess Charlotte of Wales (*m.* Leopold of Saxe-Coburg), died 1817, leaving no issue.	(died 1827, leaving no issue).	afterwards WILLIAM IV. (*m.* Adelaide of Saxe-Meiningen). Issue—2 children, both of whom died in infancy before the year 1820.	(*m.* Victoria of Saxe-Coburg). Princess VICTORIA.

Among others who saw and wrote about Her Majesty during the period of her early childhood was Leigh Hunt, the graceful essayist, and that pioneer of cheap literature, and most enterprising of publishers, Charles Knight. The account left by the latter would only lose by abridgment, and we, therefore, make no apology for quoting it in its entirety. "In the early morning," he writes,* "when the sun was scarcely high enough to have dried up the dews of Kensington's green alleys, as I passed along the broad central walk, I saw a group on the lawn before the palace, which, to my mind, was a vision of exquisite loveliness. The Duchess of Kent and her daughter, whose years then numbered nine, are breakfasting in the open air, a single page attending them at a respectful distance; the matron looking on with eyes of love, whilst the fair, soft English face is bright with smiles. The world of fashion is not yet astir. Clerks and mechanics, passing onward to their occupation, are few; and they exhibit nothing of that vulgar curiosity which I think is more commonly found in the class of the merely rich than in the ranks below them in the world's estimation. What a beautiful characteristic it seemed to me of the training of this Royal girl, that she should not have been taught to shrink from the public eye; that she should not have been burdened with a premature conception of her probable high destiny; that she

* In *Passages of a Working Life.*

should enjoy the freedom and simplicity of a child's nature; that she should not be restrained when she starts up from the breakfast-table and runs to gather a flower in the adjoining parterre; that her merry laugh should be as fearless as the notes of the thrush in the groves around her. I passed on and blessed her; and I thank God that I lived to see the golden fruits of such training."

Leigh Hunt's recollections refer to a year later, and are in a more humorous vein. He tells of the peculiar kind of personal pleasure which it gave him to see the future Queen, as she came up a cross-path from the Bayswater Gate, with a girl of about her own age by her side, whose hand she was holding

KENSINGTON PALACE.

as if she loved her. A magnificent footman in scarlet walked behind her, with the splendidest pair of calves in white stockings we ever beheld, and looking somehow like a gigantic fairy, personating for his little lady's sake the grandest kind of footman he could think of.*

This was the year that Sir Walter Scott dined with the Duchess of Kent. "I was very kindly received by Prince Leopold," he wrote in his *Journal*, under date the 19th of May, 1828, "and presented to the little Princess Victoria—the heir-apparent to the Crown, as things now stand.... This little lady is educating with much care, and watched so closely that no busy maid has a moment to whisper, 'You

* Abridged, and slightly altered.

are heir of England.' I suspect, if we could dissect the little heart, we should find some pigeon or other bird of the air had carried the matter." That Sir Walter was mistaken in this very natural suspicion will be presently seen.*

Greville is perhaps the only writer of any account who does not speak of the youthful Princess as a pretty child. He saw her in her tenth year, and describes her as "short and plain-looking;" but adds significantly, "if nature has not done much,

THE QUEEN AT THE AGE OF 10.
By permission of Messrs. H. GRAVES & Co.

fortune is likely to do a great deal more for her."† The same entertaining diarist tells of a State dinner given by George the Fourth in the summer of 1829, at which two little Royal ladies were present—the Princess Victoria and the child Queen of Portugal. The Princess had just entered upon her eleventh year, and her appearance at Court had attracted much attention. There was little doubt in people's minds, that if she lived a few years longer she would be Queen of England. The King was

* Lockhart's *Life of Scott*, vol. ix. 242, quoted in *Life of the Prince Consort*, vol. i. 3. † Greville's *Journal*, part i.

in his sixty-fifth year, wifeless and childless; the Duke of Clarence, heir-presumptive to the Throne, was childless, too, and next in succession came the Princess Victoria. When the King had first talked of giving the ball, one of the Court ladies had exclaimed, with great want of tact, "Oh do; it will be so nice to see the *two little Queens* dancing together," and the remark had greatly annoyed the King.* However, the ball came off, and the Princess is said to have quite outshone the child Queen, in spite of the great display of jewels which the latter made. The day, indeed, ended rather disastrously for the poor little Queen, for she had the misfortune to tumble down while dancing, and was led away from the gay scene in some confusion.

Our Princess did not often find herself among such gaieties, however; the disreputable Court of the worst of the Georges not being, in her mother's opinion, a suitable school-room for a young girl. Nor was the King himself able to be present at many more of these brilliant assemblages, albeit they had become a sort of necessity to him. He was ageing fast, and disquieting rumours about his health began to find expression in the newspapers. Then the end came. Little more than a twelvemonth after the ball, the following notice was posted up at the Mansion House:—

"WHITEHALL, 26th *June*, 1830.

"MY LORD,—It is my painful duty to inform you that it has pleased Almighty God to release His Majesty from his sufferings. His Majesty died at about a quarter past three o'clock this morning.

"I have the honour to be, my Lord,

"Your Lordship's obedient and faithful servant,

"ROBERT PEEL."

George the Fourth was dead, and the Princess Victoria was another step nearer the Throne.

* Greville's *Journal*, part i.

CHAPTER II.

IN THE DAYS OF WILLIAM THE FOURTH.

DURING the eleven years which we have been considering, very little of political importance had taken place. The reign of George the Fourth, which almost covers this period, was distinguished by no remarkable event—no event worthy of historical remembrance—unless, perhaps, the passing of the *Catholic Emancipation Bill*, which, from whatever point of view we choose to regard it, was certainly a measure of wide-reaching importance. Beyond this, nothing of vital moment—nothing, assuredly, of real benefit to the people—had been effected; though both the ministry under Lord Liverpool, and that under the Duke of Wellington, had had it in their power to accomplish much. Possibly the King himself had been the hindrance, for seldom had the British throne been filled by so worthless a monarch. His life was a public disgrace, and gave its colour to the society of which he was the centre. Thackeray has expressed his wonder that people should ever have tolerated him; and thirty years after the King's death, he raised the inquiry, "Would we bear him now? In this quarter of a century," continues the eloquent biographer of the Georges, "what a silent revolution has been working! how it has separated us from old times and manners! How it has changed men themselves! I can see old gentlemen now among us, of perfect good-breeding, of quiet lives, with venerable grey heads, fondling their grandchildren; and look at them, and wonder at what they were once. That gentleman of the grand old school, when he was in the 10th Hussars, and dined at the Prince's table, would fall under it night after night. Night after night, that gentleman sat at Brookes's or Raggett's over the dice. If, in the petulance of play or drink, that gentleman spoke a sharp word to his neighbour, he and the other would infallibly go out and try to shoot each other the next morning. That gentleman would drive his friend Richmond the black boxer down to Moulsey, and hold his coat, and shout and swear, and hurrah with delight, while the black man was beating Dutch Sam the Jew. That gentleman would take a manly pleasure in pulling his own coat off, and thrashing a bargeman in a street row. That gentleman has been in a watchhouse. That gentleman, so exquisitely polite with ladies in a drawing-room, so loftily courteous, if he talked now as he used among men in his youth, would swear so as to make your hair stand on end."* Such was the state of society in the days when the Queen was young, in the days of George the Fourth, the *first gentleman* (!) of Europe. Do we wonder that the pure-minded Duchess of Kent avoided the Court of such a monarch, or secluded her child from the contaminating influences of such society? Well for Queen and people to-day that she did so!

WILLIAM IV.

On ascending the throne, the new King took the title of William the Fourth; he was popularly known as the "Sailor King." A month or two after his accession, the ceremony of opening London Bridge, then just completed, took place, and was honoured by the presence of His Majesty and Queen Adelaide. Other members of the Royal Family were also present, but not the Princess Victoria or her mother. The ceremony was preceded by a grand water procession, in which

* Lectures on *The Four Georges*, *Cornhill Magazine*, Oct., 1860.

the King took part, and silver medals, struck for the occasion, were distributed with liberal hand as the State barges passed slowly from Westminster to the new bridge. The ceremony over there was a banquet, with the usual toasting and speech-making, and in due course the "loving cup" was passed round and partaken of by every member of the Royal Family present. A baronetcy was then conferred upon the Lord Mayor, and the proceedings terminated.

Next day there was a grand procession of their Majesties to the House of Lords, in which the Duchess of Kent took part. On this occasion the King gave his assent to the Dower Bill of his Royal Consort, and she on her part expressed her thanks to the two Houses of Parliament for the ample provision which they had made for her maintenance in the event of her widowhood. Somewhat later in the afternoon, the Premier presented the following message from the King, which, after passing through the hands of the Lord Chancellor, was read aloud by the Clerk at the table of the House:

"His Majesty, taking into consideration that since Parliament made provision for Her Royal Highness the Duchess of Kent, and Her Highness the Princess Alexandrina Victoria of Kent, circumstances have occurred which make it necessary that a more suitable provision should be made for Her Royal Highness the Duchess of Kent, and for the suitable education and maintenance of Her Highness the Princess Alexandrina Victoria of Kent, relies on the affection and attachment of the Commons, to take the necessary measures for making such provision."

A similar message was the same evening delivered to the House of Commons by the Chancellor of the Exchequer; and on the morrow the messages were taken into consideration in both Houses. In the House of Peers, Earl Grey informed their Lordships that, in consequence of the election of Prince Leopold to the Belgic throne, an allowance of six thousand a-year which the Prince had hitherto made to his niece was withdrawn; from which circumstance he argued the importance of making a further provision for the support of the honour and dignity of the Princess Victoria, as the heiress presumptive to the Crown. Lord Althorp in the Lower House gave the same account as an argument for granting £10,000 per annum additional to the income of the Duchess; and the resolution was agreed to.

It had previously been resolved by Parliament that, should the need arise, the Duchess of Kent should be the Guardian and Regent during the minority of the Princess, and in this Parliament was wise. On hearing of the resolution, the Dowager-Duchess of Coburg had written to her daughter in the following terms: "I should have been very sorry if the Regency had been given into other hands than yours. It would not have been a just return for your constant devotion and care to your child if this had not been done. May God give you wisdom and strength to do your duty if called upon to undertake it! May God bless and protect our little darling! If I could but once see her again! The print you sent of her is not like the picture I have. The quantity of curls hide the well-shaped head, and make it look too large for the lovely little figure."

While this Regency Bill was in progress, the Princess, then twelve years old, discovered for the first time her nearness to the throne. The Baroness Lehzen had suggested to the Duchess of Kent that the time had come to break the news to her pupil, and that she should be shown her place in the succession. The Duchess agreed, and the genealogical table was placed between the leaves of the historical book. When Dr. Davys, her instructor, was gone, the Princess Victoria opened as usual the book again, and observing the additional paper said, "I never saw that before." "It was not thought necessary you should, Princess," returned the Baroness. The child had begun to tremble, but said quietly, "I see I am nearer the throne than I thought." "So it is, Madam," answered the Baroness. A pause of some moments ensued, and then the Princess resumed, "Now many a child would boast, but they don't know the difficulty. There is much splendour, but there is more responsibility." Then she placed her small hand in that of her governess, and said earnestly, "I will be good! I understand now, why you urged me so much to learn, even Latin. My

Aunts Augusta and Mary never did; but you told me Latin is the foundation of English grammar, and of all the elegant expressions, and I learned it as you wished it, but I understand all better now." And, with that, the child repeated, "I will be good!" The Baroness then said, "But your Aunt Adelaide is still young, and may have children, and of course they would ascend the throne after their father William the Fourth, and not you, Princess." The Princess answered, "And if it was so, I should never feel disappointed, for I know by the love Aunt Adelaide bears me, how fond she is of children."*

Referring to this touching episode, Mrs. Oliphant justly says: "It is seldom that an early scene like this stands out so distinctly in the early story, even of a life destined to greatness. The hush of awe upon the child; the childish application of this great secret to the abstruse study of Latin, which was not required from the others; the immediate resolution, so simple, yet containing all the wisest sage could have counselled, or the greatest hero vowed, 'I will be good,' makes a perfect little picture. It is the clearest appearance of the future Queen in her own person that we get through the soft obscurity of those childish years."

Early in the following year (1831), the Princess made her first appearance in State since the new King's accession, at a Drawing-Room held by Queen Adelaide. Newspapers of the period are unanimous in describing it as the grandest that had been seen since the presentation of Princess Charlotte of Wales, upon the occasion of her marriage to Prince Leopold. The Princess's dress on this occasion was made entirely of articles manufactured in the United Kingdom. Her frock was of English blonde over white satin, and the madonna braids of her fair hair were fastened at the back of her head by a rich diamond agrafe. She stood on the left of Her Majesty on the throne, contemplating all that passed with much dignity, but with evident enjoyment; and was the object of universal interest and admiration.

The coronation took place in the following September, but

* *Life of the Prince Consort*, vol. i. 3.

the Princess and her mother took no part in the ceremony. Their absence occasioned much surprise, and some of the leading journals (*The Times* among the rest) openly accused the Duchess of want of respect to their Majesties, and abused her in no measured terms. A justificatory plea, however, was published, from which it was made clear that the delicate state of the health of the young Princess, who was then in the Isle of Wight, rendered it indispensable that she should avoid the fatiguing ceremony.

The Duchess and her daughter remained in the island about three months, taking up their residence at Norris Castle; and the Princess was so benefited by the change that the visit was renewed for a similar period in the year 1833. A tourist, on this occasion, happening one day to be strolling about the old churchyard at Arreton, where Leigh Richmond's "dairyman's daughter" lies buried, came upon a grassy mound, beside which a lady and a young girl were seated. The latter was reading aloud, in a full melodious voice, the touching tale of the Christian maiden. The tourist turned away, and soon after was told by the sexton that the pilgrims to that humble grave were the Duchess of Kent and Princess Victoria.

Prior to this second visit, the Princess accompanied her mother on an autumn tour through several counties of England and Wales, paying a succession of visits to the seats of different noblemen, and taking Oxford on the way. That "most loyal city" interested her greatly, and during her stay there, she received a present of a magnificent Bible, printed at the University Press, and the history of her visit printed on white satin. The Royal visitors were also welcomed by an address from the Vice-Chancellor, the dons and doctors turning out in fine style, and giving the distinguished travellers a right Royal welcome. Among the great mansions visited during this tour were Eaton Hall, the home of the Grosvenors; Chatsworth, the magnificent seat of the Cavendishes; the Earl of Lichfield's mansion at Shugborough; the Earl of Liverpool's, at Pitchford Hall; and Wytham House, the noble residence of the Earl of Abingdon. The manufacturing towns on the route were not overlooked, nor the manufactures which made them famous. At Belper, the cotton mills were inspected, and the senior partner of one of the great firms had the honour of showing his future Sovereign, by means of a model, how cotton was spun. At Bromsgrove, the Princess exhibited a keen interest in the works of the nailers, from whom she received a curious gift, in the form of a thousand little nails of all patterns, enclosed in a quill, and presented in a golden box. At Beaumaris, in Wales, she visited the Eisteddfod, and invested the musical victors with the prizes awarded for their performances.

The year following (1833) we meet with the Princess at Weymouth—in other days the favourite watering-place of good old George the Third; and then we follow her to Portsmouth, to find her once more in company with the young Queen of Portugal.

In July, 1834, the Princess, then in her fifteenth year, was confirmed according to the rites of the Church of England in the Chapel Royal, St. James's. The officiating clergyman was the Archbishop of Canterbury; and her mother, as well as the King and Queen, were present at the service. The Princess "was advancing with rapid steps to the point at which the girl leaves the child for ever behind her, and stretches forward to her crown of young womanhood. She had in her own name confirmed the baptismal vow which was supposed to consecrate her as a responsible being to the service of the King of kings. Still, she was a young creature, suffered to grow up according to a gracious natural growth, not forced into premature expansion, permitted to preserve to the last the sweet girlish trust and confidence, the mingled coyness and fearlessness, pensive dreams and merry laughter, which constitute the ineffable freshness and tender grace of youth."* Willis, the American poet, saw her in the following year in company with Queen Adelaide, and has preserved for us an account of what he saw. The two Royal ladies were leaning over a railing, listening to a ballad singer, and apparently were much interested and amused at the ballad he was singing. "Queen Adelaide," continues the American, "is undoubtedly the plainest woman in her

* Tytler's *Life of the Queen*, vol. i. 40.

dominions; but the Princess is much better looking than any picture of her in the shops, and for the heir to such a Crown as that of England, unnecessarily pretty and interesting. She will be sold, poor thing! bartered away by those great dealers in Royal hearts, whose grand calculations will not be much consolation to her if she happens to have a taste of her own." How little the plain-spoken American knew! Happily for Her Majesty, the clever poet turned out to be but an indifferent prophet.

In 1835 there was more travelling in the provinces—more entertaining of the Princess and her mother by Dukes and lesser nobles of the land—more educational visits to great centres. At Wentworth, they were entertained by the Earl Fitzwilliam; at Harewood House, by the Earl of Harewood; at Belvoir, by the Duke of Rutland. At Burghley House, the seat of the Marquis of Exeter, the arrangements in honour of the Royal guests were on a scale of exceptional grandeur. Greville was there at the time, and like a second Pepys, kept his eyes and ears attent with happiest result. "They arrived from Belvoir at three o'clock, in a heavy rain," he wrote later, "the civic authorities having turned out at Stamford to escort them and a procession of different people, all very loyal. When they had lunched, and the Mayor and his brethren had got dry, the Duchess received the Address, which was read by Lord Exeter, as Recorder. It talked of the Princess as 'destined to mount the throne of these realms.' Conroy handed the answer just as the Prime Minister does to the King. They are splendidly lodged, and great preparations have been made for their reception. The dinner at Burghley was very handsome; hall well lit, and all went off well, except that a pail of ice was landed in the Duchess's lap, which made a great bustle. Three hundred people at the ball, which was opened by Lord Exeter and the Princess, who, after dancing one dance, went to bed. They appeared at breakfast next morning at nine o'clock, and at ten set off to Holkham."* A little later we find them at Walmer Castle, the guest of the Duke of Wellington.

* *Journal*, part i., vol. ii.

The year 1836 was a more than usually eventful one to our Princess. In the month of May the Duke of Coburg paid a visit to England, together with his two sons, the Princes Ernest and Albert, and stayed a month at Kensington Palace with the Duchess of Kent. Now it was that the Princess saw for the first time her future husband. The Duchess of Kent, it will be remembered, was sister to the Duke of Saxe-Coburg, so that Victoria and Albert were first cousins. They were about of an age, having been born in the same year, though not in the same month. Singularly enough, the clergyman who had officiated at the baptism of the infant Princess in the June of that year, had also officiated at the baptism of the infant Prince in the August following. And these cousins, nearly twenty years later, were to become man and wife. Marriages, they say, are made in heaven, but sometimes they are planned on earth years before the event becomes possible, and this appears to have been the case as regards the union of the two Royal cousins, Victoria and Albert. Their grandmother, the old Duchess of Coburg, was evidently a match-maker of the most pronounced type, since even from their infancy she was known to declare, "When these two cousins grow up they must be man and wife." All the Coburg family were of the same mind, especially King Leopold, who probably rejoiced greatly now that the first important move had been taken by bringing the young couple together at Kensington. The King knew what he was doing—had taken pains to learn whatever was to be learnt about his nephew and niece—and had the highest opinion of both. Yet the great question after all was this—what opinion would the young people form of one another? and that could only be left to time and the developing influence of circumstances. So here they were at last together, under the same roof—Victoria of England and Albert of Saxe-Coburg—objects of the most anxious interest, both in the Palace home of the Princess and across the water in Belgium and Saxe-Coburg.

Baron Stockmar (the one favoured person outside the immediate family circle who was "in the secret") penned this

same year the following description of the youthful Prince:—
"Albert is a fine young fellow, well grown for his age, with agreeable and valuable qualities; and who, if things go well, may in a few years turn out a strong, handsome man, of a kindly, simple, yet dignified demeanour. Externally, therefore, he possesses all that pleases the sex, and at all times and in all countries must please. It may prove, too, a lucky circumstance, that even now he has something of an English look.

"But now the question is, 'How as to his mind?' On this point, too, one hears much to his credit. . . . He is said to be circumspect, discreet, and even now cautious. But that is not enough. He ought to have not merely great ability, but a *right* ambition, and great force of will as well."* That the Baron was afterwards well satisfied that the Prince was possessed of all those qualities which he considered necessary as the consort of the future Queen, is shown by subsequent letters, but it would be taking us too far to quote them here. There will be opportunity hereafter for discussing the Prince's character.

When an invitation from the Duchess of Kent to the Duke of Coburg and his sons had been first talked of, the Baron had wisely insisted that the object of the visit should be "kept strictly secret from the Princess as well as from the Prince, so as to leave them completely at their ease." This was done; though probably the parties most interested in this innocent arrangement *guessed* a good deal. "We may never know," says Miss Tytler, "how the Royal cousins met—whether the frank, kind, unconscious Princess came down under the wing of the Duchess as far as their entrance into the clock court, where there was a little dimness of agitation and laughing confusion, *in spite of the partial secrecy*, in two pairs of blue eyes which then encountered each other for the first time; whether the courtly company ascended in well-arranged file, or in a little friendly disorder."†

The visit as a whole seems to have passed off very well, and no sooner had the Prince left England, than King Leopold

---

* *Life of the Prince Consort*, vol. i. 4.
† Tytler's *Life of the Queen*, vol. i. 44.

wrote a letter to the Princess Victoria (who till now had been left freely to the impulse of her own inclination), informing her of his wishes on the marriage subject. The answer of the Princess was prompt, and seems to have afforded her uncle great satisfaction. It concluded thus: "I have only now to beg you, my dearest uncle, to take care of the health of one now so dear to me, and to take him under your special protection. I hope and trust all will go on prosperously and well on this subject now of so much importance to me."* When she was writing that letter the Princess was probably wearing a small enamel ring with a diamond in the centre, which Prince Albert had given her at parting.† Clearly the visit of the young Prince had been made to some purpose!

On the 21st of August the Princess and her mother were the guests of the King and Queen at Windsor Castle, where His Majesty's birthday was celebrated with Royal honours. On this occasion an unfortunate scene took place in which the King appears to have acted in a singularly unbecoming manner. Displeased at the Duchess of Kent for having kept the Princess so much from Court, he took upon himself to rebuke her at the dinner party before all his guests, at the same time making a fierce attack upon her advisers. Nothing could have been in worse taste, and certainly no rebuke was ever less merited. That the charge in itself was true we are not disposed to deny; but we maintain that the Duchess was perfectly justified in secluding her daughter as she had done, for the Court of William the Fourth was far from a desirable place for a Princess to grow up in. Her conduct, in fact, had been exemplary, while the King's rebuke was uncalled-for and inexcusably discourteous.

In spite of his choleric behaviour, however, the King was very kind in proposing the Princess's health at the banquet. The Princess was sitting opposite to him, and hung her head with maidenly modesty while the toast was being proposed. His Majesty's words were these: "And now, having given the

* *Life of the Prince Consort*, vol. i. 4.
† *Reminiscences of Court and Diplomatic Life*, vol. i. 123.

health of the oldest, I will give that of the youngest member of the Royal family. I know the interest which the public feel about her, and although I have not seen so much of her as I could have wished, I take no less interest in her, and the more I do see of her, both in public and private, the greater pleasure it will give me." The whole thing was so civil and gracious, says Greville, that it could hardly be taken ill.

On the same occasion the King expressed an earnest hope that he might live to see the majority of his niece. The wish was granted, but when the day arrived the old man remained at Windsor too ill to take any part in the festivities. His short reign was drawing rapidly to a close.

Though a man of no striking abilities, William was not a bad King, and he enjoyed a fair share of popularity. He was neither afraid nor ashamed to show his face among his subjects, a fact that could hardly be asserted of his brother, George the Fourth. Yet the early years of his reign had been years of political strife and even bloodshed in the very heart of the kingdom, which only the passing of the Reform Bill of 1832 had allayed. At one time the feverish excitement of the people had assumed a serious aspect, and rioting broke out in various parts of the country. At Derby the mob rose and committed numerous outrages, which lasted for three days, and were not put an end to without loss of life and the destruction of much valuable property. In the adjoining county the rioters attacked Nottingham Castle, and in a few hours nothing remained of the noble mansion but the scarred walls. At Beeston a silk mill and several private houses were destroyed; and at Bristol the mob held the city for several hours, causing incalculable damage, and threatening at one time to lay the whole place in ruins. On the passing of the Reform Bill, however, which extended the franchise and empowered many towns hitherto unrepresented to return members to Parliament, quiet ensued, and the Commons were at leisure to give their attention to a measure of far more importance even than the Reform Bill. Need we say that we refer to the Bill which was passed in 1833 for the abolition of slavery? This, indeed, was the monumental

Act of William's reign, and the passing of such a measure would have added lustre to any reign, however glorious. Grand old William Wilberforce, who for many years had been the political leader of the anti-slavery party in England, died in London just as the Bill was passing in Parliament. He "thanked God that he had seen the day in which England was willing to give twenty millions sterling for the abolition of slavery."

But we must return to the Princess, whose life, and not the history of political movements, we are writing. While the Sailor King was lying ill at Windsor, on the bed from which he was never to rise, the bells all over the country were ringing merry peals in honour of the coming of age of the Princess Victoria. Princesses attain their majority at eighteen, and this was the eighteenth birthday of *our* Princess. As early as six o'clock in the morning, the Union Jack was hoisted on the tower of Kensington Church, and above it floated another flag, of pure white silk, which bore upon it in letters of ethereal blue the name VICTORIA. Some minutes later the gates of Kensington Gardens were thrown open, and the public were admitted into the Royal enclosure; the reason being that at seven o'clock a serenade was to be performed under the Palace windows to awaken the Princess. Did she *need* awakening? We venture to think that long before the hour arrived—long before the gates were opened—long even before the flags were hoisted on Kensington Church, the maiden was broad awake; possibly she had not closed her eyes at all the previous night. Our curious minds would like to know whether she was lying in the same room in which, just eighteen years before, she had first opened her eyes upon the light? If so, what thoughts must have crowded upon her mind! In any case, how much she had to think upon!

But the music has begun, thirty-seven vocal and instrumental performers, in full dress, are gathered on the lawn below, and the Princess goes to the window to listen. Her appearance is the signal for an outburst of cheers from the assembled spectators, and the band must leave off till these demonstrations have subsided. How fresh, how calm, how queenly, the Royal maiden looks, as she acknowledges the bursts of welcome! It is a sight to be remembered.

Later in the day, guests, and congratulations, and splendid presents arrive at the Palace, among the latter a grand pianoforte from the King, valued at two hundred guineas. Poor King! he cannot come himself: he is too ill. In the evening there is a grand State ball at St. James's Palace, and for the first time the Princess takes precedence of her mother, occupying the central chair of state. The only shadow upon the day's festivities is the illness of the King.

The days steal on—long days, doubtless, to the suffering monarch on his dying bed at Windsor; sad days to his faithful consort, as she sits beside him, tending him with gentle and unwearying care. In this way nearly a month goes by—then comes the end.

On the 21st of June, 1837, at five o'clock in the morning, two visitors of distinction arrive before the gates of Kensington Palace. They are the Archbishop of Canterbury (Dr. Howley), and the Lord Chamberlain (the Marquis Conyngham). These two dignitaries left Windsor two hours and a-half before, and they have been travelling ever since. Only business of great urgency and importance could bring them to the Palace at such an hour. At first they can get no answer to their summons. They knock, they ring, they thump for a considerable time, before the porter at the gate is roused. At last they are admitted into the courtyard; again to be kept waiting for some minutes. Then another servant appears, who shows them into one of the lower rooms of the Palace; where they are left a second time, and apparently forgotten by everybody.

But matters of State admit of no delay, and they ring the bell—ring it rather impatiently, we may suppose. The servingman who answers them would know their wishes. Their wishes are, that the attendant on the Princess Victoria might inform Her Royal Highness that they desire an audience on business of importance. Upon this there is more delay, and another ringing to inquire the cause. The Princess's attendant presently comes in, and states that her Royal mistress is in such a sweet sleep she cannot venture to disturb her; whereupon the noble Marquis answers, "We are come on business of State to the QUEEN, and even her sleep must give way to that." That is enough. In a few minutes the Royal maiden enters, clad in a loose white nightgown and shawl, her feet in slippers, her nightcap thrown off, and her hair falling upon her shoulders. Tears are in her eyes, but she is perfectly cool and collected.

In a few words the Marquis tells the errand which brings the Archbishop and himself to the Palace, and as soon as he utters the words "Your Majesty," the maiden of eighteen, by a kind of Royal instinct, puts out her hand to him, intimating that he is to kiss hands before proceeding further. The Marquis drops on one knee, kisses her hand, and then goes on to tell her of the late King's death.[*] The Queen next presents her hand to the Archbishop who kisses it in like manner. And now, having done that which was befitting her as Queen, she retires into her womanhood, saying with touching simplicity, "I ask the prayers of your Grace on my behalf." Happy omen! Day has already dawned, and in the earliness and silence of that memorable June morning, Queen and prelate kneel together, and Victoria inaugurates her reign—the noblest reign in human history—with prayer at the footstool of the King of kings.

[*] We have blended in this narrative the familiar account by Miss Wynne, in her *Diary of a Lady of Quality*, and the shorter account by Greville, in the second part of his *Memoirs*, vol. i. 20.

CHAPTER III.

THE KING IS DEAD!—LONG LIVE THE QUEEN!

"THE death of the King of England has everywhere caused the greatest sensation.... Cousin Victoria is said to have shown astonishing self-possession. She undertakes a heavy responsibility, especially at the present moment, when parties are so excited, and all rest their hopes on her." So wrote Prince Albert of Saxe-Coburg, the Queen's future husband, on the 4th of July, 1837; and the words were no exaggeration of the truth.

Greville, than whom none could have been less disposed to record any enthusiastic admiration of royalty, was even more emphatic in his praise than the Prince. Writing of the events of the memorable day of Her Majesty's accession, he said: "The King died at twenty minutes after two yesterday morning, and the young Queen met the Council at Kensington Palace at eleven. Never was anything like the first impression she produced, or the chorus of praise and admiration which is raised about her manner and behaviour, and certainly not without justice. It was very extraordinary, and something far beyond what was looked for. Her extreme youth and inexperience, and the ignorance of the world concerning her, naturally excited intense curiosity to see how she would act on this trying occasion, and there was a considerable assemblage at the Palace, notwithstanding the short notice which was given. The first thing to be done was to teach her her lesson, which, for this purpose, Melbourne (the Prime Minister) had himself

QUEEN'S FIRST COUNCIL, HELD AT KENSINGTON PALACE, 11 A.M., 21st JUNE, 1837.

to learn. . . . She bowed to the lords, took her seat, and then read her speech in a clear, distinct, and audible voice, and without any appearance of fear or embarrassment. She was quite plainly dressed, and in mourning. After she had read her speech, and taken and signed the oath for the security of the Church of Scotland, the Privy Councillors were sworn, the two Royal dukes first by themselves; and as these two old men, her uncles, knelt before her, swearing allegiance and kissing her hand, I saw her blush up to the eyes, as if she felt the contrast between their civil and their natural relations, and this was the only sign of emotion which she evinced. Her manner to them was very graceful and engaging; she kissed them both, and rose from her chair and moved towards the Duke of Sussex, who was farthest from her, and too infirm to reach her. She seemed rather bewildered at the multitude of men who were sworn, and who came, one after another, to kiss her hand, but she did not speak to anybody, nor did she make the slightest difference in her manner, or show any in her countenance, to any individual of any rank, station, or party. I particularly watched her when Melbourne and the Minister, and the Duke of Wellington and Peel approached her. She went through the whole ceremony, occasionally looking at Melbourne for instruction when she had any doubt what to do, which hardly ever occurred, and with perfect calmness and self-possession, but at the same time with a graceful modesty and propriety particularly interesting and ingratiating."*

Our illustration of the Queen's First Council is taken from Sir David Wilkie's celebrated picture, which was painted by command of Her Majesty. In this picture the Lord Mayor (the Right Hon. T. Kelly), and the Attorney-General (Sir J. Campbell), appear among the rest, but according to Greville (who, as Clerk of the Council, must be allowed to know), they had no business to be present. The room had been cleared of all but members of the Council just before Her Majesty entered, but in the bustle and confusion incidental upon opening the doors to some late arrivals, the Crown lawyer

* Greville's *Memoirs*, part i., vol. ii.

and the chief magistrate had smuggled themselves back into the apartment, and thus they were (very improperly), spectators of what passed.*

The day following this Council the Proclamation took place in the Tapestry Room of St. James's Palace. This apartment is lofty, but not of large dimensions; and is fitted up with some gorgeous tapestries, representing the loves of Venus and Mars. The tapestries are of the time of Charles the Second; and had for many a long year lain neglected in a chest, but were placed in their present position on the occasion of the marriage of George the Fourth. Over the carved chimney-piece are some relics of the period of Henry the Eighth, notably the letters H. A. (Henry and Anne Boleyn), united by a true lover's knot. The spectacle of the Proclamation was singularly effective, and made a deep impression on those who were privileged to witness it. In the centre stood the youthful monarch, her eyes suffused with tears; profoundly sensible, we make no doubt, of the immense responsibility of her situation.

Mrs. Browning, queen of poetesses, has drawn for us the central figure of the scene with an essentially womanly touch:—

> "O maiden, heir of kings,
>   A king has left his place;
> The majesty of death has swept
>   All other from his face;
> And thou upon thy mother's breast
>   No longer lean adown,
> But take the glory for the rest,
> And rule the land that loves thee best.
>   The maiden wept;
>   She wept to wear a crown.
>   *   *   *   *
> "God bless thee, weeping Queen,
>   With blessings more Divine,
> And fill with better love than earth
>   That tender heart of thine;
> That when the thrones of earth shall be
>   As low as graves brought down,

* Greville's *Memoirs*, part i., vol. ii.

A pierced hand may give to thee
The crown which angels shout to see.
Thou wilt not weep
To wear that heavenly crown."

It was a trying moment, but there was encouragement for the young Queen in the hearty cheers of her people, which swelled up to her from the Palace courtyard.

The Duchess of Kent stood a little to the right of her daughter, and was observed to watch her with an anxious eye; her heart throbbing with feelings of natural love and pride. The President of the Council supported the Queen on her right hand, and Lord Melbourne on her left; while close behind were most of the members of the Cabinet and other high functionaries of State. In the quadrangle below, opposite the window, a band of household trumpeters and sergeant-at-arms was stationed, whose duty it was to attend the Proclamation of the Sovereign in the various parts of the metropolis; and in front of these were the crowds of densely packed spectators, principally ladies of distinction, who were hardly less demonstrative in their expressions of loyalty than the men.

Silence having been obtained, Clarenceux, King-at-Arms, attended by four pursuivants (Portcullis, Rouge Croix, Blue Mantle and Rouge Dragon) came forward, and made proclamation in the following terms:—

"PROCLAMATION.

"Whereas it hath pleased Almighty God to call to His mercy our late Sovereign Lord, King William the Fourth, of blessed memory, by whose decease the Imperial Crown of the United Kingdom of Great Britain and Ireland is solely and rightfully come to the high and mighty Princess, Alexandrina-Victoria; we, therefore, the Lords Spiritual and Temporal of this Realm, being here assisted with those of his late Majesty's Privy Council; with numbers of other principal gentlemen of quality; with the Lord Mayor, Aldermen, and Citizens of London, do now hereby, with one voice and consent of tongue and heart, publish and proclaim that the high and mighty Princess, Alexandrina-Victoria, is now, by the death of the late Sovereign of happy memory, become our only lawful and rightful liege Lady, Alexandrina-Victoria, by the Grace of God, Queen of Great Britain and Ireland, Defender of the Faith, &c., &c. To whom we acknowledge all faith, and constant obedience, with all humble and hearty affection, beseeching God, by whom Kings and Queens do reign, to bless the Royal Princess, Alexandrina-Victoria, with long and happy years to reign over us.

"GOD SAVE THE QUEEN!

"Given at our Court, at Kensington,
this 20th day of June, in the year
of our Lord, 1839, and in the first
year of our reign." *

Loud cheers again rent the air when the Proclamation had been read, and then the Queen, after repeatedly bowing her acknowledgment, withdrew from the window. With that the trumpeters blew with a will, the band struck up the National Anthem, the Park and Tower guns boomed forth, and shortly afterwards the enthusiastic spectators of the ceremony, having given exhaustive proof of the soundness of their loyal lungs, quietly dispersed.

Just a week after the Proclamation the young Queen received the following manly and sensible letter from Prince Albert:—

"BONN, 26th *June*, 1837.

"MY DEAREST COUSIN,—I must write you a few lines to present you my sincere felicitations on that change which has taken place in your life.

"Now you are Queen of the mightiest land of Europe; in

* *London Interiors*, vol. i. 163.

your hand lies the happiness of millions. May Heaven assist you and strengthen you with its strength in that high but difficult task.

"I hope that your reign may be very long, happy, and glorious, and that your efforts may be rewarded by the thankfulness and love of your subjects.

"May I pray you to think likewise sometimes of your cousins in Bonn, and to continue to them that kindness you favoured them with till now. Be assured that our minds are always with you.

"I will not be indiscreet and abuse your time. Believe me always, your Majesty's most obedient and faithful servant,

"ALBERT." *

Of the numerous deputations which waited upon Her Majesty during the early months of her reign to express their loyalty and good wishes, we cannot here speak particularly. A passing reference may be made, however, to a delegation of the Society of Friends, which was received by the Queen in one of the State apartments of St. James's Palace—the Queen Anne Chamber. The well-known objection of the Friends to uncover their heads in the presence of any but the Divine Majesty, resulted on this occasion in a singular scene. As the members of the deputation filed up the broad staircase, their broad-rimmed hats were respectfully lifted from their heads by two Yeomen of the Guard, stationed for that purpose in convenient places, and were returned to their respective owners when the interview was over. One of the delegates afterwards bore witness that the Queen was "a nice, pleasant young woman, graceful, though a little shy, and on the whole comely." The form of kissing Her Majesty's hand seems to have been submitted to with a cheerfulness that was more than Quakerly, for the good man adds, "I found that act of homage no hardship, I assure thee. It was a fair, soft, delicate little hand."

The favourable impression produced upon all minds by the general demeanour of the young Queen only deepened as the

* *Early Years of the Prince Consort,* 147.

days went by; and those who were the nearest to her person were the most struck by the sterling worth of her character. Melbourne, the Prime Minister, who had a thousand times greater opportunity of knowing what her disposition and what her capacity were than any other person, and who was not a man to be easily captivated or dazzled by superficial accomplishments or mere graces of manner, spoke highly of her sense, discretion, and good feeling; and was particularly impressed by the caution and prudence which she displayed, the former to a degree almost unnatural in one so young. It was remarked that when applications were made to Her Majesty, she seldom or never gave an immediate answer, but would say she would consider it; and it was supposed that she did this because she consulted Melbourne about everything, and waited to have her answer suggested by him. Melbourne, however, informed Greville that such was her habit even with him, and that when he talked to her upon any subject upon which an opinion was expected from her, she told him she would think it over, and let him know her sentiments the next day. *

An instance of the Queen's delicate consideration for the feelings of others, which occurred during the first week of her reign, has been recorded by Greville. "The day she went down to visit the Queen-Dowager at Windsor, to Melbourne's great surprise, she said to him, that as the flag on the Round Tower was half-mast high (a tribute of respect to the late King), and they might perhaps think it necessary to elevate it upon her arrival, it would be better to send orders beforehand not to do so." † The tender, womanly thoughtfulness of this action surely gives evidence of very admirable qualities.

Prior to the visit to Windsor, it had been the young Queen's painful task to write a letter of condolence to the Queen-Dowager, and it was remarked that the letter was addressed, "Her Majesty the Queen." Some one present, who had a right to speak (probably the Duchess of Sutherland or the Baroness Lehzen), observed that this was not correct, and that the letter should be directed, "Her Majesty the Queen-Dowager." "I

---

* Greville's *Memoirs*, part ii., vol. i.   † *Ibid.*

am aware of that," said the girl Queen; "but I will not be the first to remind her of her altered position."

In more than one place in his *Journal*, Greville has alluded to the Queen's prudence with regard to money. This prudence was shown on the occasion of the visit above referred to, when, on a proposal being made to Her Majesty that she should take into her service the late King's band, she declined to incur so great an expense without further consideration. Yet one of the first things she spoke to Melbourne about was the payment of her father's debts, which she was resolved to discharge—and eventually *did* discharge—to the last penny.* Her uncle, George the Fourth, is said to have spent £10,000 a-year for the coats on his back, and was hardly ever out of debt! What a contrast!

Towards the close of the year, the Queen paid a State visit to the city, and dined with the Lord Mayor at the Guildhall. The incidents of the Royal progress have been pleasantly sketched by a recent writer in *The Westminster Budget*.† "It was true Queen's weather on the 9th of November, 1837, albeit somewhat cold and slightly foggy in the earlier hours. The streets, from St. James's Palace to the Guildhall, were lined with police and 12th Royal Lancers. It would doubtless have been wiser to have added a regiment or two of foot soldiers, as the crowd seems to have been somewhat difficult to restrain in its exuberant loyalty. On three or four occasions during the slow journey, which lasted from 1 o'clock to 3.30 P.M., Her Majesty ordered Lord Albermarle, who rode by the side of the Duchess of Sutherland, opposite the Queen, to lower the windows and call upon the police and cavalry 'not to press too hard upon the people.' The young Queen was accompanied by several of her uncles and aunts, and by her mother, the Duchess of Kent, whose carriages, drawn by six horses and escorted by Life Guards and walking grooms, preceded the Sovereign's State coach. Twelve gorgeous footmen, walking in fours, were a few paces in front of the eight cream-coloured steeds drawing the

---

* Greville's *Memoirs*, part ii., vol. i.
† For the 21st of July, 1893.

THE KING IS DEAD!—LONG LIVE THE QUEEN! 59

cumbersome but gorgeous vehicle in which the girl Queen sat with her Master of the Horse and her Mistress of the Robes. Her Majesty wore a silken robe of pink and silver check, with silver sprays. On her head was a tiara of brilliants, and in her right hand she carried a large bouquet of white flowers. Six Royal carriages, each drawn by six horses, contained the great officers of the realm, including Prime Minister Melbourne, and Lords Palmerston, Mulgrave, and John Russell. Grooms, footmen, and yeomen of the guard were at all the wheels. In the Strand the procession was joined by the Duke of Wellington and the Archbishop of Canterbury in their state coaches, and by a large string of judges in their robes, and peers and peeresses, all in gala vehicles, and wearing orders and tiaras. There were two hundred carriages in the procession, which, with escort and attendants, covered a continuous mile and a-half of ground. At Temple Bar, the Lord Mayor and Sheriffs received the Queen, and there his lordship and a brave array of civic dignitaries, all on horseback, took position in front of the Royal carriage. The state vehicles of the municipal dignitaries closed the procession.

SIR MOSES MONTEFIORE.

"Her Majesty changed her dress at Guildhall for a dinner toilette of rich pink satin, with gold and silver ornaments, and a necklace of magnificent pearls round her shapely neck. Upon her head was a diadem of brilliants. She dined at a centre table with the Royal personages only, the Lord Mayor heading a second table, and the retiring Lord Mayor a third. The Queen herself rose and drank to the Lord Mayor, and seemed to thoroughly enjoy herself. The plate on the tables was valued at £400,000, and the chandelier in the Queen's reception-room was composed of 1000 ounces of solid gold." Before dining, the Queen conferred a baronetcy on the Lord Mayor, and knighted the two sheriffs, one of whom was Moses Montefiore, the first Jew ever knighted in England.

In the following year, some three months before the grand coronation ceremony came off, Greville had the honour of dining with the Queen at Buckingham Palace. There was a numerous party, including the Duchess of Kent, the Hanoverian Minister, Baron Münchausan, Earl Grey, and a host of other statesmen and diplomatists. "The dinner was like any other great dinner," says Greville. "After the eating was over, the Queen's health was given by Cavendish, who sat at one end of the table, and everybody got up to drink it. . . . The Queen sat for some time at table, talking away very merrily to her neighbours, and the men remained about a quarter of an hour after the ladies. When we went into the drawing-room, and huddled about the room in the sort of half-shy, half-awkward way people do, the Queen advanced to meet us, and spoke to everybody in succession, and if everybody's 'palaver' was as deeply interesting as mine, it would have been worth while to have had Gurney to take it down in shorthand. The words of kings and queens are precious, but it would be hardly fair to record a Royal after-dinner colloquy. . . . After a few insignificant questions and answers, gracious smile and inclination of head on part of Queen, profound bow on mine, she turned to Lord Grey. Directly after, I was (to my satisfaction), deposited at the whist table to make up the Duchess of Kent's party, and all the rest of the company were arranged about a large round table (the Queen on the sofa by it), where they passed about an hour and a-half in what was probably the smallest possible talk, interrupted and enlivened, however, by some songs which Lord Ossulston sang. . . . She (the Queen) is very civil to everybody, and there is more of frankness, cordiality, and good humour in her manner than of dignity. She looks and speaks cheerfully; there was nothing to criticise, nothing particularly to admire. The whole thing seemed to be dull, perhaps unavoidably so, but still so dull that it is a marvel how anybody can like such a life."*

* Greville's *Memoirs*, part ii., vol. i.

This dinner took place in March, and early in the next month there was a magnificent ball at the Palace, at which the Queen more than justified those high opinions which had been formed of her. "Her manner and bearing," says Greville, "were perfect." Among the guests was Prince Esterhazy, son of the Austrian Ambassador, better remembered for the lustre of his diamonds than the brilliancy of his attainments or the worth of his moral character. He danced with the Queen, and was afterwards present at her coronation, where his jewels created quite a stir. Her Majesty danced three dances, and seems to have been in high spirits. The simplicity and good humour which characterised her conversation, and the mingled grace and cordiality of her manners, are said to have been very captivating.

And now London began to grow busy with preparations for the Coronation. The Court tailors and dressmakers had long been hard at work; the jewellers in the west end of London were doing a great trade; the Royal cooks and confectioners stooped early and late over their culinary labours. Out of doors, carpenters were preparing all manner of wooden erections for the display of flags and bunting, and the accommodation of eager sightseers. Tickets, admitting the fortunate holders to window-sittings in houses past which the procession was to go, were selling for fabulous prices,* and business was almost at a standstill by reason of the congested state of the traffic. From one end of the route of the Royal procession to the other—*i.e.*, from the top of Piccadilly to Westminster Abbey, stretched a vast line of scaffolding, with accommodation for tens of thousands of spectators, yet all the seats were taken days before the great day arrived.

On the 27th of June (the Coronation took place on the 28th), London presented a sight such as it had seldom presented before.. "There never was anything seen like this town," wrote Greville, "it is as if the population had been on a sudden quintupled; the uproar, the confusion, the crowd, the noise, are

---

* The Chancellor of the Exchequer told Greville that £200,000 were paid for seats alone. Greville's *Memoirs*, part ii., vol. i. 108.

indescribable. Horsemen, footmen, carriages squeezed, jammed, intermingled; the pavement blocked up with timbers, hammering and knocking, and falling fragments stunning the ears and threatening the head; not a mob here and there, but the town all mob, thronging, bustling, gaping, and gazing at everything, at anything, or at nothing; the park one vast encampment, with banners floating on the tops of the tents, and still the roads are covered, the railroads loaded with arriving multitudes."*

All this was something to be written about and remembered, something to be talked of on firelight evenings years hence; but the event of which it was but the precursor, the event to which all the preparations, all the influx of people, all the unwonted excitement tended—*that* had yet to come.

The memorable day arrives. Before four o'clock on Thursday morning, the 28th of June, 1838, all London is awake. At seventeen minutes past three a Royal salute of twenty-three guns announces that the sun is rising upon the joyous day, and already eager multitudes are hurrying in the direction of the parks and of Westminster Abbey. But the loyal crowds have many hours to wait. At six o'clock the police appear and begin to clear a way for the procession. Two hours later most of the military who are to take part in the grand pageant—some squadrons of Life Guards, a troop of Lancers, and a company of Light Infantry—assemble on the parade opposite Buckingham Palace, where the uncrowned Queen is getting ready for the great occasion. Then the carriages which are to compose the cavalcade begin to appear; those of the Foreign Ambassador ranging in the south walk, and the Royal carriages in the north walk of the Mall. At ten o'clock the procession begins to move. Up to this time the day had been lowering, and it has seemed doubtful whether sunshine or rain will prevail, but just as the band of the Life Guards strikes up the National Anthem, and the Queen's coach begins to move, the sun shines out, nor hides his face again till the procession is over. At the same moment, two sailors, mounted on one of the triumphal arches,

* Greville's *Memoirs*, part ii., vol. i.

THE QUEEN TAKING OATH TO MAINTAIN THE PROTESTANT FAITH.
From the painting by Sir GEORGE HAYTER.   By permission of Messrs. H. GRAVES & Co.

run up the Royal Standard with a ringing cheer, which is instantly responded to by the multitude in a shout that swells on from the Palace to the Abbey. Marshal Soult, one of Napoleon's great generals, who appears in a cobalt-coloured equipage relieved with gold, gets an enthusiastic reception, which he acknowledges by repeated bows. Wellington and all the members of the Royal Family are also heartily received, particularly the Duchess of Kent, whose carriage is drawn by six horses and escorted by a body of Life Guards. The Queen's carriages, of which there are no less than thirteen, come last of all, save that a squadron of Life Guards closes the procession. The State coach which conveys Her Majesty is drawn by eight cream-coloured ponies, and is attended by a Yeoman of the Guard at each wheel, and two footmen at each door. Gold Stick (Viscount Combermere) and the captain of the Yeomen of the Guard (the Earl of Ilchester), ride on either side, each attended by two grooms. The occupants of the coach, beside the Queen, are the Mistress of the Robes (the Duchess of Sutherland), the Master of the Horse (Lord Albemarle), and the Captain-General of the Royal Archers (the Duke of Buccleuch).

Needless to say, the loudest, longest, heartiest welcome was reserved for Her Majesty. Words are powerless to describe the enthusiasm that her presence evoked.

> "Such a noise arose
> As shrouds at sea in the stiff tempest make,
> As loud, and to as many tunes ; hats, cloaks,
> (Jackets 'twas said) flew up, and had their faces
> Been loose this day, they had been lost."

The Queen acknowledged these demonstrations of loyalty by bowing repeatedly. It was all she could do, but the tumult of her feeling during this hurricane of welcome, who shall adequately describe?

Her Majesty's appearance in the Abbey, where some fifteen hundred specially privileged spectators were assembled, was the signal for another tremendous ovation. The vast audience simultaneously arose, and a shout "loud as from numbers without numbers," rang through the venerable arches of the Abbey, and was re-echoed by the multitude outside. The cheering was renewed as the Queen entered the choir, and took her seat in the Recognition Chair, nor did it cease till the opening of the Coronation anthem.

When this had been sung, the Queen rose to her feet, and the Archbishop of Canterbury coming towards her, and turning to the east side of the theatre, made the Recognition thus:—

"SIRS,—I here present unto you Queen Victoria, the undoubted Queen of this realm; wherefore, all you who are come this day to do your homage, are you willing to do the same?"

CROWN JEWELS.

These words he repeated at the south, west, and north sides of the theatre, Her Majesty turning with each reception to the part of the audience addressed, when loud and repeated cries of "God save Queen Victoria!" testified how willingly that homage was rendered.

After the Recognition, the Queen's "First Offering," an altar-cloth of gold, and an ingot of the precious metal weighing one pound, were placed by the Archbishop—the one on the altar, and the other in the oblation basin. Then the Litany was read by the Bishops of Worcester and St. Davids, and the choir having sung the Sanctus, the communion service was read by the Archbishop of Canterbury—or rather *begun* by his Grace, for the Bishop of Rochester read the epistle, and the Bishop of

Carlisle the Gospel. The Bishop of London then preached a sermon—"a very good sermon," says Greville—and when that was at an end the ceremony of administering the Oath was gone through. For this purpose the Queen left her chair, and approached the altar; and there, kneeling upon the cushion on the altar steps, and laying her right hand upon the Holy Gospels, she took the Coronation Oath, afterwards kissing the Book, and setting her Royal Sign manual to a transcript of the Oath, which the Lord Chamberlain held for that purpose in a silver standish. The form of words during this part of the ceremony was extremely impressive.

"Madam," said the Archbishop, advancing towards the Queen, "is your Majesty willing to take the Oath?"

"I am willing."

"Will you solemnly promise and swear to govern the people of this United Kingdom of Great Britain and Ireland, and the dominions thereto belonging, according to the statutes in Parliament agreed on, and the respective laws and customs of the same?"

The Queen answered in an audible voice, "I solemnly promise so to do."

"Will you, to your power, cause law and justice, in mercy, to be executed in all your judgments?"

"I will."

Then said the Archbishop: "Will you, to the utmost of your power, maintain the laws of God, the true profession of the Gospel, and the Protestant reformed religion established by law? And will you maintain and preserve inviolably the settlement of the united Church of England and Ireland, and the doctrine, worship, discipline and government thereof, as by law established within England and Ireland, and the territories thereunto belonging? And will you preserve unto the bishops and clergy of England and Ireland, and to the Churches there committed to their charge, all such rights and privileges as by law do or shall appertain to them or any of them?"

In a clear and steady voice the Queen replied, "All this I promise to do."

Anon came the Anointing, which took place in St. Edward's Chapel, and now the Queen took her seat for the first time in the Coronation Chair. As a preliminary to this, the Royal robe of crimson velvet which she was wearing was removed, an anthem being sung by the choir while the disrobing was in progress. Upon taking her seat, a rich cloth of gold was held over her head by four Knights of the Garter, two of whom were Dukes, and two Marquises; and then the Archbishop took the anointing spoon, previously filled from the ampulla, and anointed

THE CORONATION CHAIR.

Her Majesty on the head and hands in the form of a cross, uttering at the same time a form of words. A prayer followed, the Queen kneeling at her faldstool; and then the Regalia—the most important apparatus of the Coronation — came into prominence.

The procession and presentation of these symbolical articles were among the most interesting and singular features of the long ceremony. Each of the twelve precious emblems had a separate custodian, of whom seven were dukes, three bishops, and the rest nobles of important rank—the Prime Minister among the rest. The procession had taken place at an early stage of the proceedings, but the presentation of the Regalia to Her Majesty was reserved for now. It followed fitly upon the Anointing. No article was omitted. St. Edward's Staff—the Spurs—the Sceptre with the Cross—the Pointed Swords of Temporal and Spiritual Justice—the Pointless Sword of Mercy—the Sword of State—the Sceptre with the Dove—the Orb—St. Edward's Crown—the Patina—the Chalice—and the Bible—all were presented in turn; and then, after being placed in the Queen's right hand by the Lord Chamberlain or the Archbishop, according as the articles in question had a civil or a religious significance, they were, with one or two exceptions, deposited on the altar. Just after the Sword of Mercy had been thus presented the Queen arose, and was invested by the Dean of Westminster (or, rather, by Lord John Thynne, officiating for the Dean) with the Imperial mantle, or dalmatic robe of cloth of gold, the Lord Great Chamberlain fastening the clasps. According to Greville, there was not a little confusion during this part of the ceremony, and but for Lord Thynne and the Archbishop, who had prepared themselves by a little previous rehearsal, there might have been a serious hitch. He informs us that they made the Queen leave the Recognition Chair and enter into St. Edward's Chapel before the prayers were concluded, much to the discomfiture of the Archbishop. "She said to John Thynne, 'Pray tell me what I am to do, for they don't know'; and at the end, when the Orb was put into her hand, she said to him, 'What am I to do with it?' 'Your Majesty is to carry it, if you please, in your hand.' 'Am I?' she said; 'it is very heavy.'" *

At the fitting on of the ruby Coronation Ring there was another difficulty. The ring "was made for her little finger instead of the fourth, on which the rubric prescribes that it should be put. When the Archbishop was to put it on, she extended the former, but he said it must be on the latter. She said it was too small, and she could not get it on. He said it was right to put it there, and, as he insisted, she yielded, but

* Greville's *Memoirs*, part ii., vol. i. 107.

had first to take off her other rings, and then this was forced on; but it hurt her very much, and as soon as the ceremony was over she was obliged to bathe her finger in iced water in order to get it off." *

The Crowning, which followed closely upon the ceremony of the Ring, formed the culminating scene of all, if, indeed, we except the Enthronement. The cheering and cries of "God save the Queen," which arose from all parts of the Abbey as the Archbishop placed the Crown upon the fair young head, stirred even the pulses of the apathetic Miss Martineau. The acclamation, she says, "was very animating; and in the midst of it—in an instant of time the Peeresses were all coroneted"—all but "one beautiful creature, with transcendent complexion and form," the large braids of whose light hair would in no way permit the coronet to keep on. Meanwhile, the signal had been given outside the Abbey: the trumpets sounded, the drums began to beat, and the Tower and Park guns fired a Royal salute.

"The minster was alight that day, but not with fire, I ween,
And long-drawn glitterings swept adown that mighty aisled scene.
The priests stood stoled in their pomp, the sworded chiefs in theirs,
And so, the collared knights,—and so, the civil ministers,—
And so, the waiting lords and dames—and little pages, best
At holding trains—and legates so, from countries east and west—
So, alien princes, native peers, and high-born ladies bright,
Along whose brows the Queen's, new crowned, flashed coronets to light,—
And so, the people at the gates, with priestly hands on high,
Which bring the first anointing to all legal majesty.
And so, the Dead—who lie in rows beneath the minster floor,
There, verily an awful state maintaining evermore—

   * * * * *

And when, betwixt the quick and dead, the young fair Queen had vowed,
The living shouted, 'May she live! Victoria, live!' aloud—
And as the loyal shouts went up, true spirits prayed between,
'The blessing happy monarchs have, be thine, O crownèd Queen!'" †

* Greville's *Memoirs*, part ii., vol. i. 107.
† Mrs. Browning.

A few moments later Her Majesty removed to the Recognition Chair, on the south-east side of the Throne, the choir singing the *Te Deum*. Then, amid renewed expressions of enthusiasm from her people, she was led up to the Throne, where she took her seat, and the nobles who had borne the Regalia grouped themselves around their Queen. The Archbishop then knelt before Her Majesty, and for himself and the other Lords Spiritual pronounced the words of homage, they kneeling around him and repeating the words after him. The Lords Temporal next went through the same form, headed by the two Princes of the Blood Royal, the Dukes of Sussex and Cambridge, Her Majesty's uncles. The former was suffering from indisposition at the time, and as he was ascending the steps of the Throne, feebly and with great difficulty, the Queen, yielding to the impulse of natural affection, flung her fair arms about his neck and tenderly embraced him. The Duke was so overcome by this genuine display of feeling that he was quite unable to repress his emotion.

"The homage," says Miss Martineau, "was as pretty a sight as any: trains of Peers touching her crown and then kissing her hand. It was in the midst of that process that poor Lord Rolle's disaster sent a shock through the whole assemblage. It turned me very sick. The large, infirm old man was held up by two Peers, and had nearly reached the Royal footstool when he slipped through the hands of his supporters, and rolled over and over down the steps, lying at the bottom coiled up in his robes. He was instantly lifted up, and he tried again and again, amidst shouts of admiration of his valour. The Queen at length spoke to Lord Melbourne, who stood at her shoulder, and he bowed approval; on which she rose, leaned forward, and held out her hand to the old man, dispensing with his touching the crown. He was not hurt, and his self-quizzing on his misadventure was as brave as his behaviour at the time. A foreigner in London gravely reported to his own countrymen, what he entirely believed on the word of a wag, that the Lords Rolle held their title on the condition of performing the feat at every coronation."

An anthem followed, and then the Bishops of Carlisle and Rochester received from the altar, by the hands of the Arch-

HER MAJESTY RECEIVING THE SACRAMENT AFTER THE CORONATION IN WESTMINSTER ABBEY, JUNE 28, 1838.

bishop, the patina and chalice, which they carried into St. Edward's Chapel, and brought from thence the sacramental bread upon the patina and the wine in the chalice. Her Majesty next went to the altar, and laying aside her crown, knelt down. Then the Bishops delivered the patina and chalice into the Queen's hands; and when she had partaken of the bread and wine she handed the vessels to the Archbishop, who replaced them upon the altar. After placing her "Second Offering," a purse of gold, in the hands of the Primate, she resumed her crown and once more ascended her Throne of State. This was practically the end of the ceremony, which had lasted upwards of three hours; and between three and four o'clock Her Majesty left the Abbey and returned to the Palace with the same state as had attended her setting forth in the morning.

It was a day long to be remembered—a day that we shall probably never see the like of again—at least, in this century. "Many, very many," wrote Lord Shaftesbury (then Lord Ashley) in his diary, "were impressed. The crowds were immense, perhaps half-a-million people assembled in admiring affection and loyalty to witness the Royal procession. Both during the day and night such order and good-humour were observed as would have done honour to a private family. Even the fair Hyde Park has been quiet, decent, respectful, and safe. What a nation is this! What materials for happiness and power! What seeds of honour to God and service to man!"

"What a nation!" Ay, and what a Queen! How well she had sustained the burden of her honours throughout this long and trying day! How royally and yet with what delicate womanliness had she comported herself from first to last! "Poor little Queen!" Thomas Carlyle said of her about this time, "she is at an age at which a girl can hardly be trusted to choose a bonnet for herself, yet a task is laid upon her from which an archangel might shrink." So it was; yet this day, when the "poor little Queen" had been upon her trial, as it were, she had surpassed all expectations. Even Greville—most unenthusiastic of men—could not withhold his praise. Referring to the homage scene and Lord Rolle's misadventure he wrote:

"The Queen's first impulse was to rise, and when afterwards he came again to do homage she said, 'May I not get up and meet him?' and then rose from the throne and advanced down one or two steps to prevent his coming up, an act of graciousness and kindness which made a great sensation. It is, in fact, the remarkable union of *naïveté*, kindness, nature, good nature, with propriety and dignity, which makes her so admirable and so endearing to those about her, as she certainly is. I have been repeatedly told that they are all warmly attached to her, but that all feel the impossibility of for a moment losing sight of the respect which they owe her. She never ceases to be a Queen, but is always the most charming, cheerful, obliging, unaffected, Queen in the world." * This was high praise to fall from the lips of a shrewd, level-headed man-of-the-world like Greville, particularly as its object was a maiden of nineteen. Yet the praise was just, and posterity has feelingly endorsed it.

* Greville's *Memoirs*, part ii., vol. i. 108. In our account of the Coronation ceremony we have followed chiefly the *Annual Register* and the *Sun* for the 28th of June, 1838, incorporating facts from Miss Martineau, Greville, and others.

CHAPTER IV.

THE MAIDEN QUEEN.

VICTORIA was now Queen indeed—the Coronation Day was over and past—and the great city which had witnessed the crowning of its fair young Sovereign relapsed into its wonted seriousness and calm. Let us take advantage of the lull by glancing briefly at the state of the country over which the maiden of nineteen had been called to rule. The conditions of life at the time of the Queen's accession were very different from what they are now. The Victorian Era it must be remembered has been an era of change and an era of progress, challenging comparison, in this respect, with any of the great eras of the past, and the social life of sixty years ago bears no more resemblance to the social life of to-day than it does to the days of Anne or William of Orange. When Her Majesty came to the throne, railways and steam navigation were practically unknown; to-day, over one thousand million pounds are invested in the railways of the British Empire; and the amount invested in merchant steamers sailing under the British flag may be imagined when it is stated that the number of such vessels, from 100 tons *gross* and upwards, exceeds six thousand. On the day of the Queen's accession Sir Edwin Arnold saw lucifer matches sold in the streets as curiosities at a halfpenny each; they may now be bought anywhere at three-halfpence a dozen boxes! Our shipping is seven times as great as it was sixty years ago, and our foreign trade has quadrupled itself. In 1837 the public grants for schooling were £200,000; they have risen to more than four millions. In that day, sanitary science (which has since become so fruitful of good) had made but little headway; philanthropic work was as yet undeveloped, the children of the poor were fearfully neglected; and, not least among the many ills, negative and positive, trade was in a wretched condition. Statesmen were trying hard to shut their eyes to this latter fact; but the newspapers would not, and probably *could* not had they wished. In June, 1837, *The Manchester Courier* was lamenting this depression and the consequent scarcity of employment and low wages for the operatives, among whom distress prevailed to a deplorable extent. In the summer of the same year *The Morning Chronicle* affirmed that at Manchester there were 50,000 hands out of employ, and that most of the large establishments were working only half-time. At Wigan, 4000 weavers were totally unable to get work; and persons whose opinions could be relied upon, declared that half-a-million hands, at least, would be idle in the manufacturing districts in the very worst time of the year. The effects of the depression were even felt as far north as the Firth of Tay, and *The Fifeshire Journal* contained the gloomy confession, that "the pressure upon manufactures and commerce has at length reached our county."

Nevertheless, the new reign did not belie the favourable prognostics which the more optimistic had dared to utter concerning it, and so early as July, 1837, a hopeful Edinburgh reviewer wrote: "The new reign is beginning well. The temporary clouds, lately impending over us, have been lifted up as on its approach. It is scarcely two months since the farmer was threatened with a second 1816—the merchant with another 1825. Providentially the cornfields and Mark Lane agree in the brightness of our actual prospects. The political spectres which, for the last six years, have been stalking and gibbering in our streets, have also disappeared. During all that period we could hear nothing but one everlasting cry of 'Wolf.' The horrors of the French Revolution were daily knocking at our doors. At present, not only has the revolutionary alarm subsided, but most persons admit that history presents few national spectacles more encouraging than the manliness and moderation which marked the conduct of the English people throughout this stirring crisis; their honest consciousness of the rectitude of their purpose, and their just reliance on the stability of the institutions which they loved. With what vigour did they shift the helm and put about when they saw that the vessel of the State was almost on the breakers! How instinctively, as it were, did the good ship seem to right itself, in spite of mutineers aboard! And ever since, how steady and gallant has been its bearing over the open sea, the proof of adverse winds from opposite quarters of the heavens only serving to keep it true to its determined course."

Among these "adverse winds" which seemed to threaten at times the safety of the "vessel of State," one of the most threatening was the agitation arising out of the Chartist movement. The Chartists were so called because they drew up what they termed the People's Charter, in which they demanded universal suffrage, vote by ballot, annual parliaments, and other measures of reform—real or supposed. Some of the demagogues soon began to talk about resorting to physical force for the accomplishment of their objects, and torch-light meetings of an alarming character spread dismay on all sides. At Birmingham and Sheffield fearful riots broke out; robbery walked the streets; malcontents sought the lives of employers; and for many days both towns were in a state of uproar and confusion. At Newport, Monmouthshire, a traitorous magistrate, named Frost, put himself at the head of seven thousand rioters, and forced a conflict with the military; an act of frenzied boldness which resulted in the loss of twenty lives.

Meanwhile, however, the good of the people, and the prosperity of the country, were being promoted in other places and in less equivocal ways. In the autumn of 1838, the Anti-Corn Law Association was formed at Manchester, and the agitation which was to effect eventually the repeal of these iniquitous laws and to give to the poor an untaxed loaf, was fairly begun. It was not till 1846, however, when famine forced the hands of the then premier, Sir Robert Peel, that the tax was removed.

The League, having accomplished its work, was dissolved soon after.

Nor was this the only way in which the public good was being advanced. While the Anti-Corn Law agitation was still in its infancy, indeed, before the League itself was formed, a great impetus was given to the Temperance movement by the anti-drink crusade of the Franciscan friar, Father Mathew. This noble-minded man was a native of Tipperary, and had already won his way to the hearts of the people by the great zeal and self-sacrifice which he had shown at the outbreak of the Asiatic cholera in 1832. To enlist the energies of such a man in the cause of temperance was an object worth trying for, and he was earnestly pressed to join the movement. At last he consented; and having signed the pledge on the 10th of April, 1838, no time was lost in setting forth upon his first mission. From that moment he became the moral apostle of Ireland, and the fame of his eloquence and energy spread rapidly through the country. Thousands upon thousands rushed to sign the pledge. At Limerick a scene of indescribable excitement was presented; "at Parsonstown a military force was necessary to keep order about the chapel in which the apostle of temperance was preaching. At Nenagh, twenty thousand persons are said to have become teetotallers in one day; one hundred thousand in Galway in two days; in Loughrea, eighty thousand in two days; between that and Portumna, from one hundred and eighty thousand to two hundred thousand; and in Dublin about seventy thousand in five days." The work of Father Mathew may to some extent be estimated by the fact that whereas in the year 1837 the quantity of spirits distilled in Ireland was 11,235,635, gallons, on which a duty was paid of £1,310,824, the quantity distilled in 1841 (only four years later) was less than six-and-a-half millions, and the duty £864,726. The influence of the man was almost unbounded, and more than two million persons are said to have entirely altered their habits, as the result of his successive crusades.*

* See Ward's *Reign of Victoria*, vol. ii. 551, 552; and *Imperial Dictionary of Biography*, art. *Mathew*.

It will thus be seen that if, in one part of the United Kingdom, the social outlook at the beginning of the Queen's reign was rather gloomy, there were movements of a new and splendid order in *other* parts, in which were stimulating promises for the future.

From the young Queen, too, as we have seen, great things might be expected; and promise turned to performance as time went on. The regal and the womanly, so finely blended in her character, were often asserted in a manner to command the highest praise. She was a Queen, every inch of her; and yet, at the same time, one of the kindest and most considerate of her sex. We have an early instance of her queenliness in her dignified answer to Melbourne, when that nobleman on one occasion, having put before her a paper to sign, began to urge the *expediency* of the measure: "I have been taught, my Lord, to judge between what is right and what is wrong," she said, "but expediency is a word I neither wish to hear nor to understand." In a similar way, the touching incident of the death-warrant, recorded by Miss Greenwood, illustrates her essential womanliness. A court-martial death-warrant—the condemned person, a private who had deserted three times— was presented by the Duke of Wellington to receive Her Majesty's signature. "She shrank from the dreadful task, and with tears in her eyes, asked, 'Have you nothing to say on behalf of this man?'

"'Nothing; he has deserted three times!' replied the Iron Duke.

"'Oh, your Grace, think again!'

"'Well, your Majesty, he certainly is a bad soldier, but there was somebody who spoke as to his good character. He may be a good fellow in private life.'

"'Oh, thank you!' exclaimed the Queen, as she dashed off the word 'pardoned' on the awful parchment, and wrote beneath it her beautiful signature."

The signing of death-warrants, by-the-way, is now performed by Royal Commission, "to relieve Her Majesty," as they tell us, "of a painful duty"; but, the fact is, if we may whisper a little secret, the Queen's tender heart is not to be trusted in such an awful business.

Another interesting trait in the character of the Maiden Queen was her respect for the Lord's Day. This was shown on two or three occasions. One of her first acts was to refuse to examine on a Sunday some State papers which Melbourne had brought for her inspection. The papers were of importance, and the Premier having arrived too late on the Saturday night for the Queen to go into them then, requested that she would give them her attention on the following morning.

"To-morrow is Sunday, my Lord," replied the Queen.

"But business of State, please your Majesty," urged the Premier.

"Must be attended to, I know," answered the Queen, "and as, of course, you could not get down earlier to-night, I will, if these papers are of such vital importance, attend to them after we come from church to-morrow morning."

To-morrow morning came, and the Queen and her Court ladies went to church. The noble Viscount went too. The sermon that morning was on the obligations of the Christian Sabbath, and the statesman was taken rather by surprise. At the conclusion of the service the Queen asked him how he had liked the sermon.

"Very much, your Majesty," he replied.

"I cannot conceal from you," returned the Queen, "that last night I sent the clergyman the text from which he was to preach. I hope we shall all be the better for his words."

The day passed without a word or whisper of the papers, but at night, as the Queen was about to withdraw, she said, "To-morrow morning, my Lord, at any hour you please we will go into those papers—at seven o'clock, if you like." The urgency of the matter had, however, strangely abated, and his Lordship replied that nine o'clock would be quite early enough.

To cite another instance. It came to Her Majesty's knowledge, through the Bishop of London, that two Wesleyans belonging to the Royal band had been summarily dismissed for refusing to attend at Sunday rehearsals. Sending for the leader, the Queen inquired what had become of the two bandsmen; and on being informed that their "absurd religious scruples" were the cause of their dismissal, she commanded that they should be at once reinstated, adding, with a dignity and emphasis worthy of the occasion, "I will have no more persecution in my service for conscience' sake, and I will have no more rehearsals on Sundays."

Her Majesty's quickness of wit, of which we have already given some examples, was curiously illustrated about this time in connection with a sermon preached before her by Dean Hook, a clergyman of extreme High Church principles. In the course of his homily the Dean "told the Queen that the Church would endure let what would happen to the Throne. On her return to Buckingham House, Lord Normanby, who had been at the chapel, said to her, 'Did not your Majesty find it very hot?' She said, 'Yes, and the sermon was very hot too.'"*

In the month of this very hot sermon (July, 1838), the Maiden Queen went in person to the House of Lords to prorogue Parliament. She drove thither in state, her carriage being drawn by the cream-coloured ponies which had been used in the Coronation procession, and she must have looked very grand in her Parliamentary robes, which consisted of a surcoat, mantle, and hood of crimson velvet, furred with ermine, and bordered with gold lace. The speech from the throne, which she stood up to read, was finely delivered, and the youthfulness and grace of her person were again the subjects of loyal admiration. "The serene serious sweetness of her candid brow and clear soft eyes," says Fanny Kemble, the actress, who was present, "gave dignity to the girlish countenance, while the want of height only added to the effect of extreme youth of the round but slender person, and gracefully moulded hands and arms. The Queen's voice was exquisite, nor have I ever heard any spoken words more musical in their gentle distinctions than 'My Lords and Gentlemen,' which broke the breathless silence of the illustrious assembly, whose gaze was riveted on that fair flower of royalty. The enunciation was as perfect as the intonation

* Greville's *Memoirs*, part ii., vol. i.

was melodious, and I think it is impossible to hear a more excellent utterance than that of the Queen's English by the English Queen."

In the November of the previous year Her Majesty had *opened* Parliament in person, when the question of her income had been discussed and settled. £385,000 a-year was the sum voted in both Houses to support the dignity of the first lady in the land, and the allowance cannot be said to be illiberal. Twelve years previously Her Majesty had had to defer the purchase of a half-crown box through lack of funds!

At the time of which we have been speaking (July, 1838), Kensington Palace had been given up for some months, and the Queen now resided either at Buckingham Palace or Windsor Castle. While staying at the former she often went riding in the Park or Row, to the great delight of her subjects, whose enthusiasm had by no means died out now that the Coronation was over; and the ease and grace of her carriage were highly spoken of. Her skill as a horsewoman was not less admirable than her other accomplishments, and reflected great credit on her former riding-master, Fozard, a well-known professor in his day. The Queen had shown her consideration for him when she came to the Throne by appointing him her Royal stirrup-holder.

The Court life of the Maiden Queen, though marked by none of the extravagances of preceding reigns, gave evidence of the youthfulness of her heart and of that love of innocent gaiety which is one of the charms of girlhood. In the evenings, there were always music and singing, and not infrequently small dances, in which the Ladies-in-waiting took part. On one of these occasions the dance was kept up till dawn, and the quadrangle being then open to the east, the young Queen went out on the roof of the portico to see the sun rise, and a lovely sight it was. The great orb of light was rising behind St. Paul's, which could be distinctly seen, and Westminster Abbey and the trees in the Green Park stood out against a golden sky, beside which the myriad lights of the Palace looked dim indeed. Miss Liddell, (afterwards Lady Bloomfield) who about this time was appointed to wait upon Her Majesty, tells the following amusing story. "One day the Queen expressed a desire to hear me sing, so, in fear and trembling, I sang one of Grisi's famous airs, but omitted a shake at the end. The Queen's quick ear immediately detected the omission, and, smiling, Her Majesty said, 'Does not your sister shake, Lady Normanby?' My sister immediately answered, 'Oh yes, ma'am, she is shaking all over.' The Queen, much amused, laughed heartily at the joke."[*]

Of the Windsor life of the Maiden Queen we have a graphic picture from Greville's ready pen. "The life which the Queen leads is this: She gets up soon after eight o'clock, breakfasts in her own room, and is employed the whole morning in transacting business; she reads all the despatches, and has every matter of interest and importance in every department laid before her. At eleven or twelve Melbourne comes to her and stays an hour, more or less, according to the business he may have to transact. At two she rides with a large suite (and she likes to have it numerous); Melbourne always rides on her left hand, and the equerry-in-waiting generally on her right; she rides for two hours along the road, and the greater part of the time at a full gallop; after riding she amuses herself for the rest of the afternoon with music and singing, playing, romping with children, if there are any in the Castle (and she is so fond of them that she generally contrives to have some there), or in any other way she fancies. The hour of dinner is nominally half-past seven o'clock, soon after which time the guests assemble, but she seldom appears till near eight. The lord-in-waiting comes into the drawing-room and instructs each gentleman which lady he is to take in to dinner. When the guests are all assembled the Queen comes in, preceded by the gentlemen of her household, and followed by the Duchess of Kent and all her ladies; she speaks to each lady, bows to the men, and goes immediately into the dining-room. . . . Melbourne invariably sits on her left, no matter who may be there; she remains at table the usual time,

[*] *Reminiscences of Court and Diplomatic Life*, vol. i. 19, 20.

but does not suffer the men to sit long after her, and we were summoned to coffee in less than half-an-hour. In the drawing-room she never sits down till the men make their appearance. Coffee is served to them in the adjoining room, and then they go into the drawing-room, when she goes round and says a few words to each, of the most trivial nature, all, however, very civil and cordial in manner and expression. When this little ceremony is over, the Duchess of Kent's whist table is arranged, and then the round table is marshalled, Melbourne invariably sitting on the left hand of the Queen, and remaining there without moving till the evening is at an end. At about half-past eleven she goes to bed, or whenever the Duchess has played her usual number of rubbers, and the band have performed all the pieces on their list for the night. This is the whole history of her day; she orders and regulates every detail herself, she knows where everybody is lodged in the Castle, settles about the riding or driving, and enters into every particular with minute attention. But while she personally gives her orders to her various attendants, and does everything that is civil to all the inmates of the Castle, she really has nothing to do with anybody but Melbourne, and with him she passes (if not in *tête-à-tête*, yet in intimate communication) more hours than any two people, in any relation of life, perhaps ever do pass together besides. He is at her side for at least six hours every day—an hour in the morning, two on horseback, one at dinner, and two in the evening. This monopoly is certainly not judicious; it is not altogether consistent with social usage, and it leads to an infraction of those rules of etiquette which it is better to observe with regularity at Court."* Poor little Queen! we say again with Carlyle. What keen cold eyes are watching her!

Her attachment to Melbourne is, however, quite understandable. Ruler of a vast empire though she was, Victoria was still a woman, and women need, and ever will need, the

* Greville's *Memoirs*, part ii., vol. i. 146-148.

counsel of the stronger sex. Melbourne himself said to her the following year, when she told him of her contemplated marriage, " You will be much more comfortable ; for a woman cannot stand alone for any time, in whatever position she may be." Firmness, patience, caution, courage, resolution—all these she had, but she was weak woman still, and it was but natural that she should lean upon her chief Minister, and seek to keep him near her person. Far from endorsing the hard cavils of Greville, therefore, we heartily approve the Queen's conduct, and agree with the Duke of Wellington that Melbourne was quite right to go and stay at the Castle as he did, and that it was very fit he should instruct her in the business of government.

Not that Melbourne's counsel was always of the wisest, however. On one occasion his advice to the Queen was most unstatesmanly, and became the cause of much angry party feeling. In May, 1839, the Whig ministry, of which he was the head, tendered their resignation, and Sir Robert Peel was asked to form a new ministry. The Tory statesman was willing to do this, and no difficulty presented itself in the construction of a Cabinet until Sir Robert, guided by constitutional precedent, asked for a change of persons in the posts of the Ladies of the Bedchamber. These posts the Whig Ministers under Melbourne had entirely filled with their nearest relations, and Sir Robert could hardly be blamed for demanding their dismissal. The Queen refused to yield the point, however, and, acting under the advice of Melbourne, addressed the following note to the Tory baronet :—" The Queen, having considered the proposal made to her yesterday by Sir Robert Peel, to remove the Ladies of the Bedchamber, cannot consent to adopt a course which she conceives to be contrary to usage, and which is repugnant to her feelings." The Queen's conduct in the matter had a certain queenliness about it, but there was more of simple womanliness, and Melbourne had given her very ill advice. Peel called upon Her Majesty and tried to persuade her to change her mind, but she was firm. He brought Lord Ashley (afterwards seventh Earl of Shaftesbury) with him, thinking that as the Earl was in the habit of seeing a good deal of the Queen he might have some influence with her, but Lord Ashley made no impression. Then the Duke of Wellington and Peel went together, and persuasions were renewed, but all to no purpose. "They found her," says Greville, "firm and immovable; and not only resolved not to give way, but prepared with answers to all they said, and arguments in support of her determination. They told her that she must consider her *Ladies* in the same light as her *Lords;* she said, 'No, I have Lords besides, and these I give up to you.' And when they still pressed her, she said, 'Now, suppose the case had been reversed, that you had been in office when I had come to the Throne, and that Lord Melbourne had required this sacrifice of me.' Finding that she would not give way, Peel informed her that under these circumstances he must consult his friends," and a meeting accordingly took place the same afternoon. The Queen meanwhile sent a letter to Melbourne, "written," says Greville, "in a bitter spirit, and in a strain such as Elizabeth might have used," which Melbourne lost no time in laying before his colleagues, who had gathered in haste from all quarters. Alluding to her interview with the Duke and Peel, the Queen said, "Do not fear that I was not calm and composed. They wanted to deprive me of my Ladies, and I suppose they would deprive me next of my dressers and of my housemaids; they wished to treat me like a girl, but I will show them that I am Queen of England!" All this was very pretty and womanly, *but it was not constitutional*, and the result was inevitable. Peel declined to form a Cabinet, and the former Ministers returned to power.

Of course the Tories were greatly incensed at what had occurred, and an unfortunate Court scandal which arose about the same time roused their animosity against the Queen to the highest pitch. Into that, however, we do not propose to enter. We confine ourselves to the Bedchamber difficulty. The public, looking on with calmer eyes, saw in the Queen's unyieldingness only the pretty wilfulness of a high-spirited girl, and a wish gained ground among them, which presently found free expression in the newspapers, that Her Majesty would soon trust herself to the protection and aid of a husband.*

* Greville's *Memoirs*, part ii., vol. i. 201, 202; *Memoirs of Baron Stockmar*, vol. ii. 11-15.

CHAPTER V.

WOOED, WON, AND WEDDED.

AIDEN princesses need seldom be at a loss for husbands; the only trouble is that they cannot always choose for themselves. No less than six marriages had been contemplated for the young Princess Victoria, and, of course, the one on which she had set her own heart was opposed in quarters where opposition was no light matter. Her uncle, William the Fourth, had been specially anxious that she should marry Prince Alexander of the Netherlands, brother to the King of Holland, and, in his anxiety to effect this object, had done all in his power to prevent the Duke of Coburg's visit to England in 1836, though happily without success. The Duke, as we have seen, came over with his sons, and spent nearly four weeks at Kensington Palace with the Duchess of Kent. When, in the following year, the King died, and the Princess became Queen, opposition of every kind ceased; and only a very bold man would have now dared to press upon the young Sovereign an alliance that was uncongenial to her tastes.

Nothing so quixotic was attempted. The two who probably had the most influence with her—her mother and King Leopold—had set their wishes where her own heart was now set, and her betrothal with the Prince Albert was only a question of time. The Queen has herself drawn aside the veil, and told us what her first impressions of her cousin were. "The Prince was at that time much shorter than his brother, already very handsome, but very stout, which he entirely grew out of afterwards. He was most amiable, natural, unaffected, and merry; full of interest in everything, playing on the piano with the Princess, his cousin, drawing — in short, constantly occupied. He always paid the greatest attention to what he saw, and the Queen remembers well how intently he listened to the sermon preached in St. Paul's, when he and his father and brother accompanied the Duchess of Kent and the Princess there, on the occasion of the service attended by the children of the different charity schools. It is indeed rare to see a prince, not yet seventeen years of age, bestowing such earnest attention on a sermon."*

It will be remembered that shortly after this visit, King Leopold wrote to the Princess Victoria on the subject he had so much at heart, and that the Princess returned a very favourable answer; but it was not till nearly two years later that Prince Albert was spoken to upon the subject. The communication was made with the Queen's sanction, but the Prince was told that his extreme youth would make it necessary to postpone the marriage for a few years. This was disappointing, particularly as no actual betrothal was at present contemplated, and the Prince very naturally said, "I am ready to submit to this delay, if I have only some certain assurance to go upon. But if, after waiting, perhaps for three years, I should find that the Queen no longer desired the marriage, it would place me in a very ridiculous position, and would, to a certain extent, ruin all the prospects of my future life." His father, the Duke of Saxe-Coburg, had a positive objection to so long a delay, and was ably supported by his trusted friend, Baron Stockmar. The Baron wrote his own and the Duke's views to King Leopold, in a letter dated the 12th of September, 1838, and in the course of the letter, said, "Albert is now passed eighteen. If he waits till he is in his twenty-first, twenty-second, or twenty-third year, it will be impossible for him to

* Memorandum by the Queen, March, 1864 (see *Early Years of the Prince Consort*, 216).

begin any new career, and his whole life would be *marred* if the Queen should change her mind."*

The Queen, however, had no thought of changing her mind; and even her demand for delay was not to be taken too seriously. Probably it originated in maidenly caprice, and was not part of any definite resolve. Her Majesty has herself been pleased to acknowledge that she never entertained any serious idea of delay, and she afterwards informed the Prince that she would never have married any one else. It was a source of regret to her, however, that she had not kept up the correspondence with him after her accession as she had done before it. In the memorandum from which these facts are gleaned Her Majesty further remarks: "The only excuse the Queen can make for herself is in the fact, that the sudden change from the secluded life at Kensington to the independence of her position as Queen Regnant at the age of eighteen, put all ideas of marriage out of her mind, which she now most bitterly repents. A worse school for a young girl, or one more detrimental to all natural feelings and affections, cannot well be imagined than the position of a Queen at eighteen, without experience and without a husband to guide and support her. This the Queen can state from painful experience, and she thanks God that none of her dear daughters are exposed to such danger."

Matters were at last brought to an issue by a second visit of the young Princes to England, in the October of 1839. The uncertainty of Prince Albert's position was becoming a positive clog upon his happiness, and he had determined to end it. He afterwards acknowledged to the Queen that he came over on this second visit, "with the intention of telling her that if she could not then make up her mind she must understand that he could not now wait for a decision, as he had done at a former period when the marriage was first talked about." The Royal brothers were the bearers of a letter from the King of the Belgians, which, to one who can read between the lines, is significant enough. It ran thus:—

* *Memoirs of Baron Stockmar*, ii. 4.

"LAEKEN, 8*th October*, 1839.

"MY DEAREST VICTORIA,—Your cousins will be themselves the bearers of these lines. I recommend them to your 'bienveillance.' They are good and honest creatures, deserving your kindness, and not pedantic, but really sensible and trustworthy. I have told them that your great wish is that they should be quite 'unbefangen' (at their ease) with you.

"I am sure that if you have anything to recommend to them they will be most happy to learn it from you. . . .

"My dear Victoria,

"Your most devoted Uncle,

"LEOPOLD R."

A few days later the King wrote even more plainly, making special allusion to the younger of the two princes. "I trust they will enliven your sojourn in the old castle," he said, "and may Albert be able to strew roses without thorns on the pathway of life of our good Victoria! He is well qualified to do so."[*]

The Princes arrived at Windsor Castle on the 8th of October, and Her Majesty was waiting to receive them at the top of the staircase. The reception was most cordial. The three years since last they met had made a great difference in the appearance of Prince Albert, and the Queen was agreeably struck by the change. He had outgrown his boyish corpulency, was tall and manly, and eminently handsome. His blue eyes and expansive forehead betokened intelligence of a high order, his smile was peculiarly winning and sweet, and his manner gentle and courteous. Melbourne told the Queen that the Prince and she were strikingly like each other. The more important subject of the Prince's character may be safely left to Baron Stockmar. The Baron, it may be remembered, had cautiously reserved his opinion three years before. In the year of the second visit, however, he wrote: "The more I see of the Prince the better I esteem and love him. His intellect is so sound

[*] *Early Years*, 229.

and clear, his nature so unspoiled, so predisposed to goodness as well as truth, that only two external elements will be required to make of him a truly distinguished Prince." These external elements the Baron explains to be a proper acquaintance with the English nation and its constitution, and knowledge of the world.

On the second day after the arrival of her cousin, the Queen herself wrote to her uncle the King of the Belgians, "Albert's beauty is most striking, and he is most amiable and unaffected —in short, very *fascinating*." Then, with maidenly delicacy of feeling, she hastens to add, both "the young men are very amiable, delightful companions, and I am very happy to have them here." "Most striking," "most unaffected," "very amiable," "very fascinating." All these superlatives could point to but one conclusion : the young Queen was really in love.

Life at the Castle during the visit of the Princes was as pleasant as youth and bright spirits could make it. All sorts of amusements were devised for the occasion, and it soon became evident to others besides Uncle Leopold that Albert and Victoria were growing—or had grown—remarkably fond of one another. The brothers paid the Queen a visit every morning after breakfast, and took lunch with her and the Duchess of Kent at two o'clock. In the afternoon all four went riding, accompanied by Lord Melbourne, and most of the ladies and gentlemen in attendance, the whole party forming a large cavalcade. Dinner, which began the evening, was always a grand affair, and after dinner, on alternate evenings, there was a dance. At these dances the Queen put off the monarch and became the woman alone. She danced most frequently with Prince Albert, and showed him many attentions which she could never show to others. Poor young Queen! if she was ever to have a husband, she must do that which every woman shrinks from doing—she must herself make the proposal. One evening she took from her bosom the flower she was wearing, and presented it to the Prince. It was the pledge for which he had long waited, the assurance that she loved him before all men ; and, with ready wit, he seized a penknife, and slitting a

PRINCE ALBERT OF SAXE-COBURG AND GOTHA.

hole in his tight-fitting military jacket just above the heart, deposited the flower there.

Next day the Prince went hunting, and returned at twelve o'clock. Half-an-hour later he received a summons to the Queen's room, which he almost instantly obeyed. The Queen was alone. A unique and difficult task was before her—one of the most difficult that ever fell to the lot of woman. She had sent for the Prince that she might offer him her hand in marriage! Exactly what took place at the interview we shall never know, and too much curiosity on the subject would be unbecoming; but the Prince has lifted a corner of the curtain in one of his letters, and imagination may supply the rest. Writing to his grandmother he says: "The Queen sent for me alone to her room a few days ago, and declared to me in a genuine outburst of love and affection, that I had gained her whole heart, and would make her intensely happy if I would make her the sacrifice of sharing her life with her, for she said she looked on it as a sacrifice; the only thing which troubled her was that she did not think she was worthy of me. The joyous openness of manner in which she told me this enchanted me, and I was quite carried away by it."*

We have a glimpse from the Queen's own point of view in a letter written by Her Majesty to the King of the Belgians, on the very day that the proposal was made. "My mind is quite made up," she wrote, "and I told Albert this morning of it. The warm affection he showed me on learning this, gave me great pleasure. He seems perfection, and I think that I have the prospect of very great happiness before me. I love him more than I can say, and shall do everything in my power to render this sacrifice (for such in my opinion it is) as small as I can. . . . These last few days have passed like a dream to me, and I am so much bewildered by it all that I know hardly how to write; but I do feel very happy."† To our minds there is something extremely noble in the Queen's conduct on this occasion. It is more than womanly. The whole tone of her letter, which, unfortunately, is too long to quote, gives evidence

* *Early Years*, 239, 240. † *Ibid.* 227, 228.

of a fine sympathetic intuition, such as few natures possess, and when, a little later, we find her saying: "How I will strive to make him feel as little as possible the great sacrifice he has made! I told him it *was* a great sacrifice on his part, but he would not allow it." When, we repeat, we find the young Queen pouring out her loving heart in language so unaffectedly ingenuous, our admiration is increased, and we feel profoundly thankful that the Prince proved himself so worthy of her choice.

If the gentle Queen had tried to make her young cousins happy in the days before her betrothal, how were her efforts increased now that she stood in so much nearer and dearer a relationship to one of them! "Since this moment," wrote the Prince himself, "Victoria does whatever she fancies I should wish or like, and we talk together a great deal about our future life, which she promises me to make as happy as possible. . . . She is really most good and amiable, and I am quite sure Heaven has not given me into evil hands, and that we shall be happy together."* Among the "sights" of one kind and another which the Prince witnessed during his stay at Windsor, was a review of the 2nd Battalion of the Rifle Brigade in the Home Park by the Queen. The Queen has given, in her *Journal*, a spirited account of the review, which will be more acceptable to the reader than any paraphrase of ours. "At ten minutes to twelve I set off in my Windsor uniform and cap, on my old charger 'Leopold,' with my beloved Albert, looking so handsome in his uniform, on my right, and Sir John Macdonald, the Adjutant-General on my left; Colonel Grey and Colonel Wemyss preceding me; a guard of honour, my other gentlemen, my cousin's gentlemen, Lady Caroline Barrington, etc., for the ground. A horrid day! Cold—dreadfully blowing—and, in addition, raining hard when we had been out a few minutes. It, however, ceased when we came to the ground. I rode alone down the ranks, and then took my place, as usual, with dearest Albert on my right, and Sir John Macdonald on my left, and saw the troops march past. They afterwards manœuvred. The Rifles looked beautiful.

* *Early Years*, 240.

It was piercingly cold, and I had my cape on, which dearest Albert settled comfortably for me. He was so cold, being '*en grande tenue*,' with high boots. We cantered home again, and went in to show ourselves to poor Ernest [the Prince's brother] who had seen all from a window."*

On the 14th of November the Princes brought their eventful visit to a close, and returned to the Continent. The Queen had now another trying task before her—namely, to make known her resolve on the subject of marriage to the Privy Council. On the 23rd of the same month the Council met, eighty members—an unusually large number—being present. When they had seated themselves, the folding doors were thrown open, and the Queen entered, attired in a plain morning gown, and wearing a bracelet containing Prince Albert's picture. She hardly knew who was there, but recognised Lord Melbourne, who looked kindly at her, with tears in his eyes. She then read her short Declaration in a clear, sonorous, sweet-toned voice, but her hands trembled so excessively that Greville wondered how she was able to get through it. The Queen has hinted that the Prince's picture gave her courage. The Declaration was in these words:—

"I have caused you to be summoned at the present time in order that I may acquaint you with my resolution in a matter which deeply concerns the welfare of my people, and the happiness of my future life.

"It is my intention to ally myself in marriage with the Prince Albert of Saxe-Coburg and Gotha. Deeply impressed with the solemnity of the engagement which I am about to contract, I have not come to this decision without mature consideration, nor without feeling a strong assurance that, with the blessing of Almighty God, it will at once secure my domestic felicity, and serve the interests of my country.

* *Early Years*, 233, 234.

"I have thought fit to make this resolution known to you at the earliest period, in order that you may be apprised of a matter so highly important to me and to my kingdom, and which, I persuade myself, will be most acceptable to all my loving subjects."

Her Majesty has told us in her *Journal* that she felt most happy and thankful when her part of the task was over. Lord Lansdowne then made a little speech, in the name of the Council, in which he requested that "this most gracious and most welcome communication might be printed," and the Queen, having bowed her assent, placed the paper in his hands and withdrew. The whole proceedings had not lasted above two or three minutes.

In the January of the following year (1840), Her Majesty opened Parliament in person, and the announcement of the forthcoming marriage formed part of the Queen's Speech. The congratulations on all sides were warm and cordial. Sir Robert Peel, speaking for the Opposition, only stated the truth when he declared that the Queen had the singular good fortune to be able to gratify her private feelings while she performed her public duty, and to obtain the best guarantee for happiness by contracting an alliance founded on affection.* Of how few Royal marriages could this be said!

The Prince, accompanied by his father and brother, arrived at Dover on the 6th of February, and stayed there the night. He then proceeded to Canterbury, where also he spent a night, travelling on by easy stages, as it had been arranged that he should not appear at Buckingham Palace till the 8th. All the villages turned out to welcome him, and at the cathedral city just named, he was received with special enthusiasm. The town was illuminated in the evening, and great crowds assembled before the hotel, cheering vociferously. From this place the Prince sent on his valet with his favourite greyhound, Eôs; and the Queen speaks in her *Journal* of the pleasure which the sight

* *Early Years*, 270.

of the faithful animal gave her, the evening before the arrival of its master. The Royal party arrived at the Palace at half-past four o'clock in the afternoon on the day arranged, and were received at the hall-door by the Queen and the Duchess of Kent, attended by the whole household.*

The marriage was fixed for the 10th of February, and as the happy day drew near the excitement of the people became intense. They had heartily approved of the match from the first, partly on political grounds, but more especially because the betrothed couple were known to be really attached to one another. Dickens threw himself into the excitement with his accustomed heartiness, and penned some extraordinary letters, in which the great event of the season was ludicrously referred to. "Society is unhinged here by Her Majesty's marriage," he says in one of them, "and I am sorry to say that I have fallen hopelessly in love with the Queen, and wander up and down with vague and dismal thoughts of running away to some uninhabited island with a maid of honour, to be entrapped by conspiracy for that purpose."† In another he writes: "I am utterly lost in misery, and can do nothing. I have been reading *Oliver*, *Pickwick*, and *Nickleby* to get my thoughts together for the new effort, but all in vain—

> 'My heart is at Windsor,
> My heart isn't here;
> My heart is at Windsor
> A following my dear.'" ‡

A letter of a very different kind was written by the Royal bridegroom himself on the morning of his wedding-day. It was to his grandmother, the Dowager-Duchess of Coburg, and ran thus: "In less than three hours I shall stand before the altar with my dear bride! In these solemn moments I must once more ask your blessing, which I am well assured I shall receive, and which will be my safeguard and my future joy! I must end. God help me!"§ A youth of twenty-one who could pen such a letter had princely qualities of the right sort.

* *Early Years*, 304–306. † Foster's *Life of Dickens*, i. 195.
‡ *Ibid.* 196. § *Early Years*, 308, 309.

The marriage was, of course, a very grand affair, but unfortunately the day was dark and stormy—"a dreadful day," says Greville, "with torrents of rain and violent gusts of wind."* Nevertheless, the crowds that collected in St. James's Park to catch a sight of the procession were immense. Even the trees of the Park were laden with spectators, and now and again a bough would snap and bring to earth its weight of living fruit. The immediate road for the procession—viz., the Mall from Buckingham Palace to St. James's—was kept clear with great difficulty, so numerous were the attempts from the pressure without to break through on the line, in order to secure more favourable points of view. The Prince was the first to arrive, attended by a small escort of Horse Guards, but the windows of his carriage being closed, he was scarcely recognised, and there was but slight applause. A quarter of an hour later, however, the band in front of the Palace struck up the National Anthem, and the fact that the Bride had entered her carriage and was on her way to St. James's, spread quickly through the vast concourse of people, and was received with tremendous shouts. The *cortége* of Her Majesty was attended by a full guard of honour, but the carriages, seven in number, were drawn by only two horses each. "The Queen," says Mrs. Oliphant, "was extremely pale as she passed along under the gaze of multitudes, her mother by her side, crowned with nothing but those pure flowers which are dedicated to the day of bridal, and not even permitted the luxury of a veil over her drooping face. The lace fell about her, but left her Royal countenance unveiled." Her carriage drew up at the Palace entrance at ten minutes past twelve o'clock.

At twenty-five minutes past twelve, a flourish of trumpets and drums announced that the procession of the Royal bridegroom had begun its movement, and the Prince was greeted with loud clapping of hands from the gentlemen and enthusiastic waving of handkerchiefs from the assembled ladies as he passed along towards the Chapel. He wore the uniform of a Field-Marshal in the British army; and over his shoulders was hung

* Greville's *Memoirs*, part ii., vol. i. 267.

the collar of the Garter, surmounted by two white rosettes. His form, dress, and demeanour were much admired; and he seemed greatly pleased by the cordial expressions of good-will with which he was received. As he entered the chapel a voluntary was performed on the organ by Sir George Smart.

A few minutes passed away, and then a buzz of excitement told that the Bride's procession had begun to move. Every person rose as the doors were again opened, and the procession came in with slow and solemn steps. All the female Royalties—the Princess Sophia of Gloucester, the two Princesses Augusta, the Duchess of Cambridge, and the pretty little Princess Mary—were heartily cheered; and a specially warm welcome awaited the Bride's mother, the Duchess of Kent, towards whom the liveliest sympathy was manifested. It is said that she appeared somewhat disconsolate and distressed, and need we be surprised? "The mother who gives a daughter away, even to the best of sons, resigns the first place in that daughter's heart, the first right to her time, thoughts, and confidence;" and the Duchess must have felt this. The Duke of Sussex—always and deservedly popular—came next, and seemed in excellent spirits. On him devolved the important duty of giving away the Royal bride. Then came Melbourne, bearing the sword of State; but he passed almost unnoticed, for all eyes were now centred upon the chief figure in the procession, the Bride herself, who came immediately after the Prime Minister, her train borne by twelve noble maidens—peers' daughters every one of them. Her Majesty seemed anxious and excited, and was paler than usual; and she looked neither to the right hand nor to the left as she passed on into the Chapel. Her dress was of rich white satin trimmed with orange blossoms, and a diamond necklace encircled her fair neck. On her head she wore a wreath of the same blossoms, and over them a magnificent veil of Honiton lace, of the value of £1000. The bridesmaids and trainbearers were similarly attired, save that they had no veils.

The wedding ceremony in the Chapel Royal went off without a hitch, and the Queen's demeanour throughout was touchingly womanly. When all had taken their places and silence

THE QUEEN'S MARRIAGE TO PRINCE ALBERT, IN THE CHAPEL OF ST. JAMES'S PALACE, FEB. 10, 1840.
After the picture by Sir George Hayter, R.A. By permission of Messrs. Henry Graves & Co.

was restored, she rose, and, with the Prince, advanced to the steps of the altar, where the Archbishop of Canterbury and the Bishop of London were already waiting. The pale young Bride was once again the cynosure of all eyes. Bowing her head upon her hand, she remained for a few moments in silent prayer; and then the Archbishop began the marriage service in the usual words. Nothing was omitted from the beautiful liturgy —nothing added. The names of the bridegroom and the bride were mentioned simply as "Albert" and "Victoria"; and the Queen of the greatest Empire in the world promised to *obey* and *serve* as well as to love and honour the man to whom her troth was plighted. It was afterwards observed by one who was present at the ceremony that Her Majesty's expression of the words "love, cherish, and obey," and the confiding look with which they were accompanied, were inimitably chaste and beautiful. At the supremely interesting moment when the Prince placed the wedding ring—a plain gold one—on the Queen's finger, the Earl of Uxbridge gave the signal, and the cannon fired the Royal salute. The Tower artillery answered by firing alternately with the Park guns, and all the bells in London and Westminster rang out a joyous peal, announcing to every citizen in the metropolis that Her Majesty was a wedded wife.

"She vows to love who vowed to rule, the chosen at her side,
  Let none say 'God preserve the Queen,' but rather 'Bless the Bride,'
None blow the trump, none bend the knee, none violate the dream
Wherein no monarch but a wife, she to herself may seem;
Or if you say, 'Preserve the Queen,' oh, breath it inward, low—
She is a *woman* and *beloved*, and 'tis enough but so.
Count it enough, thou noble Prince, who tak'st her by the hand,
And claimest for thy lady-love our Lady of the land.
And since, Prince Albert, men have called thy spirit high and rare,
And true to truth and brave for truth as some at Augsberg were,
We charge thee by thy lofty thoughts and by thy poet-mind,
Which not by glory and degree takes pleasure of mankind,
Esteem that wedded hand less dear for sceptre than for ring,
And hold her uncrowned womanhood to be the Royal thing."*

       * Mrs. Browning.

The Queen returned to the Palace, no longer pale and anxious-looking, but "with a joyous and open countenance, flushed, perhaps, in the slightest degree;" and the sun, which had hidden its face till now, beamed its welcome on the newly-wedded pair. The breakfast was served in the State dining-room of the Palace, which was hung with white for the occasion, and profusely decorated with white flowers. The bride's-cake was a sight to behold—wonderful alike in dimensions and design. It measured three yards in circumference, and weighed 300 pounds; and quires of foolscap might be filled in describing the pretty devices which it bore. Among the rest were images of Prince Albert and the Queen; the former with a dog at his feet—in token of fidelity; the latter with a pair of turtle-doves—emblems of love and felicity. Britannia stood at the top of the cake, in act of blessing the Royal couple, but the artist who had the designing of the figure made the singular mistake of representing the "ruler of the waves" in the costume of Ancient Rome!

Upon leaving the Palace for Windsor the Queen and her young husband were well received; but "they went off," says Greville, "in very poor and shabby style. Instead of the new chariot in which most married people are accustomed to dash along, they were in one of the old travelling coaches, the postillions in undress liveries and with a small escort, three other coaches with post-horses following."* The Queen wore a white satin pelisse edged with swansdown, and a white bonnet tastefully trimmed with white ostrich plumes. The Prince was in a fur-trimmed coat with deep collar, and wore—or rather carried—a high-crowned hat, for the article in question was more frequently in his hand than on his head, so repeatedly did he raise it in response to the cheers of the multitudes. The long route of twenty-two miles was literally thronged with spectators, and V's and A's and other decorations were plentiful all the way. The Queen was in high spirits. "Our reception," she afterwards wrote, was "most enthusiastic, hearty, and gratifying in every way, the people quite

* Greville's *Memoirs*, part ii., vol. i. 267.

deafening us with their cheers—horsemen, etc., going along with us."

By the time the Royal borough was reached, night, though not darkness, had fallen upon the waiting multitudes in the streets. The town was one blaze of light, for the illuminations had been prepared on a scale of more than wonted magnificence. The enthusiasm here surpassed everything. The Eton boys specially distinguished themselves, and their loyalty did not pass unnoticed by Her Majesty. "They accompanied the carriage to the Castle," she wrote, "cheering and shouting as only schoolboys can. They swarmed up the mound as the carriage entered the Quadrangle; they made the old Castle ring again with their acclamations." It was a pleasing close to a memorable and happy day.

Many years have rolled by since the troth of these Royal lovers was plighted, and the boys who followed the bridal pair to the Castle gates are boys no longer. They are old men now, or else are in their graves. But the central object of that day's rejoicings is still with us. The gentle Lady who wielded the sceptre of Britain then still wields it: nor is she less beloved by her people than in the day of her espousals. Yet time with her, too, has wrought changes. The snows of age are on the brow that wears the crown; and, alas! there is a vacant seat beside the throne.

CHAPTER VI.

THE HOME IN THE PALACE (1840-1848).

THE Queen realised in Prince Albert all, and more than all, her fondest hopes had imagined; and it would be difficult to find anywhere in history a picture of domestic felicity to equal that which their wedded life presents. If ever there was perfect happiness on earth, it was in the palace home of Queen Victoria in those twenty years before her widowhood. Never did woman dote more fondly upon a husband; never did wife fulfil more thoroughly and whole-heartedly her marriage vows. One single extract from her *Journal* is incidental proof of this. "I told Albert that formerly I was too happy to go to London, and wretched to leave it, and how since the blessed hour of my marriage, and still more since the summer, I dislike it, and am unhappy to leave the country, and would be content and happy never to go to town. The solid pleasures of a peaceful, quiet, yet merry life in the country, with my inestimable husband and friend, my all-in-all, are far more durable than the amusements of London, though we don't despise or dislike them sometimes." * Another entry, belonging to an earlier date, exhibits this intensity of devotion in an even stronger light. It refers to the Prince's parting with his father, the Duke of Saxe-Coburg, who returned to the Continent a fortnight after the Royal marriage. "He (Prince Albert) said to her that I had never known a

* *Early Years*, 338.

father, and could not therefore feel what he did. His childhood had been very happy. Ernest, he said, was now the only one remaining here of all his earliest ties and recollections; but if I continued to love him as I did now, I could make up for all. . . . Oh! how I did feel for my dearest, precious husband at this moment! Father, brother, friends, country, all has he left, and all for me. God grant that I may be the happy person, the *most* happy person, to make this dearest, blessed being happy and contented. What is in my power to make him happy I will do." * Such glimpses of the deep inward life of our gracious Queen should be very dear to the hearts of her loyal subjects.

That interesting volume, *The Early Years of the Prince Consort*, compiled under the direction of Her Majesty, contains a long and pleasant chapter on the first year of their wedded life. Levees, presentations, addresses, drawing-rooms, and great dinners followed the marriage in rapid succession, the dinners being often succeeded by little dances, which were usually prolonged to a late hour, and were at first somewhat trying to the Prince. Late hours at night led naturally to late hours in the morning; and breakfast was seldom over before eleven o'clock. The Queen, in a memorandum written since the Prince's death, takes all the blame of this injurious habit on herself.

Easter of 1840 was spent at the Castle, where the Queen and Prince took the Sacrament together for the first time in St. George's Chapel. Her Majesty tells us that "the Prince had a very strong feeling about the solemnity of this act, and did not like to appear in company either the evening before or on day on which he took it, and he and the Queen almost always dined alone on these occasions." † On the Easter Monday an accident happened to the Prince, which might have been fatal, but fortunately only resulted in torn clothes and a few contusions. His horse, a handsome but very vicious thorough-bred, suddenly bolted, and the Prince, after turning the animal several times in a vain endeavour to stop it, was at last knocked off by a tree

* *Early Years*, 312, 313. † *Ibid.* 331.

against which he brushed in passing. The Queen, who had seen from a window the beginning of the affair, ran anxiously to the Prince's room in hopes of seeing something further, but horse and rider were by that time out of sight. It was a great relief to her when one of the grooms-in-waiting rode back and she heard him say that the Prince was not hurt. "It was a frightful fall," the loyal-hearted Wife wrote in her *Journal,* "and might (I shudder to think of the danger my dearest, precious, inestimable husband was in) have been nearly fatal! . . . Oh, how thankful I felt that it was no worse! His anxiety was all for me, not for himself." *

About this time the Queen was taking lessons in singing from Signor Lablache, and the Prince, who was himself an accomplished musician, often joined in them. At other times they would play on the organ together in the Prince's drawing-room at Buckingham Palace; or, if they were at Windsor, she would sit near him, a tranced and happy listener, while he played alone on the large organ in the music-room. † Their fondness for sacred music, as well as the genuineness of their feeling for sacred things generally, is evidenced by the following entry in the Queen's *Journal,* "We two dined together, as Albert likes being quite alone before he takes the Sacrament; we played part of Mozart's Requiem, and then he read to me out of the *Stunden der Andocht* (Hours of Devotion), the article on Selbsterkenutniss (Self-knowledge)." ‡

Her Majesty's birthday (the 24th of May) was kept at Claremont that year, a place dear to her from her childhood, and the Prince and she were "able to take charming walks in the pretty grounds and neighbourhood." But they were back again at Buckingham Palace before the end of the month, and on the 1st of June we find the Prince presiding at a meeting of the Society for the Abolition of Slavery, at which he delivered a speech in English, his own composition, which had the double merit of being short and to the point. "He was very nervous before

---

* *Early Years,* 332-334.
† Since converted into a private chapel.
‡ *Early Years,* 332.

he went," says the Queen, "and had repeated his speech to me in the morning by heart." *

It was on the 10th of this month that the miserable potboy, Oxford, made his cowardly attempt to shoot the Queen. The facts are given by Greville in his usual vivid and easy style.

"On Wednesday afternoon, as the Queen and Prince Albert were driving in a low carriage up Constitution Hill, about four or five in the afternoon, they were shot at by a lad of eighteen years old, who fired two pistols at them successively, neither shots taking effect. He was in the Green Park without the rails, and as he was only a few yards from the carriage, and, moreover, very cool and collected, it is marvellous he should have missed his aim. In a few moments the young man was seized, without any attempt on his part to escape or to deny the deed, and was carried off to prison. The Queen, who appeared perfectly cool, and not the least alarmed, instantly drove to the Duchess of Kent's to anticipate any report that might reach her mother, and, having done so, she continued her drive and went to the Park. By this time the attempt upon her life had become generally known, and she was received with the utmost enthusiasm by the immense crowd that was congregated in carriages, on horseback, and on foot. All the equestrians formed themselves into an escort, and attended her back to the Palace, cheering vehemently, while she acknowledged, with great appearance of feeling, these loyal manifestations. She behaved on this occasion with perfect courage and self-possession, and exceeding propriety; and the assembled multitude, being a high-class mob, evinced a lively and spontaneous feeling for her—a depth of interest which, however natural under such circumstances, must be very gratifying to her, and was satisfactory to witness." †
The perpetrator of the outrage was, of course, brought to trial, when it soon became clear that the crime had no political significance, but had merely originated in a morbid craving for notoriety. The youth, according to Greville, "conducted himself during the examination with acuteness, and cross-examined

---

* *Early Years*, 341, and *Speeches and Addresses of the Prince Consort*, 81, 82.   † Greville's *Memoirs*, part ii., vol. i. 288.

the witnesses (a good many of whom were produced) with some talent;" nevertheless, a plea of insanity was set up, and effect having been given to it by the jury, the culprit was committed to a lunatic asylum for life. Years after he was released, on a promise to go to Australia, where, so late as 1882, he was earning an honest livelihood as a house painter.

For several years after Oxford's attempt, a large volunteer body-guard escorted the Queen from the Park to the Palace gates, whenever she went riding or driving; and her appearance anywhere in public was the signal for a loyal demonstration. On the night of the attempt, the National Anthem was played at all the theatres amidst unbounded enthusiasm, and the scene at the Opera-House when Her Majesty appeared there, a day or two afterwards, beggars description. As the Queen entered the Royal box, the whole house rose, and waving hats and handkerchiefs, cheered deliriously for several minutes. Then the orchestra struck up the National Anthem, and the vast audience still standing and facing Her Majesty, sang the stirring ode as perhaps it had never been sung before.

Of the numerous Court and fashionable gaieties which marked the first year of the Queen's marriage, it is needless to speak particularly. There is a terrible sameness about such things, and the reader would soon be as weary of hearing about them as those who indulge in them feel in the gaieties themselves. It will be more interesting to turn to an account, from Her Majesty's own pen, of the ordinary mode of life at the Palace. "At this time the Prince and Queen seem to have spent their day much as follows: they breakfasted at nine, and took a walk every morning soon afterwards. Then came the usual amount of business (far less heavy, however, than now); besides which they drew and etched a great deal together, which was a source of great amusement, having the plates 'bit' in the house. Luncheon followed at the usual hour of two o'clock. Lord Melbourne, who was generally staying in the house, came to the Queen in the afternoon, and between five and six the Prince usually drove her out in a pony phaeton. If the Prince did not drive the Queen, he rode, in which case she took a drive with the Duchess of Kent or the ladies. The Prince also read aloud most days to the Queen. The dinner was at eight o'clock, and always with the company. In the evening the Prince frequently played at double chess, a game of which he was very fond, and which he played extremely well. At first the Queen tried to get rid of the bad custom, prevailing only in this country, of the gentlemen remaining, after the ladies had left, in the dining-room. But Lord Melbourne advised against it, and the Prince himself thought it better not to make any change. The hours, however, were never late of an evening, and it was very seldom that the party had not broken up by eleven o'clock."*

Interesting specimens of the etched work to which Her Majesty refers, as produced about this time, have appeared in various publications; and some of them show careful drawing of a difficult kind. The actual immersing of the plates in the acid bath was not done by the Queen, but by a Miss Skerrett, one of the Queen's first dressers, though she never acted in that capacity. It was Miss Skerrett who communicated with the artists, wrote letters to tradespeople, etc.; and her services were greatly valued by the Queen.

When in town, the Prince would sometimes go out riding in the morning without the Queen, and accompanied only by his equerry. He was a man who loved to learn, and his observant eye took note of everything of an informing character as he rode along. He paid no visits in general society, but was to be found at the studios of artists, at museums of art or science, and at institutions for good and benevolent purposes. "He would frequently return to luncheon at a great pace, and would always come through the Queen's dressing-room, where she generally was at that time, with that bright, loving smile with which he ever greeted her; telling her where he had been— what new buildings he had seen—what studios, etc., he had visited. Riding for mere riding's sake he disliked, and said, '*Es ennuyirt mich so*' ("It bores me so.')" †

On the 11th of August, the Queen prorogued Parliament in

* *Early Years*, 348–350.
† Memorandum by the Queen in *Early Years*, 355.

person, and next day the Court left London for Windsor. Here were spent three very happy months, the Prince, as usual, finding plenty to do. He formed a pretty little stud of all the Arab horses which the Queen had received as presents; and superintended the building of some new stables and a riding-school at the Castle. Under his directions, too, a long stretch of greensward on the top of the Castle-hill was laid out in pleasure-grounds, with plants, etc.; and he exerted himself, fortunately, with success, to preserve from demolition the fishing temple near by, and George the Fourth's Cottage, which were both to have been taken away.*

The Prince's birthday (August 26th) fell on one of these happy Windsor days, and was kept up with much innocent merriment. In the morning he was awakened by a reveille, composed by a Coburg musician, and then all the family staying at the Castle breakfasted together at Adelaide Cottage, which lies at the foot of the hill on which the ancient borough stands. The children of the Queen's half-sister, Feodora, already a familiar name to the reader, were dressed as Coburg peasants, and looked delightfully funny. In the afternoon, which was as bright and sunny as an English August afternoon might be expected to be, the Prince drove the Queen through the park in a phaeton; and in the evening there was a grand dinner.†

As autumn stole on, and the evenings began to draw in, the character of their pleasures changed a little. Less time was given to garden-planning and other outdoor pursuits, and more to indoor recreations, such as music and etching. Lady Lyttleton, writing from Windsor Castle in the October of this year, speaks enthusiastically of the Prince's skill as an organist, and we can readily understand the delight which the Queen (herself a true musician) must have felt in listening to him. Her Ladyship says: "Yesterday evening, as I was sitting here comfortably after the drive, by candle-light, reading M. Guizot, suddenly there arose from the room beneath, oh, such sounds! . . . It was Prince Albert, dear Prince Albert, playing on the

* *Early Years*, 357.   † *Ibid.* 365.

organ; and with such master skill, as it appeared to me, modulating so learnedly, winding through every kind of bass and chord, till he wound up into the most perfect cadence; and then off again, louder and then softer. . . . I ventured at dinner to ask him what I had heard: 'Oh, my organ! a new possession of mine. I am so fond of the organ! It is the first of instruments; the only instrument for expressing one's feelings' (I thought, are they not good feelings that the *organ* expresses?) 'And it teaches to play; for on the organ *a mistake!* oh, such misery!' and he quite shuddered at the thought of the sostenuto discord." *

About the middle of November, the Court returned to London, and on the 21st of the month, the Queen's first child, the Princess Royal, was born at Buckingham Palace. The Prince would naturally have preferred a son, but even the wishes of princes cannot be consulted in such matters. "For a moment only," says the Queen, "was he disappointed at its being a daughter and not a son;" and it is gratifying to learn that his care and devotion to Her Majesty during the time of her confinement to her room, "were quite beyond expression." † He sat beside her in the darkened chamber, read to her, and wrote for her. "No one but himself ever lifted her from her bed to her sofa, and he always helped to wheel her on her bed or sofa into the next room. For this purpose he would come instantly when sent for from any part of the house." In short, his care of the Queen, to use Her Majesty's own words, "was like that of a mother, nor could there be a kinder, wiser, or more judicious nurse." ‡ As time went on, and more little baby faces came to gladden the home circle, his devotion in this respect never ceased—never even diminished.

On the occasion which we are now considering, the Prince's care was requited by the speedy recovery of the Queen; and the Court was able to return to Windsor in good time for the Christmas holidays. All was happiness, "and the dear delights

---

* *Life of the Prince Consort*, vol. i. 15.
† *Early Years*, 365.   ‡ *Ibid.* 366.

THE CHRISTENING OF THE PRINCESS ROYAL IN BUCKINGHAM PALACE, FEBRUARY 10, 1841.

of home had been made more precious by the young life, which now gave it a new and tenderer charm. Christmas was the favourite festival of the Prince, who clung to the kindly custom of his native country, which makes it a day for the interchange of gifts, as marks of affection and goodwill. The Queen fully shared his feelings in this respect, and the same usage was then introduced into their home, and was ever afterwards continued."*
Her own room and the Prince's were made bright with Christmas trees, on or beside which the presents were placed, some for the family and others for the members of the household, for the Queen believed in a community of happiness, and Christmas was not "merry Christmas" to her unless those about her were "merry" too. Be sure, the little Princess was held up in the arms of her fond mother, to look at the gay-coloured candles and the gift-laden boughs! Be sure that a little dimpled hand was guided to the bending branch whereon the presents for baby Victoria hung! Her little Highness doubtless enjoyed the fun as much as anybody, for she was an intelligent baby we are told, and "very merry."

The christening took place the following year, on the anniversary of the Queen's marriage, and went off very well. The Princess "behaved with great propriety," said her father, "and like a Christian. She was awake but did not cry at all, and seemed to crow with immense satisfaction at the lights and brilliant uniforms, for she is very intelligent and observing." †
The day before the christening, the Queen had had a nasty fright by seeing her idolised husband fall through the ice in Buckingham Palace Gardens while skating. He was figuring gracefully not far from the Queen, who was standing on the bank with one of her ladies, when, to adopt the Prince's own account, he "fell plump into the water, and had to swim for two or three minutes in order to get out." "Victoria," he continues, "was the only person who had presence of mind to lend me assistance, her lady being more occupied in screaming for help. The shock from the cold was extremely painful, and I cannot thank Heaven enough, that I escaped with nothing

* *Life of the Prince Consort*, vol. i. 17. † *Ibid.* 17.

more than a severe cold. They had, it seems, broken the ice recently at that particular spot, and it had frozen over again, so that it was impossible to distinguish the place."*

Such were the home events of the first year of the Queen's wedded life. We have dwelt upon them at greater length than we shall be able to dwell upon succeeding events, and for this no apology is needed. The first few months of married life have an interest of their own, and that interest is not diminished when one of the wedded lovers is Queen of England. We have seen what happiness strewed the path of the young Queen and her husband, and have seen, too (conspicuously in the Queen's own case), that that happiness was based upon ardent love and the truest unselfishness. It was, indeed, an encouraging beginning.

The following year, in so far as the domestic events of the Queen's life are concerned, is chiefly memorable for the birth of a male heir to the British crown. On the 9th of November, 1841, the Prince of Wales was born at Buckingham Palace, and the cherished hope of Her Majesty and the Prince Consort was fulfilled. The Tower guns boomed forth the announcement of the new arrival just as the Lord Mayor's procession was setting out from Guildhall. Though the Queen's recovery was again rapid, she was not able to leave her room till after the birthday of the Princess Royal, so the little Princess—" Pussy " was her name at that time—had to be brought in to receive the birthday wishes and kisses of her fond mother. Her Majesty has not forgotten to record the pleasant incident, as the following quotation will show :—" Albert brought in dearest little Pussy, in such a smart white merino dress trimmed with blue, which Mama had given her, and a pretty cap, and placed her on my bed, seating himself next to her, and she was very dear and good. And as my precious, invaluable Albert sat there, and our little love between us, I felt quite moved with happiness and gratitude to God." †

When Her Majesty was well enough to move, the Court returned to Windsor, much to the delight of the Queen and the

* *Life of the Prince Consort*, vol. i. 17. † *Ibid.* vol. i. 21.

Prince, who felt, as the former told King Leopold, like prisoners freed from a dungeon. "I wonder very much," wrote the Queen in the same letter, "whom our little boy will be like. You will understand how fervent are my prayers, and I am sure everybody's must be, to see him resemble his father in *every, every* respect, both in body and mind! Oh, my dearest uncle, I am sure if you knew how happy, how blessed I feel, and how proud in possessing such a perfect being as my husband, and if you think that you have been instrumental in bringing about this union, it must gladden your heart!" *

There were two little ones to think about now, when hanging the toys on the Royal Christmas-tree. The Prince Consort felt the joy of this no less than the Queen Mother, and writing to his father during the festal season, he says, with genuine feeling: "This is the dear Christmas Eve, on which I have so often listened with impatience for your step, which was to usher us into the gift-room. To-day I have two children of my own to make gifts to, who, they know not why, are full of happy wonder at the German Christmas-tree and its radiant candles." †

The christening of the new baby was, of course, a grand affair, and the King of Prussia, the most powerful Protestant potentate in Europe, came over specially for the occasion. In fact, he was one of the infant Prince's godfathers. The ceremony took place in St. George's Chapel, Windsor, on the 25th of January, 1842, at one o'clock in the afternoon. The sponsors, six in number, stood on the right side of the communion table; the Queen, Prince Albert, the infant Prince, the rest of the Royal Family and the Court, on the left side. Immediately behind the Queen stood the Duke of Wellington, bearing the great sword of State. The Archbishop of Canterbury read the service, and performed it very well, though he appeared nervous. The little Prince—whom a witness of the ceremony described as a beautiful baby, with fine large eyes, and as lively and intelligent-looking as an eight-months' old child—was taken from the nurse's arms by the Duchess of Buccleuch, and handed to the Archbishop, who went through the necessary

* *Life of the Prince Consort*, vol. i. 22.   † *Ibid.* vol. i. 22.

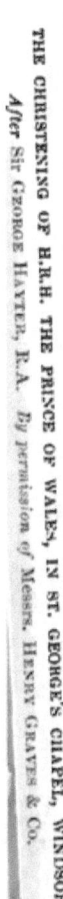

THE CHRISTENING OF H.R.H. THE PRINCE OF WALES, IN ST. GEORGE'S CHAPEL, WINDSOR.
After Sir George Hayter, R.A. *By permission of* Messrs. Henry Graves & Co.

form, but held the baby as though he were afraid of breaking it, and seemed greatly relieved when the child was safely out of his arms again. Then the choir sang the Hallelujah chorus, and the service concluded.*

The London season that year was a gay one, but it was gaiety in the midst of sadness and discontent. Trade was in a wretched state, thousands were out of employment, and the Chartist movement, of which we have elsewhere spoken,† was then in its strength. In order, as it was said, to give an impetus to trade, the wheel of fashionable pleasure was set spinning at a great rate, and dinners, concerts, balls, followed each other in rapid succession. At one of these great displays—a ball given at Covent Garden Theatre for the relief of the Spitalfields weavers—the Queen and the Prince appeared in State, and the affair was a great success. But the great show of the season was the magnificent *Bal Costumé*, popularly known as "the Queen's Plantagenet Ball," which was given at Buckingham Palace a fortnight earlier. "This," said the Prince, in a letter to the Duchess of Saxe-Gotha, " we have organised with the view of helping trade in London, which is greatly depressed. We are to represent Edward III. and Queen Philippa, and the whole Court is to appear in the Court dress of that period. The Duchess of Cambridge is to head a procession of 120 persons, intended to represent France, Italy, and Spain."‡ Her Majesty's dress on this occasion was entirely composed of the manufactures of Spitalfields, and must have cost several hundred pounds, for it was heavy with gold and silver brocade. The jewels that sparkled on the band of her stomacher were worth thousands more. Her hair was folded *à la Clovis*, and was surmounted by a light crown of gold, in which there was but one stone—a diamond. But that diamond shone like a star, and was valued at ten thousand pounds.

"The leading feature of the ball," says a contemporary newspaper,§ "was the assemblage and meeting of the Courts of

---

* *Reminiscences of Court and Diplomatic Life*, vol. i. 34–36.
† Page 76.   ‡ *Life of the Prince Consort*, vol. i. 23.
§ Quoted in Tytler's *Life of the Queen*, 162–164.

Anne of Brittany (the Duchess of Cambridge) and Edward III. and Philippa. A separate entrance to the Palace was set apart for the Court of Brittany, the Duchess of Cambridge assembling her Court in one of the lower rooms of the Palace, while the Queen and Prince Albert, surrounded by a numerous and brilliant circle, prepared to receive Her Royal Highness in the Throne-room, which was altered so as to be made as much as possible to harmonise with the period. The throne was removed and another erected, copied from an authentic source in the time of Edward III. . . . At the back of the throne were emblazoned the royal arms of England in silver. Seated on this throne, Her Majesty and Prince Albert awaited the arrival of the Court of Anne of Brittany. . . . About half-past ten, the heralds marshalled the procession from the lower suite of rooms up the grand white marble staircase, and by the Green Drawing-room to the Throne-room, all the State-rooms having been thrown open and brilliantly illuminated. The Duchess of Cambridge entered, magnificently dressed as Anne of Brittany, led by the Duke of Beaufort, richly clad as Louis XII., and followed by her Court. . . . Each gentleman, leading a lady, passed before the Queen and Prince Albert, and did obeisance." Specially noteworthy among the many noteworthy figures was that of Chaucer, impersonated by Monckton Milnes, the poet, afterwards Lord Houghton. Bulwer Lytton, the novelist, was also present, in the dress of a gentleman of the period, a doublet of dark velvet, slashed with white satin. The Queen retired at three o'clock, but the dancing was kept up for an hour after her withdrawal; and it was broad daylight before the last guest left the Palace. Thus closed the most splendid and unique fête of the season—indeed, of the reign. Probably there is nothing in English history to compare with it, unless the Field of the Cloth of Gold. "The Powder Ball" at Buckingham Palace, in 1845, when all the guests dressed in the style of 1750, was certainly inferior to it.

Before the month was out, the public were thrown into a fresh fever of excitement by the news of another attempt to shoot the Queen. On Sunday, the 29th, as the Queen and

Prince were returning from the Chapel Royal, St. James's, and when the carriage was nearly opposite Stafford House, a man stepped out from the crowd and fired a pistol full at Her Majesty. The Prince turned to her and asked, "Did you hear that?" but the Queen had been bowing to the people on the other side of the carriage, and had heard nothing. "I may be mistaken," said the Prince, "but I am sure I saw some one take aim at us." Singularly enough he had been the only one of the party to witness the occurrence, and both the Queen and Prince deemed it advisable to keep the matter a profound secret. Still more singularly, the incident had been witnessed by only one in the crowd, a boy of fourteen, and thus the would-be assassin got away. Her Majesty was now harassed by the disquieting thought that the act might be at any moment repeated; but that did not deter her from driving out the next day, an act which Greville characterises as "brave but imprudent."* However, she was careful to save others from unnecessary exposure, and her female attendants were not a little surprised when they were forbidden to accompany her.

The act *was* repeated. "We drove out at four," the Prince afterwards wrote to his father, "giving orders to drive faster than usual, and for the two equerries, Colonel Wylde and Colonel Arbuthnot, to ride close to the carriage. You may imagine that our minds were not very easy. We looked behind every tree, and I cast my eyes round in search of the rascal's face. We, however, got safely through the parks and drove towards Hampstead. The weather was superb, and hosts of people on foot. On our way home, as we were approaching the Palace, between the Green Park and the Garden Wall, a shot was fired at us at about five paces off. It was the fellow with the same pistol—a little swarthy, ill-looking rascal. The shot must have passed under the carriage, for he lowered his hand. We felt as if a load had been taken off our hearts, and we thanked the Almighty for having preserved us a second time from so great a danger."† That evening the Queen said to one of her

---

* Greville's *Memoirs*, part ii., vol. ii. 96.
† *Life of the Prince Consort*, vol. i. 124.

maids of honour, Miss Liddell (afterwards Lady Bloomfield), "I dare say, Georgy, you were surprised at not driving with me this afternoon, but the fact is that, as we returned from church yesterday, a man presented a pistol at the carriage window, which flashed in the pan; we were so taken by surprise that he had time to escape, so I knew what was hanging over me, and was determined to expose no life but my own."* The new seeker after notoriety proved to be a carpenter's son, named Francis. He was condemned to death, but the sentence was afterwards commuted, and he was transported beyond seas.

The very day that the commutation was made known, the Queen's life was a third time threatened. The wretch in this case was a chemist's assistant named Bean—a hunchback. His pistol, which was found to contain powder, paper, and some pieces of a clay pipe, providentially missed fire. On hearing of the attempt, Sir Robert Peel hurried up from Cambridge to consult with the Prince as to the steps to be taken. "During their interview," says Sir Theodore Martin, "Her Majesty entered the room, when the Minister, in public so cold and self-commanding, in reality so full of genuine feeling, out of his very manliness was unable to control his emotion, and burst into tears."† The law, which had hitherto given a certain kind of dignity to crimes of this kind, by the very magnitude of the punishment awarded, was now amended; and a Bill was hurried through Parliament, making such attempts punishable as high misdemeanours, by transportation for seven years, or imprisonment, with or without hard labour, for a term not exceeding three years; the culprit to be publicly or privately whipped as often and in such manner and form as the court should direct, not exceeding thrice. Under this new law, Bean was tried on the 25th of August, and sentenced to eighteen months' imprisonment.

After Bean's attempt little happened for some years to disturb the tranquillity of the Palace home, unless, indeed, the retirement from the Queen's service of her old friend and governess,

---

* *Reminiscences of Court and Diplomatic Life*, vol. i. 45, 46.
† *Life of the Prince Consort*, vol. i. 24.

the Baroness Lehzen. Greville's *Journal* has the following entry under date of the 5th of October, 1842 :—" The Baroness Lehzen has left Windsor Castle, and is gone abroad for her health (as she says), to stay five or six months, but it is supposed never to return. This lady, who is much beloved by the women and much esteemed and liked by all who frequent the Court, who is very intelligent, and has been a faithful and devoted servant to the Queen from her birth, has for some time been supposed to be obnoxious to the Prince, and as he is now all-powerful her retirement was not unexpected."* Whatever truth there may have been in the rumour, it is certain the Baroness did *not* return, and the Queen did not see her again till 1845, when they met at Gotha. She died in 1870 at the advanced age of 87.

If distinctions could be made where happiness was so uniform, probably the Queen's brightest times were the autumn and winter months spent at Windsor, when the restraints demanded by Court life in London were to some extent laid aside; and she and the Prince were able to give themselves up, almost unreservedly, to the pure pleasures of a country life. "Now I am free; now I can breathe," Prince Albert used to say on getting back into the country; and the Queen shared his feelings, and grew fonder and fonder of the old Castle with every visit. At the end of 1840 the Prince had established a model farm at Windsor, and till the close of his life he continued to take the most lively interest in the breeding of stock, and in the introduction of agricultural improvements.†

Of course there were guests and great dinners enough during these Windsor days—times of regal gaiety and splendour, when silks would rustle and jewels flash, and the plate and china rooms of the Castle would be made to bring forth of their best. Then the tables would groan beneath their burden of gold plate —goblets and massive plates and dishes all of the precious metal, some of them the work of the great Florentine Benvenuto Cellini. Then the costly services of Sèvres and old Chelsea

---

* Greville's *Memoirs*, part iii., vol. ii. 110.
† *Life of the Prince Consort*, vol. i. 32.

china would be seen; and from the Royal kitchen what miracles of the culinary art would go forth!

Sometimes the Queen would dine in private, but seldom for two days running, though on one occasion she did so, contrary to her own wishes. Imagine the consternation of the Maids of Honour, when, having just finished their soup and fish, a message came to them from the Queen to know who gave the order that they were to dine without her! They stared at each other, and at last discovered that one of the pages had been the cause of the mistake. Her Majesty and the Prince took the matter in good part, and the incident formed a pleasant break in the monotony of the Court.

In these days the Queen appears to have taken interest in everything, and was herself the very soul of fun. One day we find her polkaing with the Countess Wratislaw, and making that lady give her a regular dancing lesson; another, she gets all her ladies to dance a reel, and looks on, laughing heartily. On another occasion the Prince and one of her Maids of Honour yield her great amusement by spinning rings and counters. "The Queen," says the maid in question, Miss Liddell, "supplied me with her different rings, and gave the history of each. One, a small enamel with a tiny diamond in the centre, the Prince gave her the first time he came to England, when he was sixteen. Another beautiful emerald serpent he gave her after they were engaged. The next, the Queen said, 'was my wedding ring,' which she has never taken off; and yesterday, when a cast was taken of her hand, Her Majesty was in an agony lest the ring should come off with the plaster."*

Of an evening the Queen would frequently get one of her ladies to play to her—not tinkling, pretty music, but difficult classical pieces and grand overtures. One night the piece was Beethoven's "Septuor," the pianists Miss Paget and Miss Liddell, and when they came to the last bar the Queen expressed her pleasure that they were playing together, and observed that had either of them gone wrong the piece would have been spoilt. "I enjoy nothing so much," says Miss

* *Reminiscences of Court and Diplomatic Life*, vol. i. 123, 125.

Liddell, "as seeing the Queen in that nice quiet way, and I often wish that those who don't know Her Majesty could see how kind and gracious she is when she is perfectly at her ease, and able to throw off the restraint and form which must and ought to be observed when she is in public."*

Incidents such as these do not, however, bring us into the innermost circle of happiness—the circle of the family—that sacred sphere where love reigns alone, and the laughter of merry children is the sweetest music of all. To gratify ourselves with a sight of such felicity we must step up into the nursery and take a peep at the Royal babies. Yonder is the little Princess Royal, now in her second year. She is growing a fine child, and runs about and talks at a great rate. She is delighted with two new frocks which her grandmother, the Duchess of Kent, has given her for a Christmas-box; and takes them, first one and then the other, and holds them up to be admired. An intelligent child and very fat; her dress, a dark blue velvet frock, muslin sleeves gathered tight to the chubby arms, yellow kid mittens, and the daintiest little white shoes. The Prince of Wales is a fine little fellow, too, and well-behaved; his large eyes and curly hair give promise of the handsome man into which he will grow. Neither of the children is averse to a romp, and when one of the ladies spins a round ivory counter for their amusement they go off into fits of laughter.† Here are children healthy, happy, and good-tempered—surely we have been inspecting a model nursery!

The Princess Royal was an astonishing child, even as a baby. One day she was introduced to the old Duke of Wellington—always a welcome friend at Victoria's Court. She put out her hand to him, much as her mother might have done in the old days at Kensington, and the grey-haired veteran bent down in the most gallant manner and kissed it, telling her at the same time to remember him.

On another occasion she was called upon to thank a certain major for a box of toys which he had sent her. She did so

* *Reminiscences of Court and Diplomatic Life*, vol. i. 131, 132.
† *Ibid.* vol. i. 51, 52, 98.

very prettily, and on being brought back to the Queen's room, Her Majesty turned round to her and said, "Well, Pussy, what did you say?" The child—she was only two and a-half years old at the time—answered readily, "I said—I said my speech."*

The Princess was quick to assert her dignity, too, if she saw occasion. The Queen took her out for a drive one day, and happened to call her, as she often did, "Missy." The child took no notice the first time, but the next she looked up very indignantly, and said to her mother, "I'm not missy, I'm the Princess Royal." In her third year she could speak French fluently, and knew how to turn her knowledge to some account. Once, when a Maid of Honour happened to disturb her while poring over a book, she motioned the disturber away with her infantine hand, and said sedately : "*N'approchez pas moi, moi ne veut pas vous.*"†

Another instance of her early linguistic cleverness is recorded by the Queen. "Our Pussette," she wrote to the King of the Belgians, "learns a verse of Lamartine by heart, which ends with '*Le tableau se déroule à mes pieds*' (The picture unrolls itself at my feet). To show how well she understood this difficult line, I must tell you the following *bon-mot*. When she was riding on her pony, and looking at the cows and sheep, she turned to Madame Charrier (her governess) and said, '*Voilà le tableau qui se déroule à mes pieds?*' Is not this extraordinary for a child of three years?" ‡

The fertility of the Princess's imagination was likewise remarkable, and must often have afforded considerable diversion to her parents. An entry in Lady Bloomfield's *Journal*, under date the 26th of August, 1843, relates to a striking exhibition of this quality. "We drove with the Queen and the little Princess yesterday. The latter chattered the whole time, and was very amusing. Prince Albert rode away to look at a house he is having built, and the carriage stood still till he returned. The Queen was talking to us, and not taking any notice of the Princess, who suddenly

---

* *Reminiscences of Court and Diplomatic Life*, vol. i. 99.
† *Ibid.* vol. i. 63, 64. ‡ *Life of the Prince Consort*, vol. i. 33.

exclaimed, 'There's a cat under the trees!'—fertile imagination on her part, as there was nothing of the kind; but having succeeded in attracting attention, she quietly said, 'Cat come out to look at the Queen, I suppose.'" Lady Bloomfield goes on to tell how that the Princess then took a fancy to some heather at the side of the road, and asked Lady Dunmore to get her some. Lady Dunmore observed she could not do that, as they were driving too fast; so the Princess answered, "No, *you* can't, but *those girls* might get out and get me some"—meaning the fair diarist and Miss Paget!*

Before this time, the advent of a second little Princess had added one more to the Royal nursery. The new-comer was the Princess Alice—whose goodness in after years endeared her to all hearts in a very special manner. She was born on the 25th of April, 1843, and the Queen a fortnight later described her as "a pretty and large baby," and expressed a conviction that she would be the beauty of the family. A year later her father expressed the same thought; in view of which encomiums we are hardly surprised to find the Queen adding "she was a very vain little person"! Before the close of the forties the nursery echoed to the shouts and merry laughter of three more baby-arrivals—a Prince and two Princesses. Prince Alfred (afterwards Duke of Edinburgh, and then of Coburg) came first—" a real darling baby," says Lady Bloomfield, plump, healthy, and rosy, with large blue eyes and dark hair. Her Majesty had his cap taken off to show her Maids of Honour the hair, and when the lady just named was tying on the little cap again, the Queen laughed and said, "Oh, Georgy understands all about babies, she has so many nephews and nieces; pray, how many have you now, my dear?" Lady Bloomfield expressed her belief that she had forty-six, but added that she was not quite sure.† It is said that the Queen incurred a fine of 7s. 6d. for having allowed six weeks to elapse before registering the Prince,

* *Reminiscences of Court and Diplomatic Life*, vol. i. 68, 69.
† *Ibid.* vol. i. 109.

but we rather doubt the story. After Prince Alfred came Princess Helena (now Princess Christian), who was born at Osborne on the 25th of May, 1846, and then in March, 1848, the Princess Louise was born at Buckingham Palace.*

In March, 1844, the Queen and Prince Albert had their first separation from one another since their marriage. The Prince's father had died a few weeks before, and matters of business made it necessary that he should go to Coburg for a few days. The Queen urged him to the step, though at real pain to herself; for they had not been one day apart since their marriage. He left England on the 28th of March, and next day Lady Lyttleton wrote from Buckingham Palace: "The Queen has been behaving like a pattern wife, as she is, about the Prince's tour; so feeling, and so wretched, and yet so unselfish; encouraging him to go, and putting the best face upon it to the last moment. . . . We all feel sadly wicked and unnatural in his absence, and I am actually counting the days on my part, as Her Majesty is on hers." Tender letters, however, passed between the Royal pair, and none knew better than the Prince how to cheer the drooping spirits of the wife who loved him so devotedly. On the first day of his absence he wrote from Dover Harbour: "Poor child! you will, while I write, be getting ready for luncheon, and you will find a place vacant where I sat yesterday. In your heart, however, I hope my place will not be vacant. I at least have you on board with me in spirit. I reiterate my entreaty, 'Bear up!' and do not give way to low spirits, but try to occupy yourself as much as possible. You are even now half-a-day nearer to seeing me again; by the time you get this letter you will be a whole one —thirteen more, and I am again within your arms."†

On the 11th of April the Prince returned to England, arriving at Windsor Castle in the evening. The entry in his *Diary* for that day is delightfully laconic: "Crossed on the 11th. I arrived at six o'clock in the evening at Windsor. *Great joy.*" It would be interesting to have the entry from the Queen's *Journal* of the same date to place beside it.

* *Life of the Prince Consort*, vol. i. 35.   † *Ibid.* vol. i. 35.

Her Majesty's birthday that year was a day of happy surprises. Unknown to the Queen, the Prince had commissioned two celebrated artists—Mr. (afterwards Sir Charles) Eastlake, and Thorburn, the miniature painter—to paint for him—the one, a small cabinet picture of angels, the other, a portrait of himself in armour, to be ready by the 24th of May. The future President of the Academy thus refers to his part in this pleasing episode in a letter to a friend: "On the 5th of March the Prince asked me if I could paint a little picture of angels, such as I had introduced in the fresco—and which, he added, the Queen admired much—by the 24th of May (this is the day by which I am to do a picture for Her Majesty), as he wished to present it to the Queen on her birthday. I said I thought it was His Royal Highness's birthday. 'No,' he said, 'that was in August.' I promised to do the picture, and if I finish both, which I shall do if I live, the result will be curious. Each means a surprise to the other, and the same painter is selected."*

Thorburn's portrait of the Prince was in his best style—a work worthy to rank with the finest specimens of Venetian art—and the Queen was overjoyed with the present. She considered it—and still considers it—the best portrait ever painted of her husband. The birthday, as usual, was spent at Claremont, and Lady Lyttleton thus refers to the occasion: "The Prince has given the Queen a portrait of himself, by Thorburn, most beautiful indeed. Quite his gravest, manliest look, and done when he was rather tanned, as he was on his return, *in armour* (which is according to an old wish of the Queen's); the painting is quite magnificent, and so bold and free that he says the lower part of the face was done in half-an-hour, and it is full of genius and admirably like. Then there is . . . such a lovely group of angels painted for *to-day* by Eastlake, offering a medallion, with *Heil und Segen* (Health and Blessing) on it! All placed in a room turned into a bower by dint of enormous garlands."†

On the 28th of October of this year, the City—indeed, the

* *Life of the Prince Consort*, vol. i. 36.   † *Ibid.* vol. i. 36.

whole way from the Mansion House to Buckingham Palace—was crowded to see the Queen pass in state to the Royal Exchange, then just completed. The Prince Consort had laid the foundation stone of the building two years before, and the Queen had now come to open it. The day passed off very well — fine weather, no accidents, and great enthusiasm. The procession was met at Temple Bar by the Lord Mayor and Aldermen, and then there was a grand luncheon in the Banqueting-hall of the new building. The Lord Mayor got himself into a terrible hobble, however, just before the procession reached Temple Bar—the situation reminding one of the Mayor of Plymouth (in *Water Babies*), who got trapped in a lobster-hole when out fishing. His Worship, it appears, had drawn a pair of jack-boots over his shoes and stockings as a protection from the mud, and just as the famous glass-coach, with Her Majesty inside, was approaching he found to his horror that he could not get the boots off again. He managed to remove one of them, but the other stuck fast. Imagine the situation! The chief magistrate of the City of London precariously sustained on one leg, and clinging with pathetic earnestness to a friendly support, while several men tug frantically at the stubborn boot! Human labour, alas! was wasted, and while the men tugged, the State-carriage was coming nearer and nearer. At last, in an agony of desperation, the Mayor gasped out, "Let go! I'll put the other boot on again!" And put it on he did, and in jack-boots his Worship figured in the procession, and thus booted he sat down at the banquet and took luncheon with the Queen of England!*

Whether Her Majesty noticed the condition of the Lord Mayor's pedal extremities we are not informed, but she thought the ceremony a big success, and writing next day to the King of the Belgians, she said: "Nothing ever went off better; and the procession there, as well as the proceedings at the Royal Exchange, were splendid and royal in the extreme. It was a fine and gratifying sight to see the myriads of people assembled, more than at the Coronation even, and all in

* *Reminiscences of Court and Diplomatic Life*, vol. i. 109–113.

such good humour and so loyal. I seldom remember being so pleased with any public show, and my beloved Albert was most enthusiastically received by the people. . . . The articles in the papers, too, are most kind and gratifying. They say no Sovereign was ever more loved than I am (I am bold enough to add), and *this* because of our happy domestic home, and the good example it presents."*

These concluding remarks are very true. The home life of the Queen was the great secret of her enormous popularity, therein affording a striking contrast to that of her uncle, George the Fourth. Some lines of Tennyson, written six or seven years later, were already true of Her Majesty, as they have remained true ever since.

> " Her court was pure ; her life serene ;
> God gave her peace ; her land reposed ;
> A thousand claims to reverence closed
> In her as Mother, Wife, and Queen."

But we must hasten on.

A week or two after the opening of the Royal Exchange, there was a pretty little review of the Guards and Blues in Windsor Park, in honour of the Prince of Wales' birthday. It was true Queen's weather; the day bright and warm, and more like May than November. The troops marched past the Queen and Prince, presenting arms, and afterwards fired a *feu de joie*. The Royal children behaved in a most exemplary manner, and the soldiers had a good view of them as they marched past. "The Princess Royal was the only one who appeared a little frightened at the firing, and towards the end, when the band struck up 'God save the Queen,' she thought, poor child, that it was going to begin again, so she put her little hands to her ears, which shocked the Queen dreadfully." The Princess Alice was exceptionally good—standing all the time, and never once moving.†

In the following year, the great domestic event was the

---

* *Life of the Prince Consort*, vol. i. 41.
† *Reminiscences of Court and Diplomatic Life*, vol. i. 124.

purchase of Osborne—now Her Majesty's favourite residence, if we except Balmoral. Almost ever since her marriage, the Queen had had a great desire to have a place of her own, a private residence to which she could escape for a time from the oppressive splendour of the Court, and live a retired and simple life with the rest of mankind. The estate of Osborne, recommended to her by Sir Robert Peel, appeared to answer all the requirements of such a wish, and in March, 1845, the purchase had been made. Uncle Leopold was, of course, one of the first to be told of the purchase. "It sounds so pleasant" the Queen wrote to him, not without a touch of irony, "to have a place of one's own, quiet and retired, and free from all Woods and Forests and other charming departments, which really are the plague of one's life."* Her delight on entering into her new possession is expressed in another letter to the King, a few days later. "It is impossible to see a prettier place, with woods and valleys, and points of view, which would be beautiful anywhere; but when these are combined with the sea (to which the woods grow down), and a beach which is quite private, it is really everything one could wish."† Various additions were made to the property from time to time, new plantations were formed, and the gardens were laid out with great taste and care under the direction of the Prince Consort. The result was worthy of the effort. The vigorous luxuriance of the conifers and flowering shrubs which he planted became in time a sight to feast the eye; and the place grew in beauty and charm every year. The woods were a favourite resort for birds, and especially for nightingales, whose song the Prince preferred before all others. The Queen has told us of the happy peaceful walks she used to take with him in the Osborne woods, and how the Prince would whistle to the nightingales in their own peculiar long note, which they invariably answered. At night he would stand on the balcony listening to them.‡ Their life at Osborne was, indeed, simplicity itself, and what with country

---

* *Life of the Prince Consort*, vol. i. 42.
† *Ibid.*
‡ *Early Years of the Prince Consort*, 195.

air and sea-bathing, the Royal children throve and grew strong, delighting the hearts of their parents by their health and high spirits. Writing to the Dowager-Duchess of Coburg in the year 1847, Prince Albert says: "You really should, some day, take courage to trust yourself to the unstable element the sea, were it only to have a peep at our little folks. When we are in the Isle of Wight, where we are not surrounded by a Court and its formalities, our life is so quiet and simple that it would not fatigue you."*

OSBORNE HOUSE.

But not only were the grounds extended and improved. Building operations on a large scale were begun, and a new and more commodious residence presently arose in place of the old. In the year 1846, that portion of the present mansion which contains the Royal apartments, and which is known as the Pavilion, was completed and occupied; but the rest was not finished till 1851. The mansion is in the Italian style, and a queenlier structure could not be imagined.

* *Life of the Prince Consort*, vol. i. 78.

It is well depicted in the accompanying illustration, which conveys a better idea of its architectural features than a laboured description would give. In front of the mansion are terraces, flower-beds, lawns and park; sculpture, vases, fountains, and ornamental waters; shady places and winding paths, where myrtles and magnolias, camellia bushes and ilexes flourish in all their beauty. The place, indeed, is a terrestrial paradise.

Lady Lyttleton has penned a charming account of the first day in the new home—a family picture that leaves nothing to be desired. "Our first night in this house is well past. Nobody smelt paint or caught cold, and the worst is over. It was a most amusing event coming here to dinner. Everything in the house is quite new, and the drawing-room looked very handsome; the windows lighted by the brilliant lamps in the room must have been seen far out at sea. I was pleased by one little thing. After dinner we were to drink the Queen and Prince's health as a *house-warming*. And after it the Prince said, very naturally and simply, but seriously: 'We have a hymn' (he called it a *psalm*) 'in Germany for such occasions, it begins—' and then he repeated two lines in German, which I could not quote right, meaning a prayer to 'bless our going out and coming in;' it was dry and quaint, being Luther's—we all perceived that he was feeling it."* The hymn, of which we translate a single verse, is an amplification of Psalm cxxi. 8:—

> Lord, with Thy favour us endow,
>   Our going out, our entering bless:
>   Bless Thou our daily bread; nor less
> Whate'er we do, whate'er allow.
>   Bless, when the pains of death o'ertake us
>   And blissful heirs of Heaven make us.

Could a happier or more suitable way have been chosen of celebrating such an occasion?

It was at Osborne, if we mistake not—and about this time—that Lady Lyttleton sketched that delightful little picture of the Princess Alice, on her fourth birthday, which lies before us

* *Life of the Prince Consort*, vol. i. 57, 58.

in the memorial volume of the lamented Princess. "Dear Princess Alice is too pretty, in her low frock and pearl necklace, tripping about and blushing and smiling at her honours. The whole family, indeed, appear to advantage on birthdays; no tradesman or country squire can keep one with such hearty simple affection and enjoyment. *One* present I think we shall all wish to live farther off: a live lamb, all over pink ribbons and bells. He is already the greatest pet, as one may suppose. Princess Alice's pet lamb is the cause of many tears. He will not take to his mistress, but runs away lustily, and will soon butt at her, though she is most coaxy, and said to him in her sweetest tones, after kissing his nose often : 'Milly, *dear* Milly! *do* you like me?'"* Kind little heart! We love to think of the dead Princess as she was in the days of her happy childhood, when her mother was still young, and the family circle as yet had known no break. In one of these childhood days the Prince of Wales—full of mischief no doubt, as boys usually are—made a joke about the great height of one of the Queen's dressers, whereupon his little sister, thinking that the remark might have caused annoyance, said to her brother, but so that the dresser should hear it: "It is very nice to be tall; papa would like us all to be tall." This was her way always. Whenever she suspected that anybody's feelings had been hurt, she tried to make things smooth again. "At Christmas-time," says Madame Müller, who formerly held a post in the Queen's household, "she was most anxious to give pleasure to everybody, and bought presents for each with her own pocket-money. She once gave me a little pin-cushion, and on another occasion a basket, and wrote on a little card with a coloured border (always in German for me), 'For dear Frida, from Alice,' and brought it to me on Christmas-Eve. I felt that she had thought how much I must have missed my home that day."†

It has been said that the Queen was very strict with her children. She may have been; but she was not too strict. If all mothers exhibited a tithe of the strong common sense which

* *Princess Alice*, 6. † *Ibid*. 7, 8.

the Queen has ever shown in this particular, the world would be a much better place than it is. The Queen's great maxim ever was, and we know this on her own authority, "that the children should be brought up as simply, and in as domestic a way as possible; that (not interfering with their lessons) they should be as much as possible with their parents, and learn to place their greatest confidence in them in all things." As to religious training, she held that that was best which was given to a child, day by day, at its mother's knees. "I am quite clear," she wrote, when this important question was under consideration in relation to the Princess Royal, "that she should be taught to have great reverence for God and for religion, but that she should have the feeling of devotion and love which our Heavenly Father encourages His earthly children to have for Him, and not one of fear and trembling; and that the thoughts of death and an after life should not be represented in an alarming and forbidding view, and that she should be made to know *as yet* no difference of creeds, and not think that she can only pray on her knees, or that those who do not kneel are less fervent and devout in their prayers."* If the training of children, carried on on these lines is to be denominated "strict," then by all means let us introduce the golden rule of "strictness" into all our homes. We shall be gainers by it; and the fruit of the training will be seen in such characters as the Princess Alice, who, it should be remembered, never found her early life a burden, but could write, even in her days of wedded felicity: "I can look back to my childhood and girlhood as the happiest time of my life."†

* *Life of the Prince Consort*, vol. ii. 31. † *Princess Alice*, 1.

CHAPTER VII.

THE QUEEN AS GUEST AND GUEST-RECEIVER
(1840–1848).

DURING the first years of her reign the Queen travelled a good deal more than she has done since; and not the least interesting portion of Her Majesty's life is that which relates to her visits to her own subjects in various parts of the country. Needless to say, she visited in London too; but the published details of such visits are rare, and, for the most part, uninteresting. Perhaps, if we except the Royal palaces, no place in London saw more of the young Queen than Stafford House, that historic mansion which Rogers, the banker poet, declared to be superior to all the palaces of Europe. Among the pictures in this superb mansion "hangs," says Lord Ronald Gower,* "a brilliant water-colour drawing by Eugene Lami, representing one of the many occasions on which the Queen— then in the early happy days of her reign—honoured Stafford House by her presence. It was during one of these receptions that Her Majesty, on entering the great hall, paid her hostess a compliment worthy of Louis XIV.: 'I have come from my house to your palace!' In Lami's drawing the grand staircase is shown crowded with guests, and the spacious hall a blaze of light. The artist has chosen the moment when the Queen, escorted by her host and hostess, is descending the staircase." It may not be generally known that Stafford House in less than thirty years will revert to the Crown. It will then doubtless

* *My Reminiscences*, vol. i. 2.

become a Royal residence, and not improbably will have to house the Duke of York if he then be Prince of Wales.

The first Royal progress which the Queen made in company with Prince Albert was in the summer of 1841, the chief places visited being Nuneham (the Archbishop of York's residence), Oxford, Woburn Abbey (the seat of the Russells), Panshanger (the seat of Earl Cowper), Brocket Hall (Lord Melbourne's), and Hatfield, the magnificent estate of the Marquis of Salisbury. Everywhere along their route the Royal travellers were met by the warmest expressions of loyalty. Their carriage was frequently surrounded by supplementary escorts, improvised by the enthusiasm of the farmers, etc., though it should be stated that these well-meaning yeomanry were occasionally a source of some discomfort to the Queen. Thus, at Dunstable, "numbers of farmers," Her Majesty records, "rode with us, and they nearly smothered us with dust;" and again, when driving out from Woburn Abbey, "a crowd of good loyal people rode with us part of the way. They so pressed and pushed, that it was as if we were hunting."* The latter place was reached on the 27th of July. It "is really very beautiful," the Prince wrote to the Duchess of Kent, "and as complete and comfortable as possible. Yesterday we arrived here, and to-day we make an excursion to Brocket to Lord Melbourne, who is rather nervous about it. . . . H. has already lost his hat from the carriage, sat down upon a basket of strawberries, mistaken ice at dinner for bread, and thrust his fingers into it, etc., etc."† Who the luckless H. was we are not informed.

In 1843 the Queen and Prince paid interesting visits to the Isle of Wight, Dartmouth, Plymouth, Falmouth, etc., going from place to place in their yacht *Victoria and Albert*. Greville, who went over the yacht while it was lying at Plymouth, describes it as luxuriously fitted up, but adds that everything was "sacrificed to the comfort of the Court, the whole ship's company being crammed into wretched dog-holes, officers included;"‡ but it should be added that the blame of this rested

---

* *Life of the Prince Consort*, vol. i. 19.   † *Ibid.*
‡ Greville's *Memoirs*, part ii., vol. ii. 196.

with the Admiralty, not the Queen. Her Majesty made a small collection of flowers at each place they went to, which were dried and kept as mementoes. Upon leaving Falmouth for Tréport, on a visit of which we shall have to speak hereafter, an amusing incident occurred. Lady Canning and Miss Liddell had settled themselves in a sheltered place on deck, protected by the paddle-box, and had been seated there some time, when the Queen came on deck and remarked what a comfortable place they had chosen. Her Majesty sent for her camp-stool and settled herself beside them; and all three were composedly working away at some plaited paper bonnets, when they observed a commotion among the sailors. The men had gathered in little knots and were talking together in a mysterious manner. Presently an officer came up to the distinguished plaiters, looking rather puzzled; but his courage seemed to forsake him, and he went away again. Then another approached, with the same puzzled look; but he also appeared to lose heart, and walked away as the first had done. At last the captain, Lord Adolphus FitzClarence, drew near, whereupon the Queen inquired what was the matter, adding, with a sly smile, that she hoped there was not going to be a mutiny on board. Lord Adolphus laughed, but remarked that he really did not know what *would* happen unless Her Majesty would be graciously pleased to move her seat. "Move my seat," said the Queen; "why should I? What possible harm can I be doing here?" "Well, ma'am," said Lord Adolphus, "the fact is, your Majesty is unwittingly closing up the door of the place where the grog tubs are kept, and so the men cannot have their grog!" "Oh, very well," said the Queen, "I will move on one condition—that you bring me a glass of grog." This was accordingly done, and after tasting it the Queen said, "I am afraid I can only make the same remark I did once before, that I think it would be very good if it were stronger!" This, of course, delighted the men, and the little incident caused much amusement on board.*

This year there was another grand progress through the country, when Drayton, Birmingham, Chatsworth, Belvoir,

---

* *Reminiscences of Court and Diplomatic Life*, vol. i. 76, 77.

Chesterfield, and other places were visited. Her Majesty's stay at Drayton Hall, the seat of Sir Robert Peel, gave much pleasure to the great statesman, but can scarcely have strengthened his political position as Prince Albert imagined it would. While here the Queen quite dispensed with formalities, chatting freely with everybody, playing at patience with the ladies, etc., etc. At dinner she looked charming, we are told, in a pink silk gown with three flounces. Next morning the Queen went out walking, and visited the farm, dairy, kitchen garden, and other parts of the baronet's estate. At Chatsworth the reception of the Royal travellers eclipsed everything. The Duke of Devonshire met the Queen at the station, and brought her in his own coach-and-six, with a coach-and-four following, and eight outriders. There was a ball in the grand banqueting-hall the same night, when the Queen danced a country dance with Lord Leveson, and afterwards waltzed with the Prince. The grounds were brilliantly illuminated, and the play of the green and red lights on the fountains and cascades is said to have had a charmingly fairy-like effect. Having seen the whole place covered with innumerable lamps and all the materials of the illuminations, "the guests were astonished and delighted when they got up the following morning," says Greville, "not to find a vestige of them left, and the whole garden as trim and neat as if nothing had occurred. This was accomplished by Paxton, who got 200 men, set them to work, and worked with them the whole night till they had cleared away everything belonging to the exhibition of the preceding night."* At Chesterfield, where the enthusiasm was very great, Her Majesty stood on a chair to look out of a high window, an incident trivial in itself, but which drew from one of her ladies the remark that Her Majesty took such very tight hold of her hand in mounting, that it was evident she was not used to getting on chairs.

In the following year (1844) the Queen paid a visit to Lord Exeter at Burghley. She passed through Northampton on her way thither, and her reception at this city—albeit a stronghold of radicalism—was very cheering. The triumphal arches were

* Greville's *Memoirs*, part ii., vol. ii. 216.

numerous and handsome, the houses were decorated with flags, banners, and evergreens, and enthusiastic crowds lined the streets. As it was getting dark when the Queen arrived at Burghley she was not shown over the historic old mansion till the following day, when Lord Exeter himself acted as guide. In the course of their perambulations they had to pass through a certain gentleman's room, "and lo! his best wig and whiskers were put on a block on the drawers." Fortunately the owner of these capillary appendages was not present when the discovery was made. At Burghley, as at Chatsworth, the ball in honour of the Royal visit was on a grand scale, but the lady just quoted thought it rather dull; and perhaps the Queen thought the same, for she did not dance.*

In the following January there was a visit to the Duke of Buckingham at Stowe, the neighbours and tenants being admitted into the park in great numbers to witness the Queen's arrival. There was nothing specially remarkable about this visit, unless the prodigious slaughter of hares and pheasants in the Duke's preserves, where the accumulation of game was so enormous that the Prince hit almost everything he fired at.

But a visit of real importance was to follow. Before the month was out the Queen and Prince were the guests of the Duke of Wellington at Strathfieldsaye. The curiosity manifested by the public on this occasion was only equalled by the zeal of the newspapers to satisfy it. The place was beset with tourists, who hung about the gates, and, in some cases, even wandered into the private grounds and stared in at the windows. Reporters and country editors flocked into the neighbourhood, and, in their eagerness for "copy," waylaid the Duke's servants and besought them—if not with tears in their eyes, at least with bribes in their hands, to be communicative. One daring young journalist on the staff of a popular paper actually sent a message to the Duke, requesting the honour of an interview, the public being so interested in all that was going on under his Grace's roof. The answer he received was short but unfavourable. "Field-Marshal the Duke of Wellington presents his compli-

* *Reminiscences of Court and Diplomatic Life*, vol. i. 129, 130.

ments to Mr. ——, and begs to say he does not see what his house at Strathfieldsaye has to do with the public press." A notice ("writ satirical," as Artemus Ward would say) was also stuck up in the grounds, desiring that people who wished to see the house would drive up to the hall door and ring the bell, but that they were to abstain from walking on the flagstones and looking in at the windows. The visit was of a more private and informal character than is usual on such occasions, Her Majesty desiring to mark in a special manner her sense of the great services which the Duke had rendered to his country and the Crown. The soldier-like regularity—and we might almost say the clockwork monotony—which were characteristic of the Duke, were very marked during the Queen's stay at Strathfieldsaye. The Prince Consort's secretary, Mr. Anson, writes: "The Duke takes the Queen in to dinner, and sits by Her Majesty, and after dinner gets up and says, 'With your Majesty's permission, I give the health of Her Majesty,' and then the same for the Prince. They then adjourn to the library, and the Duke sits on the sofa by the Queen for the rest of the evening, until eleven o'clock, the Prince and the gentlemen being scattered about the library or the billiard-room, which opens into it. In a large conservatory beyond, the band of the Duke's Grenadier regiment plays through the evening."*

During the eight years which we are considering there were also two visits to Cambridge, one in 1843 and the other in 1847. On the first occasion, the degree of LL.D. was conferred upon Prince Albert by the University, and on the second occasion he was installed as Chancellor. The Queen and Prince were shown over the Woodwardian Museum of the University during the earlier visit, and Professor Sedgewick has given an amusing account of what took place. "I received a formidable note from our Master," says the eminent geologist, "telling me of an intended Royal visit to the Woodwardian den of wild beasts, immediately after Prince Albert's degree, and enjoining me to clear a passage by the side entrance through the old Divinity Schools. This threw me off my balance, for since the building

* *Life of the Prince Consort*, vol. i. 42.

of the new library this place of ancient theological disputation has been converted into a kind of lumber-room, and was filled from end to end with every kind of unclean thing. Mops, slop-pails, chimney-pots, ladders, broken benches, rejected broken cabinets, two long ladders, and an old rusty scythe were the things that met the eye, and all covered with half-an-inch of venerable dust. There is at the end of the room a kind of gallery or gangway by which the undergraduates used to find their way to my lecture-room, but this was also full of every kind of rubbish and abomination. We did our best—soon tumbled all impediments into the area below, spread huge mats over the slop-pails, etc., and in a time incredibly short a goodly red carpet was spread along the gangway, and thence down my lecture-room to the door of the museum; but still there was a dreadful evil to encounter. What we had done brought out such a rank compound of villainous smells that even my plebeian nose was sorely put to it; so I went to a chemist's, procured certain bottles of sweet odours, and sprinkled them cunningly where most wanted.

"Inside the Museum all was previously in order, and inside the entrance door from the gangway was a huge picture of the Megatherium, under which the Queen must pass to the Museum, and at that place I was to receive Her Majesty. So I dusted my outer garments and ran to the Senate House, and I was just in time to see the Prince take his degree and join in the acclamations. This ended, I ran back to the feet of the Megatherium, and in a few minutes the Royal party entered the mysterious gangway above described. They halted, I half thought in a spirit of mischief, to contemplate the furniture of the schools; and the Vice-Chancellor (Whewell) pointed out the beauties of the dirty spot, where Queen Bess had sat 250 years before, when she presided at the Divinity Act. A few steps more brought them under the feet of the Megatherium. I bowed as low as my anatomy would let me, and Queen and Prince bowed again most graciously, and so began Act First. The Queen seemed happy and well pleased, and was mightily taken with one or two of my monsters, especially with the

Plesiosaurus and gigantic stag. The subject was new to her; but the Prince evidently had a good general knowledge of the old world; and not only asked good questions, and listened with great courtesy to all I had to say, but in one or two instances helped me on by pointing to the rare things in my collection, especially in that part of it which contains the German fossils. I thought myself very fortunate in being able to exhibit the finest collection of German fossils to be seen in England. They fairly went the round of the Museum, neither of them seemed in a hurry, and the Queen was quite happy to hear her husband talk about a novel subject with so much knowledge and spirit.

"He called her back once or twice to look at a fine impression of a dragon-fly which I have in the solenhope state. Having glanced at the long succession of our fossils, from the youngest to the oldest, the party again moved into the lecture-room. The Queen was again mightily taken with the long neck of the Plesiosaurus; under it was a fine head of an Ichthyosaurus, which I had just been unpacking. I did not know anything about it, as I had myself never seen its face before, for it arrived in my absence. The Queen asked what it was. I told her as plainly as I could. She then asked whence it came; and what do you think I said? That I did not know the exact place, but I believe it came as a delegate from the monsters of the lower world to greet Her Majesty on her arrival at the University. I did not repeat this till I found that I had been overheard, and that my impertinence had been talked of among my Cambridge friends. All was, however, taken in good part, and soon afterwards the Royal party approached the mysterious gangway. The Queen and Prince bowed, the Megatherium packed up his legs close under the abdominal region of his august body, the Royal pageant passed under, and was soon out of my sight and welcomed by the cheers of the multitudes before the Library.

"I will only add that I went through every kind of backward movement to the admiration of all beholders, only having once trodden on the hinder part of my cassock, and never once having fallen during my retrogradations before the face of the Queen.

In short, had I been a king crab, I could not have walked backwards better." *

The second visit to Cambridge, which extended over two days, was a time of much pleasure to Her Majesty. "To see my Albert honoured and esteemed, as he deserves," she wrote, "gives me the deepest satisfaction"; and this, of course, was the object of the visit. Nothing was wanting to make the occasion a real success. The aged poet, Wordsworth, wrote an Installation Ode, which was skilfully set to music, and sung on the second day with striking effect. The weather was perfect on both days, "the sky very blue; the sun very, very hot." "At Tottenham," writes the Queen, "we took the Eastern Counties Railway—the great railway king, Mr. Hudson himself, going with us—and reached Cambridge Station at one." Madam Bunsen, wife of the celebrated Chevalier Bunsen, was with the Royal party, and has described in an animated letter the reception accorded to the illustrious visitors all along the route. "As we shot along, every station and bridge and resting-place and spot of shade was peopled with eager faces watching for the Queen, and decorated with flowers, but the brightest and gayest and most excited assemblage was at the Cambridge Station itself, and from thence along the streets to Trinity College the degree of ornament and crowd and animation was always increasing. I think I never saw so many children before in one morning. I felt so much moved at the spectacle of such a mass of life collected together and animated by one feeling, and that a joyous one, that I was at a loss to conceive 'how any woman's sides can bear the beating of so strong a throb' as must attend the consciousness of being the object of that excitement, and the centre of attraction of all those eyes." †

Of course the chief interest centred around the ceremony which had brought the Queen to Cambridge, namely, the Installation of the Prince as Chancellor. This, as we have already intimated, was reserved for the second day of the visit; but soon after the arrival of the Royal party, Her Majesty received an address from the new Chancellor in the Great Hall

* *Life of the Prince Consort* vol. i. 32. † *Ibid.* 67.

of Trinity—a somewhat novel experience both for Queen and
Prince. A few minutes after Her Majesty had placed herself
on the throne, the Chancellor entered in a handsome dress of
black and gold, with a long train held up by two gentlemen
of his household, and bowed gracefully to the Queen. He
then read his address, and the Queen read an answer, expressing,
we need scarcely say, entire approbation of the choice made by
the University. The command of countenance in both is said
to have been admirable; and it was only when all the Heads of
Houses had kissed her hand, "which they did with exquisite
variety of awkwardness," that she smiled upon the Prince. "I
cannot say," wrote Her Majesty, "how it agitated and embar-
rassed me to have to receive this address, and hear it read by my
beloved Albert, who walked in at the head of the University,
and who looked dear and beautiful in his robes. . . . He went
through it admirably—almost absurd, however, as it was for
us." *

Next day the ceremony of Installation took place in the
Senate House of the University, which was packed to suffoca-
tion. After some preliminaries the Installation Ode was performed amidst immense applause, the rendering of the following
lines being specially admired:—

> "Albert, in thy race we cherish
> A nation's strength, that will not perish
> While England's sceptred line
> True to the King of kings is found;
> Like that wise ancestor of thine
> Who threw the Saxon Shield o'er Luther's life,
> When first above the yells of bigot strife
> The trumpet of the Living Word
> Assumed a voice of deep portentous sound
> From gladdened Elbe to startled Tiber heard."

A banquet and reception followed; and then, the public proceedings of the day being ended, the Queen and Prince took a
quiet stroll by the river in the cool of the evening. "We walked
through the small garden," says Her Majesty, "and could not

* *Life of the Prince Consort*, vol. i. 67.

at first find our way, after which we discovered the right road, and walked along the beautiful avenues of lime-trees in the grounds of St. John's College, along the water and over the bridges. All was so pretty and picturesque—in particular, that one covered bridge of St. John's, which is like the Bridge of Sighs at Venice. We stopped to listen to the distant hum of the town; and nothing seemed wanting, but some singing, which everywhere but here in this country we should have heard. A lattice opened, and we could fancy a lady appearing, and listening to a serenade."*

In August and September of 1846 the Queen and Prince went on two very pleasant yachting excursions, of which Her Majesty has published an account in her *Leaves from the Journal of our Life in the Highlands*. The Royal children accompanied them. On the first excursion the chief places visited were Dartmouth, Plymouth, and Guernsey; on the second, Jersey and the Cornish coast. Her Majesty was not one to be deterred by bad weather if there was anything of interest or beauty to be seen; and we find her again and again exposing her Royal person in the most reckless and surprising manner. Of this, one instance will suffice. As the yacht was entering Dartmouth Harbour, the rain was pouring in torrents, and the deck swimming with water, yet she would not go below, but stood with her children—all under umbrellas—admiring the wooded rocks, and church, and castle. Surely the love of nature here displayed is of a quite unusual kind.†

On entering Plymouth Sound "we steamed," writes the Queen, "up the Tamar, going first a little way up the St. German's river, which has very pretty wooded banks. Trematon Castle to the right, which belongs to Bertie [the Prince of Wales] as Duke of Cornwall, and Jats to the left, are extremely pretty. We stopped here, and afterwards turned back and went up the Tamar, which at first seemed flat; but as we proceeded the scenery became quite beautiful—richly wooded hills, the trees growing down into the water, and the river winding so much as to have the effect of a lake. . . . The finest parts

* *Life of the Prince Consort*, vol. i. 67.   † *Leaves*, 280.

HER MAJESTY IN ST. GEORGE'S CHAPEL, WINDSOR, 1846.
From the painting by H. E. DAWE.

begin about Saltash, which is a small but prettily built town. ... [At Tavy] ... the river becomes very beautiful. We passed numbers of mines at work ... [At Cothele] we landed, and drove up a steep hill under fine trees to the very curious old House of Cothele, where we got out of the carriage. ... It stands in the same state as it was in the time of Henry VII., and is in great preservation—the old rooms being hung with arras, etc."* At Plymouth, the Queen was received by Lord Mount Edgecumbe, but the Prince had started off early in the morning to go to Dartmoor Forest. "There were crowds where we landed," writes the Queen, "and I feel so shy and put out without Albert."†

At St. Pierre in Guernsey the Queen was much struck by the high, bright-coloured houses built down almost to the sea; and with the rocky islands of Herm and Jethou, which form conspicuous objects from the harbour. "We both sketched," says Her Majesty, "and at a quarter to nine got into our barge with our ladies. The pier and shore were lined with crowds of people, and with ladies dressed in white, singing, 'God save the Queen,' and strewing the ground with flowers. ... The people were extremely well-behaved and friendly, and received us very warmly as we drove through the narrow streets, which were decorated with flowers and flags, and lined with the Guernsey militia, 2000 strong, with their several bands. Some of the militia were mounted."‡ At St. Helier's, Jersey, the people were also most enthusiastic, "though not more so than the good Guernsey people." The decorations and triumphal arches were well done, and there were numberless kind inscriptions. A seat in one of the streets was filled by Frenchwomen from Trouville, the white handkerchiefs which formed their head-dress giving them a very picturesque appearance. At St. Michael's Mount, the Cornish pilcher fishermen came round in their large boats, and anchored near the Royal yacht. The Queen found them very noisy and talkative,—jabbering away in a kind of English hard to be understood. Accompanied by the Prince she went up the Mount, and ascended to the tower

* *Leaves*, 282, 283.   † *Ibid.* 284.   ‡ *Ibid.* 288-290.

of the old castle, on the top of which is "St. Michael's Chair," an object of interest to lovers. The fable is that whoever gets first into the chair will have at home the government of the house, and the old housekeeper told the Queen that many a couple "does go there!" but the Prince and Lord Spencer declared that it was the awkwardest place imaginable to get at.* Near Falmouth the Royal party got into the barge and rowed near to the shore in order to see a net drawn. This diversion was the suggestion of a worthy Quaker, who "proposed," says the Queen, "to put in his net and draw, that we might see all sorts of fish caught; but when it was drawn there was not one fish! So," adds Her Majesty laconically, "we went back to the *Fairy*." The following day they were shown over the Restormel Iron Mine, belonging to the Duchy of Cornwall, by a Mr. Taylor, one of the "adventurers" of the mine. "Albert and I got into one of the trucks," says the Royal diarist, "and were dragged in by miners, Mr. Taylor walking behind us. The miners wear a curious woollen dress [and a broad-rimmed cap with rounded crown]; and they generally have a candlestick in front of the cap. This time candlesticks were stuck along the sides of the mine, and those who did not drag or push the truck carried lights. Albert and the gentlemen wore miners' hats. There was no room for any one to pass between the trucks and the rock, and only just room enough to hold up one's head, and not always that. It had a most curious effect, and there was something unearthly about this lit-up cavern-like place. We got out and scrambled a little way to see the veins of ore, and Albert knocked off some pieces; but in general it is blown by gunpowder, being so hard."† On the 9th of September, the second of these delightful yachting excursions came to a close, and the Royal party returned to Osborne.

Our account of the Queen's holiday visits among her subjects, during the period which we have been considering, would be very imperfect did we omit to mention Her Majesty's three visits to Scotland, in the years 1842, 1844, and 1847. This was before the Queen had a home of her own among the Scotch

* *Leaves*, 298, 299, 301, 302. † *Ibid.* 307-309.

Highlands, for the lease of Balmoral was not acquired till the autumn of 1848. On each occasion the journey thither was made by sea—indeed, the third visit was little more than a tour round the West Coast of Scotland, though the Royal party stayed a week at Ardverikie, the seat of Lord Abercorn.

The first trip, in August of 1842, was as happy as any of which the Queen has written. She was in high spirits all the time, and Lord Fitz-Clarence told Greville that "nothing could be more agreeable and amiable than she was, and the Prince too, on board the yacht; conversing all the time with perfect ease and good humour, and on all subjects; taking great interest and very curious about everything in the ship, dining on deck in the midst of the sailors, making them dance, talking to the boatswain, and, in short, doing everything that was popular and ingratiating. Her chief fault, in little things and in great," adds Greville, who is nothing if he is not critical, "seems to be impatience; in sea phrase, she always wants to *go ahead;* she can't bear contradiction nor to be thwarted."* To tell of all the places touched at or visited on this first trip to the land of Bruce and Walter Scott would swell this volume beyond all reasonable limits; but, as we have already said, the time spent there was an extremely happy one. We have evidence of this no less from the Prince Consort's letters than from the Queen's *Journal*, for the Prince writes:—"Scotland has made a most favourable impression upon us both. The country is full of beauty, of a severe and grand character; perfect for sports of all kinds, and the air remarkably pure and light in comparison with what we have here [*i.e.*, at Windsor]. The people are more natural, and marked by that honesty and sympathy which always distinguish the inhabitants of mountainous countries, who live far away from towns. There is, moreover, no country where historical traditions are preserved with such fidelity, or to the same extent. Every spot is connected with some interesting historical fact, and with most of these Sir Walter Scott's accurate descriptions have made us familiar. The finest points we visited were

* Greville's *Memoirs*, vol. ii. 108.

Perth, Loch Leven, Scone, Dunkeld, Taymouth, Killin, Loch Tay, Loch Earn, Glen Ogle, Drummond Castle, Stirling, and Linlithgow."* At Dalkeith House, the Queen tasted oatmeal porridge for the first time, and thought it very good; she also discovered a weakness for "finnan haddies."† Of course she was taken over Edinburgh Castle, and shown the Regalia and the room in which James VI. of Scotland and First of England was born,—"such a very, very small room," remarks Her Majesty, "with an old prayer written on the wall."‡ At Scone she was shown a sycamore tree which that king had planted, and the mound was pointed out to her on which the ancient Scotch kings were always crowned.§ At Dunkeld, which was gay with Highland pipers and triumphal arches, the short stay of the Royal visitors was tinged with sadness. "Poor Lord Glenlyon received us," wrote the Queen, "but he had suddenly become totally blind. . . . He was led about by his wife; it was very melancholy."‖ At Taymouth, a castellated mansion, beautifully situated among high, wooded hills, the reception was on a grand scale. "There were a number of Lord Breadalbane's Highlanders, all in the Campbell tartan, drawn up in front of the house, with Lord Breadalbane himself in a Highland dress at their head, a few of Sir Neil Menzies' men (in the Menzies' red and white tartan), a number of pipers playing, and a company of the 92nd Higlanders, also in kilts. The firing of the guns, the cheering of the great crowd, the picturesqueness of the dresses, the beauty of the surrounding country, with its rich background of wooded hills, altogether formed one of the finest scenes imaginable. It seemed," says Her Majesty, "as if a great chieftain in olden feudal times was receiving his sovereign." After dinner the grounds were splendidly illuminated; festoons of coloured lights hung from the railings, and the words, "Welcome Victoria—Albert," were written in lamps upon the ground. A torchlight dance of Highlanders, to the sound of bagpipes, ended the day.¶ This first tour in Scotland lasted only

* *Life of the Prince Consort*, vol. i. 25.
† *Leaves*, 9.   ‡ *Ibid.* 16.   § *Ibid.* 19.
‖ *Ibid.* 21.   ¶ *Ibid.* 23–25.

a fortnight, but in that short time no less than 656 post-horses are said to have been employed.

During the visit in 1844, the Queen and Prince stayed at Blair Castle, the seat of the Duke of Athole, where the Prince had some excellent sport. The Queen often accompanied him on his shooting expeditions, and on these occasions her patience was sometimes put to the proof in a way and with results that would doubtless have surprised Mr. Greville. Her Majesty told Lady Bloomfield that she was out deer-stalking one day for nine hours, when she was not allowed to speak above a whisper, and had to hide among the rocks and heather for fear of disturbing the herd.* She has also given a spirited account of one of these expeditions in her own *Journal*. " We sat down on the ground, Lady Canning and I sketching, and Sandy and Mr. Oswald . . . lying on the grass and looking through glasses. After waiting again some time " [they had previously been made to wait in the carriage for fear of alarming the deer] " we were told in a mysterious whisper that ' they were coming,' and indeed a great herd *did* appear on the brow of the hill, and came running down a good way, when most provokingly two men who were walking on the road—which they had no business to have done—suddenly came in sight, and then the herd all ran back again, and the sport was spoilt . . . my poor Albert had not even fired one shot for fear of spoiling the whole thing, but had been running about a good deal."†

The short stay at Blair Castle gave the Queen much enjoyment, and when she visited the Duke seventeen years afterwards, the happy time all came back to her. The hall—the staircase—the stag's horns in the corridors of the castle, the faces of the Duke and the "dear Duchess"—the handsome old rooms in which at this time she lived, and in one of which " Vicky [the Princess Royal] slept in two chairs," the child at that time being scarcely four years old—all these things were recalled to remembrance, and have now found permanent record in the published *Leaves* of the Royal *Journal*. ‡ On the 1st of

---

* *Reminiscences of Court and Diplomatic Life*, vol. i. 125.
† *Leaves*, 56, 57. ‡ *Ibid.* 230.

October, the Queen left Blair Castle with many regrets, her noble host accompanying her as far as Dundee, where the Royal yacht was in waiting. "Oh! the dear hills," she wrote in her *Diary* that day, "it made me very sad to leave them behind!"*

The visit to Scotland in 1847 consisted of a tour round the West Coast, and a run inland to Loch Laggan. The Royal party embarked at Osborne on the 11th of August, and did not set foot on Scottish soil till the 17th. They touched at St. Mary's (the largest of the Scilly Islands), Milford Haven, and Douglas (Isle of Man), but the Queen only went on shore at St. Mary's. She drove through the place, which reminded her of a small fishing town, and then round the fortifications of the castle, which bears the date of one of the Edwards. "Here," writes Her Majesty, "there is a pretty walk overhanging the sea; the rock being covered with fern, and heath, and furze," while "the extensive view of the islands and rocks around is very beautiful."† At Milford Haven "numbers of boats came out, with Welsh-women in their curious high-crowned hats;" and one extremely pretty dairymaid, in complete Welsh costume, was brought on board for the Queen to see. At night the town was illuminated, and bonfires were burning along the coast. As the Royal yacht entered the Menai Straits, they got a fine view of Snowdon; and then, a little later, Caernarvon came in sight, with its grand old castle perched high up on the rocks. They passed under the Menai Bridge, and here there were crowds of loyal people in steamers and boats, who cheered tremendously, while bands on board some of the vessels played "God save the Queen." Shortly after leaving Penrhyn, the paddle-wheel broke down, and two full hours were spent in setting it right. Then they steamed on again towards the Isle of Man, which was reached in three or four hours. The first place sighted was the town of Douglas, with its picturesque castle and lighthouse. The rocks were covered with people, but no lengthy stoppage was made here; and in a few more hours the Scotch coast was well within view.‡

At about eight in the morning (17th August) they were close

* *Leaves*, 62.   † *Ibid.* 69, 70.   ‡ *Ibid.* 71–74.

to Ailsa Craig, "the formation of which," notes the Queen, "is very curious. There were thousands and thousands of birds—gannets—on the rocks, and we fired a gun off three times in order to bring them in reach of shot," but the attempt was a failure. Holy Island, Brodick Bay, and Goatfell were all passed in turn; and then the Isle of Bute was sighted, and they entered the Firth of Clyde. At Dumbarton Castle, on the Clyde, they landed, and went over the historic old place. "Its situation" (we again quote from the Royal *Journal*) "is very fine, the rock rising straight out of the river, the mountains all round, and the town of Dumbarton behind it, making it very picturesque. . . . Wallace was confined here; and it was one of the last castles which held out for Mary Queen of Scots." On continuing their journey they but retraced their course a little, and then steamed past Greenock and Rosencath (the seat of the Duke of Argyll), and so to Loch Long. Here the Queen had a very good sight of the mountain called *The Cobbler*, the top of which resembles a man sitting and mending a shoe.*

At Inveraray Castle, with its square turrets and pinewood environment, the Royal visitors again landed, and were received in true Highland fashion by the Duke and Duchess of Argyll, and others of the old nobility of Scotland. "The pipers walked before the carriage," writes the Queen, "and the Highlanders on either side, as we approached the house. Outside stood the Marquis of Lorne, just two years old, a dear, white, fat, fair little fellow, with reddish hair, but very delicate features, like both his father and mother; he is such a merry, independent, little child."† The Royal party lunched at the Castle, and then re-embarked in the yacht.

At the Crinan Canal, which connects Loch Fyne with Loch Crinan, a magnificently decorated barge, drawn by three horses, ridden by postillions in scarlet, was awaiting them, into which the Royal party stepped, and so were drawn along from end to end of the canal—a curious process, observes the Queen, but tedious. Next day more interesting places were passed—Oban, with the ruins of Dunollie Castle, Kerrara, the Lady's Rock

* *Leaves*, 75-79.   † *Ibid.* 81.

("on which a M'Lean left his wife, hoping she would be washed away," but the lady was saved), through the Sound of Mull, and so out into the Gulf of the Hebrides, with its score of rocky islands, great and small. At three o'clock in the afternoon they anchored at Staffa, and paid a visit to the far-famed Fingal's Cave, with its great vaulted hall and wonderful basaltic columns, against which the lonely sea beats with metallic sound. "It was the first time," says Her Majesty, "the British standard, with a Queen of Great Britain, and her husband and children, had ever entered Fingal's Cave, and the men gave three cheers, which sounded very impressive there."*

A wet morning followed, the precursor of many wet days, and though the weather cleared for a few hours before and after noon, the evening closed in cold and showery. They were able to get some fine views of the scenery about Lochs Linnhe and Eil, however, and during an interval of sunshine the Prince landed and paid a hurried visit to Glencoe, famous for its beautiful scenery, and still more for the horrible massacre of the Macdonalds in William the Third's time.† At Fort-William the voyage came to an end, for here the Royal party landed, and proceeded inland to Loch Laggan. On the borders of the Loch is Ardverikie, the seat of Lord Abercorn, whose guests they were to be. Unfortunately, the whole week of their stay there was miserably wet, and we can offer no better reason for saying nothing about the visit than by quoting the Queen's own words: "There is little to say of our stay at Ardverikie; the country is very fine, but the weather was most dreadful."‡

When next we see the Queen in Scotland it will be in her own home at Balmoral; but for that we must refer the reader to another chapter.

A visit of far greater importance than any to which we have yet referred—one, indeed, of considerable political importance—was paid by the Queen during the period under consideration: we refer to Her Majesty's visit to King Louis Philippe of France at the Chateau d'Eu, in September, 1843. The King himself met the Royal party off Tréport, being rowed to the

* *Leaves*, 83–86.   † *Ibid.* 86.   ‡ *Ibid.* 89.

yacht *Victoria and Albert* in a grand barge with many oars, the oarsmen in white, with red sashes, and red ribbons round their hats. "The good, kind King was standing on the boat," writes Her Majesty, "and so impatient to get out, that it was very difficult to prevent him, and to get him to wait till the boat was close enough. He got out, and came up as quickly as possible, and embraced me warmly. It was a fine and really affecting sight, and the emotion which it caused I shall never forget. . . . The King expressed again and again how delighted he was to see me."* There was a great crowd of people assembled on the shore, including two Queens (the Queen of France and the Queen of the Belgians) the whole of the French Court, and soldiers *ad libitum*. The splendour of the reception, and the cheering of the troops and people, who rent the air with cries of "*Vive la Reine!*" almost overcame Her Majesty, and were the pleasant prelude to nearly a week of new and joyful experiences. There is not much to tell, however. The greater part of the time was spent in such rural pleasures as the neighbouring villages and forests afforded—picnic parties under the trees, country fêtes, and so forth. On the 7th of September the Queen took leave of her hosts, and returned with the rest of her party to England.

A day or two later, Her Majesty again left her native shores on a visit to the King and Queen of the Belgians, at Laeken. One delightful day was spent at Bruges, the quaint and venerable seat of the merchant princes of the Middle Ages. "Never had the old city presented a more brilliant or animated appearance than on the present occasion when the Royal visitors made their progress through its streets. As Queen Victoria and the Prince passed through the Grand Place, which they did several times during the day, the bells in the great tower or belfry above the Cloth Hall pealed forth 'Rule Britannia,' 'God save the Queen,' and other English airs. Ghent, another ancient and venerable city, was visited on the following day, and the Queen was deeply interested by the University, the convent of Belgian nuns, and the Cathedral of

* *Life of the Prince Consort*, vol. i. 29, 30.

St. Bavon. At the last-named place she inspected the celebrated font in which the Emperor Charles V. was christened. On a triumphal arch in one of the principal streets were inscriptions pointing out the fact that the city had been visited by Philippa of Hainault, Queen of England, in 1343, and, after the lapse of exactly five centuries, by another Queen of England." *

Germany, Prince Albert's fatherland, was first visited by Her Majesty in 1845. The holiday was a very memorable one, and extended over the best part of a month. At the university town of Bonn, where the Prince had spent many of his student days, the enthusiasm of the people was specially marked. They "cheered us," writes the Queen, "and dear Albert most particularly, who is beloved here; and the band played a 'Dusch' [or flourish of trumpets] at the same time." The Royal visitors also drove with the King and Queen of Prussia to the house which Prince Albert had occupied while at Bonn. "It was such a pleasure for me to be able to see this house," writes the fond wife; "we went all over it, and it is just as it was, in no way altered."†

On the 11th of August, the King of Prussia gave a grand banquet to his guests, whose health he proposed in the following words:—"Gentlemen,—Fill your glasses! There is a word of inexpressible sweetness to British as well as to German hearts. Thirty years ago it echoed on the heights of Waterloo from British and German tongues, after days of hot and desperate fighting, to mark the glorious triumph of our brotherhood in arms. Now it resounds on the banks of our fair Rhine, amid the blessings of that peace which was the hallowed fruit of the great conflict. That word is *Victoria!* Gentlemen, drink to the health of Her Majesty the Queen of the United Kingdom of Great Britain and Ireland [*bowing graciously to the Queen*], and [*making his glass ring, according to German wont, against the glass of Prince Albert*] to that of her august Consort."‡

"The Queen," writes Baron Bunsen, who was present, "bowed at the first word, but much lower at the second. Her eyes brightened through tears, and, as the King was taking his seat

---
* *Life of Queen Victoria*, 90.
† *Life of the Prince Consort*, vol. i. 46. ‡ *Ibid.* vol. i. 46.

again, she rose and bent towards him, and kissed his cheek, then took her seat again with a beaming countenance."* Cologne was *en fête* on the night of the banquet, and the Royalties went thither to see the illuminations, which were on a grand scale. The city was ablaze with light, the air alive with rockets, and the fine cathedral appeared to glow with fire.

The short month in Germany was well spent. No time was wasted, and the Queen and Prince seem to have been equally delighted with their holiday. There was a glorious trip up the Rhine, visits to Coburg, Gotha, and the Thuringian Forest, and then a second trip on the queen of rivers. One specially memorable day was spent at Rosenau, a lovely spot in the Coburg region, and the birthplace of Prince Albert. "How happy, how joyful we were on awaking," writes the Queen, "to feel ourselves here, at the dear Rosenau, my Albert's birthplace, the place he most loves. . . . He was so, so happy to be here with me. It is like a beautiful dream. . . . Before breakfast we went upstairs to where my dearest Albert and Ernest used to live. It is quite in the roof, with a tiny little bedroom on each side, in one of which they both used to sleep with Florschutz their tutor. The view is beautiful, and the paper is still full of holes from their fencing; and the very same table is there on which they were dressed when little."†

The Queen was greatly struck by the simplicity of the country people, with whom she frequently conversed, and who were as good-natured and friendly as they were simple. Her Majesty was sketching in a field on one occasion, when one or two of the women, who were making hay, came close up to her, and said in the most unaffected manner, "*Guten Abend*" (good evening). The Queen returned the salutation, and added some remarks about the weather, whereupon one of the women began to talk to her quite freely, and afterwards shook her by the hand! On Prince Albert's birthday (26th of August), the peasants turned out in gala dress, the men with ribbons and flowers in their hats, and the women crowned with floral wreaths. They presented a wreath to the Prince, and a nose-

* *Life of the Prince Consort*, vol. i. 46.   † *Ibid.* 48.

gay to the Queen, and the man who handed the latter, said: " I congratulate you on your husband's birthday, and wish that he may live for many and many a year, and that you may soon come back!" They then joined in some rustic dances, singing and shouting after the manner of their country.

Before returning to England the Queen and Prince paid another visit to the King of France at Tréport and Eu, but they only slept one night at the Château. On the 10th of September the long and happy tour came to a close, and about noon on that day they disembarked at Osborne. As they drove up to the house they were greeted with loving welcomes, "for there," writes Her Majesty, " looking like roses, so well, and so fat, stood the four children, . . . much pleased to see us."*

To speak of only a tithe of the Royal and distinguished persons who were the guests of the Queen during the years 1840 to 1848, would be a long task, and we do not propose to attempt it. Among the rest were four notable visits of kings —the King of Prussia in 1842, the King of Hanover in 1843, and the Kings of Saxony and France in 1844. Then there was the visit of the Emperor Nicholas of Russia in the year last named, which was, perhaps, the most interesting of all.

The King of Prussia, as has been stated in an earlier chapter, came over for the christening of the Prince of Wales. The stay was short, but he made the most of it. One day he attended service at St. Paul's, and afterwards lunched with the Lord Mayor; another day he went to Westminster Abbey, where he inquired curiously for local details of the Queen's coronation. On the 2nd of February he called upon Mrs. Fry, the prisoners' friend, with whom he went to Coldbath Fields prison—the oddest thing that he did, according of Greville.†
Next day he went in state to the House of Lords to see the Queen open Parliament, an event of which the Baroness Bunsen has left an animated description. "On Thursday, the 3rd of February, was the opening of Parliament—the great scene from which I had expected most, and was not disappointed. The

---

* *Life of the Prince Consort*, vol. i. 52.
† Greville's *Memoirs*, part ii., vol. ii. 79, 81.

throngs in the streets, in the windows, on every spot where foot could stand—all looking so pleased—the splendid Horse Guards, the Grenadier Guards—of whom it might be said, as the King did on another occasion, 'An appearance so fine you know not how to believe it true'—the Yeomen of the Body Guard; then, in the House of Lords, the Peers in their robes, the beautifully-dressed ladies, with many, many beautiful faces; last, the procession of the Queen's entry, and herself, looking worthy and fit to be the converging point of so many rays of grandeur. . . . The composure with which she filled the throne, while awaiting the Commons, was a test of character—no fidget and no apathy. Then her voice and enunciation could not be more perfect. In short, it could not be said that *she did well*, but she *was* the Queen; she was, and felt herself to be, the acknowledged chief among grand national realities."* The King of Prussia, who was accommodated with a chair near the Woolsack, contemplated the bright scene with evident interest and pleasure. On the 4th of February he went away, "mightily pleased," says Greville, "with his reception by Queen and all classes of people, from highest to lowest; splendid entertainments from the rich, and hearty acclamations from the poor. . . . He made magnificent presents at parting to all the Officers of the Royal Household: snuff-boxes of 500 guineas a-piece to the Lord Chamberlain, Master of the Horse, and Lord Steward; boxes and watches to others, and he left £1500 with Charles Murray to be distributed among the three classes of servants at the Palace."†

The Emperor of Russia's short stay in England, in June, 1844, was marked by the same activity as the earlier visit of his neighbour, the Prussian King. "On Monday he went to Windsor, Tuesday to Ascot, Wednesday they gave him a review, which went off very badly, owing to mistakes and bad arrangement, but with which he expressed himself very well satisfied. The sight was pretty; glorious weather, 3000 or 4000 Guards, Horse, Foot, and Artillery, in the Park, the Queen, *en calèche*, with a brilliant suite. It was striking when

* *Life of the Prince Consort*, vol. i. 22.
† Greville's *Memoirs*, part ii., vol. ii. 81, 82.

the Duke [of Wellington] went and put himself at the head of his regiment, marched past and saluted the Queen and Emperor. The air resounded with acclamations as the old warrior passed, and the Emperor rode up to him and shook him by the hand. He did the same by the Prince and Duke of Cambridge as they respectively marched by at the head of their regiments, but neither of them was so cheered as the Duke. There was a blunder about the artillery. The Queen cannot endure firing, and the Duke had ordered that the guns should not be fired till she left the ground. By some mistake contrary orders were given, and they advanced and fired not far from Her Majesty. The Duke was furious, and would not be pacified, though Emperor, Queen, and Prince did their best to appease him; he blew up, and swore lustily, and ordered the luckless artillery into the rear."*

The leave-taking between the Queen and her Imperial guest appears to have been quite an affecting scene. "At a little before five," writes Her Majesty, "we went down to wait in the small drawing-room with the children. Not long after the Emperor came in, and spoke to them; and then with a sigh and with much emotion, which took all the harshness of his countenance away, he said, 'I take my leave, madam, with a swelling heart; and deeply moved by your kindness. You may be sure, madam, that I may at all times be relied upon as your most devoted servant. God bless you!' And again he kissed my hand and pressed it, and I kissed him. He kissed the children most affectionately, saying, 'God bless them, and make you happy in them!' He wanted me not to go farther, saying, 'I beseech you! go no farther! I will throw myself at your knees; pray let me lead you to your room!' But, of course, I would not consent, and took his arm to go to the hall. . . . At the top of the few steps leading to the lower hall, he again took most kindly leave, and his voice betrayed his emotion; he kissed my hand and we embraced. When I saw him at the door I went down the steps, and from the carriage he begged I would not stand there; but I did, and saw him drive off with Albert for Woolwich."†

* Greville's *Memoirs*, part ii., vol. ii. 243, 244.
† *Life of the Prince Consort*, vol. i. 37.

We will conclude with a word or two about the visit of the King of France to the Queen in October, 1844. Louis Philippe was the first French Sovereign ever received as a guest at the English Court, and, as might be supposed, the public were not a little interested in the event. It was known, too, that Philippe had passed through many vicissitudes of fortune—at one time teaching in a school of the Grisons for twenty pence a-day, when he had had to brush his own shoes, and perform other menial duties—and that increased the popular desire to see him. He did not visit London, however, for fear of giving offence to his own people, the Queen not having honoured the French capital with her presence when she was his guest in France the year before. The King's reception at Windsor has been described by Lady Lyttleton in her usually light and happy manner. Writing from the Castle on the 8th of October, she says: " At two o'clock he arrived, this curious King; worth seeing if ever a body was! The Queen having graciously permitted me to be present, I joined the Court in the corridor, and we waited an hour, and then the Queen of England came out of her room, to go and receive the King of France; the first time in history! Her Majesty had not long to wait (in the Armoury). . . . And from the Armoury, amidst all the old trophies and knights' armour, and Nelson's bust, and Marlborough's flag and Wellington's, we saw the first of the escort enter the quadrangle, and down flew the Queen, and we after her, to the outside of the door on the pavement of the quadrangle, just in time to see the escort clattering up, and the carriage close behind. The old man was much moved, I think, and his hand rather shook as he alighted; his hat quite off, and grey hair seen. His countenance is striking, much better than the portraits, and his embrace of the Queen was very parental and nice."*

Next day they were driven to neighbouring places — Twickenham, Staines, Chertsey, Claremont, and Hampton Court; most of them familiar spots to the King, who had lived at Twickenham between the years 1797 and 1807.

* *Life of the Prince Consort*, vol. i. 40.

At Hampton Court he was shown over Wolsey's Hall and all the rooms of the Palace, and remained there a considerable time. The historical collection of pictures seems to have been his chief attraction, and he made notes in his catalogue of those masterpieces which he specially admired, intending to have copies made of them for Versailles. Next day he was invested with the Order of the Garter in the Garter Room of Windsor Castle, Prince Albert and the Duke of Cambridge introducing him. "When he approached," notes the Queen in her *Journal*, "we all rose, and the King bowed in due form as he came up. I turned to him and said, 'I have the pleasure of announcing to your Majesty that you are elected a Knight of the Most Noble Order of the Garter.' Albert then placed the garter round the King's leg. I pulled it through while the admonition was being read, and the King said to me, 'I wish to kiss this hand,' which he did afterwards, and I embraced him. The Duke of Cambridge assisted me in placing the ribband over the King's shoulder; after which I embraced him again, and he embraced Albert. The King then walked round the table, shaking hands with each of the Knights, after which they were called over, and we accompanied the King to his rooms, where he again and again thanked us for our kindness."*

The only other noteworthy event during Louis Philippe's stay was the visit of the Lord Mayor and Corporation to Windsor, in full civic state—"an unprecedented departure from their established rule," says Sir Theodore Martin—in order to present an address of congratulation to the King. His reply—which, according to the usual custom, had been prepared for him—was written in such execrable English, and, moreover, was so outrageously French in tone, that the poor King was obliged at the last moment to sit down and dash off another. The Queen and Prince Albert happened to enter his room while he was bemoaning the situation, and kindly rendered him every assistance. "'Twas my good star that brought you to my room at that moment," he afterwards told them.

* *Life of the Prince Consort*, vol. i. 40.

CHAPTER VIII.

BALMORAL DAYS AND OTHER MATTERS.
(1848–1860.)

IT was stated, in a former chapter, that the lease of Balmoral, the Queen's Scottish home, was acquired in the autumn of 1848; and as we have now reached that year, and desire in the present chapter to treat of the domestic events of Victoria's life during the ensuing twelve or thirteen years, it may be well first to speak a little of a place where so much of that time was spent.

Balmoral is situated in the East Highlands, in the valley of the Dee, and its neighbourhood is esteemed one of the driest and healthiest in the world. The rain-clouds from the Atlantic discharge before they reach this favoured spot, and the moisture from the few showers that do visit it is soon absorbed by the gravelly soil. And beautiful indeed is the sight when a shower *has* fallen. Such diaphanous shadows! such lights! such radiant glow of colour!

Millais has likened Scotland to a wet pebble, and the simile is very applicable to the scenery about Balmoral, when heath and bush, and fern and bracken are drenched with the morning dew. But the neighbourhood is glorious under any aspect: whether in spring, when the birches are in tender leaf, and the thorn-bushes bursting into yellow bloom—or in summer, when the young blossoms of the heather are pink upon the hills—or in autumn, when dale and mountain have a glory of their own, and the heath has a purple hue, and the birch leaves change to gold, and the rowan berries are a bright scarlet—yes, even in winter, when the trees are swept of their leaves, and the landscape is white with snow; for Balmoral has no dull pictures to present. The Royal estate has its wilder aspects, too—corries and crags; romantic glens and rushing streams; lonely passes and shaggy woods. Deer and other game are plentiful, and close by the largest of the "shiels" or hunting-lodges is a loch with a small islet, where cormorants, gossanders, and other sea-birds occasionally breed.

The Queen's first impressions of Balmoral are briefly related in her *Journal* for the 8th of September, 1848. "We arrived at Balmoral at a quarter to three. It is a pretty little castle in the old Scottish style. There is a picturesque tower and garden in front, with a high wooded hill; at the back there is wood down to the Dee, and the hills rise all around. . . . We lunched almost immediately; and at half-past four we walked out, and went up to the top of the wooded hill opposite our windows, where there is a cairn, and up which there is a pretty winding path. The view from here, looking down upon the house, is charming. To the left you look towards the beautiful hills surrounding Loch-na-gar, and to the right, towards Ballater, to the glen (or valley) along which the Dee winds, with beautiful wooded hills, which reminded us very much of the Thüringerwald. It was so calm, and so solitary, it did one good as one gazed around, and the pure mountain air was most refreshing. All seemed to breathe freedom and peace, and to make one forget the world and its sad turmoils. The scenery is wild, and yet not desolate . . . the soil is delightful. We walked beside the Dee, a beautiful rapid stream, which is close behind the house. The view of the hills towards Invercauld is exceedingly fine."*

During the Queen's first brief stay in Balmoral she made an ascent of Loch-na-gar. It was a toilsome but enjoyable climb, and the Prince shot some ptarmigan on the way; but when they reached the top a thick mist obscured the

* *Leaves*, 101, 102.

scene, and they had to return home disappointed. The Prince, we may here remark, was very fond of sport, and a good shot. Writing to the Dowager-Duchess of Coburg, he said, "We have withdrawn for a short time into a complete mountain solitude, where one rarely sees a human face, where the snow already covers the mountain tops, and the wild deer come creeping stealthily round the house. I, naughty man, have also been creeping stealthily after the harmless stags, and to-day I shot two red deer—at least, I hope so, for they are not yet found. . . ."* A day or two later he won great praise from the keepers by bringing down "a royal" stag. "It was Her Majesty's coming out that brought the good luck," said Macdonald, the head keeper, and then the knowing Scot informed the Queen that she had "a lucky foot!" †

The following autumn the Royal party were again at Balmoral, crossing to Scotland from Ireland, and visiting Glasgow and Perth on the way. They made a short stay at Alt-na-Giuthasach, and had some pleasant rowing on Loch Muick. "The scenery is beautiful here," writes the Queen, "so wild and grand—real severe Highland scenery, with trees in the hollow. We had several scrambles in and out of the boat and along the shore, and saw three hawks, and caught seventy trout." ‡ Dhu Loch was also visited, the journey being made over a treacherous and precipitous road, the Queen riding on a troublesome little pony, which took fright at the bogs. In speaking of the bad road, an old gillie amused the Prince by saying, "It's something steep and something rough," and "this is the only best"—meaning that it was very bad. §

At Balmoral, as at Windsor and Osborne, the Queen studied the interests of those about her no less than her own, and in all her efforts for the good of the tenantry she was ably supported by her husband. "School-houses were erected and teachers appointed for the education of the young; and to give a taste for reading, and increase still more the means of information, an excellent library, the joint-gift of Her Majesty

---

* *Life of the Prince Consort*, vol. ii. 19.   † *Leaves*, 110.
‡ *Ibid.* 113.   § *Ibid.* 119.

the Queen and the Prince, was established at Balmoral, and thrown open not only to tenants and servants, but to all in the neighbourhood. . . . Moreover, he [the Prince] saw the advantage of encouraging tradesmen and labourers of good character to settle upon his estates. Houses and gardens, with a croft, where it could be conveniently added, for the keep of a cow, were provided at a very moderate rent for the blacksmith, the carpenter, shoemaker, tailor, and general merchant. Similar encouragement was given to the steady labourer, and the extensive works thus undertaken were carried on over a series of years, so as to give constant employment."*

Greville, who slept for two nights at Balmoral in the year 1849, gives a pleasant picture of the life there. "Much as I dislike Courts, and all that appertains to them, I am glad to have made this expedition, and to have seen the Queen and Prince in their Highland retreat, where they certainly appear to great advantage. The place is very pretty, the house very small. They live there without any state whatever; they live not merely like private gentlefolks, but like very small gentlefolks, small house, small rooms, small establishment. There are no soldiers, and the whole guard of the Sovereign and the whole Royal Family is a single policeman, who walks about the grounds to keep off impertinent intruders or improper characters. Their attendants consisted of Lady Douro and Miss Dawson, Lady and Maid of Honour; George Anson (the Prince's private secretary) and Gordon; Birch, the Prince of Wales's tutor; and Miss Hildyard, the governess of the children. They live with the greatest simplicity and ease. The Prince shoots every morning, returns to luncheon, and then they walk and drive. The Queen is running in and out of the house all day long, and often goes about alone, walks into the cottages, and sits down and chats with the old women. . . . After luncheon we went to the Highland Gathering at Braemar—the Queen, the Prince, four children, and two ladies

---

* The above facts were communicated to Mr. Morton, the author of *The Prince Consort's Farms*, by Dr. Robertson, who was steward of the estate in the Prince's time.

in one pony carriage; John Russell, Mr. Birch, Miss Hildyard, and I in another; Anson and Gordon on the box; one groom, no more. The Gathering was at the old Castle of Braemar, and a pretty sight enough. We returned as we came, and then everybody strolled about till dinner. We were only nine people, and it was all very easy and really agreeable, the Queen in very good humour and talkative; the Prince still more so, and talking very well; no form, and everybody seemed at their ease. In the evening we withdrew to the only room there is besides the dining-room, which serves for billiards, library (hardly any books in it), and drawing-room. The Queen and Prince and her Ladies and Gordon soon went back to the dining-room, where they had a Highland dancing-master, who gave them lessons in reels. We (John Russell and I) were not admitted to this exercise, so we played at billiards. In process of time they came back, when there was a little talk, and soon after they went to bed."*

In the autumn of 1850 the Queen made the ascent of Ben-na-Bhourd, in the neighbourhood of Balmoral, a mountain 3940 feet high, and was rewarded with a splendid view from the summit. She also attended another gathering of clans at Braemar, at which the Duffs and Farquharsons were present. There were the usual games of "putting the stone," "throwing the hammer" and "caber," and racing up the hill of Craig Cheunnich. Next day she watched some "salmon-leistering" in the Dee. Some of the men, provided with poles and spears, got into the river, and began walking up it, poking, as they went, under all the stones, with the view of driving the salmon to a part of the river where they were to be netted. The effect was very picturesque—about one hundred men wading through the river, all very much excited. Two of them got out of their depth, and one, who could not swim, would have been drowned, had not Dr. Robertson, the steward of the Balmoral estate, gone to his rescue. The Queen says she was much frightened, and "grasped Lord Carlisle's arm in great agony." At this part of the river the first salmon was speared, and afterwards they

* Greville's *Memoirs*, part ii., vol. iii. 295–297.

walked on to a ford or quarry, where, by means of spear or net, seven more were caught. The Prince went into the river with the rest, but caught nothing.* Later in the day, the Forbeses of Strathdon passed through the Royal grounds, by permission of the Queen, the pipers going in front. "When they came to the Dee," writes the Prince Consort, "our people (of Strath Dee) offered to carry them across the river, and did so, whereupon they drank to the health of Victoria and the inmates of Balmoral in whisky (*Schnapps*), but as there was no cup to be had, their chief, Captain Forbes, pulled off his shoe, and he and his fifty men drank out of it."†

A day or two after this, the Royal party made another excursion to Loch Muick. The alder-trees and mountain-ash were in full fruit, and their boughs hung gracefully over the water's edge. "The moon rose," says the Queen, "and was beautifully reflected on the lake, which, with its steep green hills, looked lovely. To add to the beauty, poetry, and wildness of the scene, Cotes (a piper) played in the boat; the men, who row very quickly and well, giving an occasional shout when he played a reel. It reminded me of Sir Walter Scott's lines in *The Lady of the Lake*:—

> "'Ever, as on they bore, more loud
> And louder rang the pibroch proud.
> At first the sound, by distance tame,
> Mellowed along the waters came,
> And, lingering long by cape and bay,
> Wailed every harsher note away.'

We were home at a little past seven; and it was so still and pretty as we entered the wood, and saw the light flickering from our humble little abode."‡

In 1851, the year of the Great Exhibition, the whole of September and the first week of October were spent at Balmoral, but the Queen makes no mention of this visit in the published part of her *Journal*. The next year, Her Majesty ac-

---

* *Leaves*, 123, 125, 126.
† *Life of the Prince Consort*, vol. ii. 55.   ‡ *Leaves*, 129, 130.

quired the fee-simple of the property, and thus the beautiful estate became her "very own." The event was commemorated by the erection of a cairn on the top of Craig Gowan, to which the Queen and Prince, and then the Royal children, in order of age, each contributed a stone. Afterwards, every lady and gentleman placed one, and then all came forward together and repeated the contribution. In this way, stone by stone, the cairn was raised, and when it was about seven or eight feet high, the Prince ascended the pile and added the top-stone, amidst ringing cheers. "It was a gay, pretty, and touching sight," observes the Queen, "and I felt almost inclined to cry. The view was so beautiful over the dear hills; the day so fine; the whole so *gemüthlich*.* May God bless this place, and allow us yet to see it and enjoy it many a long year!"†

If the great outlay involved in the purchase of the estate and the building of the new castle necessitated a heavy pull on the Royal purse, this was compensated for in measure by a most unexpected legacy. A barrister, named Nield, of miserly and penurious habits, having scraped together an enormous fortune, died and left it all to the Queen. "It is astonishing," wrote Her Majesty to the King of the Belgians, "but it is satisfactory, to see that people have so much confidence that it (the money) will not be thrown away, and so it certainly will not be. I am very curious to hear, however, what led this old gentleman to do it." Curiosity was satisfied a few days later when the Archdeacon of Bedford, one of the executors, waited upon the Queen at Balmoral, and made known to her the particulars of the will. The barrister, it seems, had succeeded to a large fortune on the death of his father, and this fortune "had accumulated in his hands, while he denied himself all but the barest necessaries. If he had relations, he knew nothing of them, or they of him"; and so he had struck upon the singular idea of bequeathing his vast wealth to the Queen of England.‡

This same autumn the Royal Family attended a torchlight

---

* An untranslatable word: "agreeable" weakly expresses the meaning.

† *Leaves*, 140, 141.   ‡ *Life of the Prince Consort*, vol. ii. 78.

ball at Corriemulzie, when, we are told, the Queen wore a white bonnet, a dress of grey watered silk, and a plaid scarf, the latter thrown over her shoulder, Highland fashion. On this occasion a reel was danced by eight Highlanders, with torches in their hands; and there were also some sword dances. The music for the evening was supplied by seven pipers, the Queen's own piper, Mackay, leading.*

About a week after the ball, the news reached Balmoral of the death of the Duke of Wellington. Her Majesty had driven to the Glas Alt, and was just sitting down to sketch by the wildly-picturesque Dhu Loch, when the letter from Lord Derby containing the fatal news was placed in her hands. "God's will be done!" she wrote in her *Journal* that evening. "The day must have come: the Duke was eighty-three. It is well for him that he has been taken when still in the possession of his great mind, and without a long illness—but what a loss! ... The Crown never possessed—and, I fear, never *will*—so devoted, loyal, and faithful a subject, so staunch a supporter!"†

The Glas Alt, above referred to, was ever a favourite spot with the Queen. One year—probably the year of the Corriemulzie ball—"there came," says an old inhabitant, "a memorable storm. The countryside was buried under snow, and the roads packed solidly with the same. The Queen (who dearly loves the wintry aspect of the hills) seized her opportunity. Fifty men were set 'to cast the road' to the Glas Alt Shiel—*i.e.*, to clear it from snow. A sledge was sent up from Windsor, and Her Majesty drove thither, and saw it for once in all the beauty and grandeur of its winter attire." ‡

The autumn visits to Balmoral in the two succeeding years may be passed over more rapidly, though that in 1853 has an interest of its own. It was then that the foundation of the new and existing Castle was laid, the Queen performing the ceremony. In the following year, her *Journal* records a visit to the Scotch kirk in the neighbourhood of Balmoral. Fine old Norman Macleod was the preacher, and the Queen describes his

---

* *Leaves*, 131, 132, 133. † *Ibid.* 136, 137, 138.
‡ *The Queen at Balmoral*, 160.

sermon as simple, eloquent, and beautifully argued. "Mr. Macleod showed in the sermon how we *all* tried to please *self*, and live for *that*, and in so doing found no rest. Christ had come not only to die for us, but to show how we were to live. The second prayer was very touching; his allusions to us were simple, saying, after his mention of us, 'Bless their children.' It gave me a lump in my throat."*

When Her Majesty next visited the Highlands, the new Castle was almost finished, and the day after her arrival (the 8th of September, 1855) the Royal Family moved in and took possession. "When we entered the hall," says the Queen, "an old shoe was thrown after us for good luck." The Castle, which is built of light grey granite of a fine quality, stands upon a "haugh," or open space, by the Dee, the hills receding for background. Byron's "Dark Lochnagar," 3800 feet high, closes the vista to the south. The architecture is in the old Scotch baronial style, with round turrets and extinguisher tops, and with crow-stepped gables. The great tower is the clock-tower, one hundred feet high, from the flagstaff of which the Royal Standard floats when the Queen is in residence. There is room in the Castle for the accommodation of one hundred and thirty persons. The beauty of the surroundings of this truly Royal residence is beyond all praise. The Dee in the more immediate vicinity is bordered by large trees, under which runs a foot-path; and so near is the house to the river, that from any part of it, if the windows be open, the rush of its waters is heard. Looking from the drawing-room windows, the eye wanders over flower-beds and terraces, across the river to the forests beyond, on up the strath, where hill overlaps hill, to the far-off Braes o' Mar. This is the view seen from the Queen's own sitting-room, and it is one very dear to Her Majesty.† After contemplating such a scene, we are not surprised that the Queen should write of her Scotch home: "Every year my heart becomes more fixed in this dear paradise, and so much more so now, that *all* has become my dearest Albert's *own* creation, own work, own build-

* *Leaves*, 144, 147.
† Abridged from Humphrey's *The Queen at Balmoral*, 10–17.

ing, own laying out, as at Osborne; and his great taste, and the impress of his dear hand, have been stamped everywhere."*

It was at Balmoral, and during the first month of residence at the new Castle, that the Princess Royal became engaged to the Crown Prince of Prussia, afterwards, for so short a period, Emperor of Germany. The Princess was only sixteen at the time, but the lovers were not married till more than two years later. Prince Frederick first made known his wishes to the Queen and Prince Consort on the 20th of September, but they were undecided, on account of the Princess's extreme youth, whether to sanction his speaking to her then or to urge delay. "However," writes the Queen, "we felt it was better he should do so; and during our ride up Craig-na-Ban this afternoon (29th September), he picked a piece of white heather (the emblem of 'good luck') which he gave to her; and this enabled him to made an allusion to his hopes and wishes, as they rode down Glen Girnoch."† "Victoria is greatly excited," wrote her father about the same time, "still all goes smoothly and prudently. The Prince is really in love, and the little lady does her best to please him." ‡

An accident which happened to the Princess Royal in the following year might, but for timely assistance, have destroyed all the hopes of the youthful lovers. The Princess was sealing a letter at her table when her sleeve caught fire at the candle. Fortunately, Miss Hildyard was seated at the same table, and at once sprang forward and extinguished the flames. The arm was severely burned, but only the upper skin was injured, and the young lady soon got all right again. This event happened at Buckingham Palace, however, and we have not yet done with Balmoral.

The chief event in 1857 was the opening of a new bridge over the Linn of Dee. A triumphal arch was erected near the spot, where the Queen was received by Lord and Lady Fife; the pipers were playing gaily, and the road was lined with Duff men. On the bridge being declared open, whisky was

---

* *Leaves*, 158. † *Ibid.* 154.
‡ *Life of the Prince Consort*, vol. iii. 63.

handed round (the Scotch can do nothing without whisky), and every one drank prosperity to the new structure.* In the same month, the Queen paid numerous visits to the cottages on the estates, distributing warm petticoats and other useful presents. "We went . . . to Mrs. Symons's . . . who had an 'unwell boy,'" writes Her Majesty, "then across a little burn to another old woman's; and afterwards peeped into Blair the fiddler's." A Mrs. Grant, mother of one of the Queen's gillies, told the Queen that she was "happy to see her looking so nice," and afterwards, in referring to the Princess Royal's approaching marriage, "I'm very sorry, and I think she's sorry hersel'." Fearing that she had "put her foot in it" (to use a familiar expression), the old lady added, "I'm very sorry I said that, but I meant no harm; I always say just what I think, not what is fut" (fit).†

There was much shooting in these days, and wherever the Prince with his guns was seen, the Queen, for a moral certainty, was not far off. On one of these occasions—in September, 1858—they came to a place where the long grass was very wet, and she was carried over it on a plaid by two of the gillies. "After this," writes Her Majesty, "we walked on for a beat quite round Carrop; and the view was glorious. A little shower of snow had fallen, but was succeeded by brilliant sunshine. The hills were covered with snow, the golden birch-trees on the lower brown hills, and the bright afternoon sky, were indescribably beautiful." ‡ The scene reminded the Queen of Clough's fine description :—

"The gorgeous bright October,
Then when brackens are changed, and heather blooms are faded,
And amid russet of heather and fern, green trees are bonnie ;
Alders are green, and oaks ; the rowan, scarlet and yellow ;
One great glory of broad gold pieces appears the aspen,
And the jewels of gold that were hung in the hair of the birch-tree,
Pendulous, here and there, her coronet, necklace, and earrings,
Cover her now, o'er and o'er; she is weary and scatters them from her."§

* *Leaves*, 159.   † *Ibid.* 161–163.   ‡ *Ibid.* 169.
§ *The Bothie of Tober-na-Vuolich.*

The following autumn the Queen ascended Morven, 2700 feet high, and Ben Muich Dhui, 4297 feet, and had a long and pleasurable drive to Inchroy. She was also present at a fête given to the members of the British Association, where she saw and conversed with Professor Owen, Sir David Brewster, Sir John Roscoe, and other eminent scientists of a bygone generation. There were the usual exhibition of Highland skill — "throwing the hammer," "tossing the caber," and "putting the stone," while reels and other dances formed an important element in the festivities. When the judges had to decide to whom to award the prizes in the famous "Ghillie Callum" dance, they could not make up their minds. "It was danced over and over again," says the Queen, "and at last they left out the best dancer of all. They said he danced 'too well'!" * During the fête, news was brought of the finding of the remains of Sir John Franklin, the Arctic explorer.

In the year 1860, the Queen went on what she calls her "first great expedition" from Balmoral. In this tour they went as far as Glen Fishie and Grantown, the latter place nearly thirty miles from Balmoral as the crow flies; but the route taken was very circuitous, and the expedition lasted two days. The Royal tourists travelled incognito as "Lord and Lady Churchill and party," but "Brown once forgot this," says the Queen, "and called me 'Your Majesty' as I was getting into the carriage; and Grant, on the box, once called Albert, 'Your Royal Highness,' which set us off laughing, but no one observed it." The one night away from home was spent at the inn at Grantown, where "a ringletted woman" waited upon them, and their dinner was soup, hodge-podge, mutton-broth, fowl, roast lamb and potatoes, with cranberry tart for second course. Their identity was not suspected till the following day, when they drove back through the town. "Evidently," writes the Queen, "the murder was out, for all the people were in the street, and the landlady waved her pocket-handkerchief, and the ringletted maid (who had curl-papers in the morning) waved a flag from the window." This

* *Leaves*, 172–188.

was not a remarkably grand reception for the Queen of England, but we doubt not, it was unimpeachably loyal. "We heard since," adds the Queen, "that the secret came out through a man recognising Albert in the street yesterday morning; then the crown on the dog-cart made them think that it was some one from Balmoral, though they never suspected that it would be ourselves. 'The lady must be terrible rich,' the woman observed, as I had so many gold rings on my fingers! . . . When they heard who it was, they were ready to drop with astonishment and fright."*

It would have been interesting to have gone over a little of the ground traversed on this amusing expedition, but we must pause. We have now treated at considerable length of the Queen's life at Balmoral till the autumn of 1860, and the reader will hardly blame us for lingering so long over scenes so enthralling. We will now retrace our steps, and consider the other events of a domestic character which come within the scope of the present chapter.

In all the years that we are considering the Queen and Prince Albert were never apart for long together. They had no such trying separation as that of 1844, when the Prince was away in Coburg for twelve days (unless, indeed, in the summer of 1858);† but even his shortest absences were felt, and both in 1849, when he went to lay the foundation-stone of the Great Grimsby Docks, and in 1859, when he went to Aberdeen to preside at the meeting of the British Association, the Queen was unhappy till his return. From the former place—or, rather, from Brocklesby, the seat of Lord Yarborough, the Prince sent a playful note to appease the wife-like anxiety. "Your faithful husband," he wrote, "agreeably to your wishes, reports—1. That he is still alive; 2. That he has discovered the North Pole from Lincoln Cathedral, but without finding either Captain Ross or Sir John Franklin; 3. That he has arrived at Brocklesby, and received the address; 4. That he subsequently rode out,

---

* *Leaves*, 189-203.

† When the Prince went to Germany for eight or nine days, the Queen remaining in England.

and got home quite covered with snow, and with icicles on his nose; 5. That the messenger is waiting to carry off this letter, which you will have in Windsor by the morning; 6. Last, not least (in the Dinner-speeches' phrase), that he loves his wife, and remains her devoted husband."

Tragedy treads upon the heels of comedy. Within little more than a month of the Prince's visit to Grimsby, public indignation was aroused by the report of a fresh attempt to shoot the Queen. The report was true, but fortunately the pistol with which the attempt was made was loaded only with powder. Her Majesty was driving down Constitution Hill at the time, with three of her children, the Prince riding in advance. The man was promptly seized, and, but for the protection of the police, would have been torn in pieces by the mob which gathered quickly on the report of the firearm. The Queen never for a moment lost her self-command, but motioning the coachman to drive on, engaged her children in conversation. The would-be assassin proved to be an Irishman, named William Hamilton, who had worked as a bricklayer's labourer both in France and England, but latterly had been earning a scanty livelihood by doing odd jobs. He was tried under the new Act, and sentenced to seven years' transportation.

A year later, as the Queen was leaving Cambridge House, a mad lieutenant, named Robert Pate, started forward, and struck Her Majesty across the face with a cane. Happily, the force of the blow was broken by the bonnet, but the forehead was severely bruised, and, as might be supposed, Her Majesty's nerves were much shaken by the occurrence. Pate maintained the closest silence as to his motives, but no doubts were entertained of his insanity. His eccentricities were well known to his friends, and had been the cause of his retirement from the army. Nevertheless, the jury refused to accept the plea, and a brutal sentence of seven years' transportation was passed upon him.

Meanwhile, death had been busy in the circle of the Queen's friends. In November, 1848, her old and valued counsellor, Lord Melbourne, passed away; and in the following

October she received a severe shock by the sudden death of Prince Albert's secretary, Mr. Anson. He had been with the Prince ever since the Royal marriage, and was a man deeply and deservedly esteemed. Writing of his death, Lady Lyttleton says: "Every face shows how much has been felt; the Prince and Queen in floods of tears, and quite shut up. It is to them a heavy loss indeed; irreparable."* Before the year was out the Dowager-Queen Adelaide, widow of William the Fourth, was laid beside her husband; and the Queen had to lament the snapping of another link which bound her to the past. "I know," she wrote to her uncle at Brussels, "how truly you will grieve with us for the loss of our dearly beloved Queen Adelaide, though for her we must not repine. Though we daily expected this sad event, yet it came as suddenly, when it did come, as if she had never been ill, and I can hardly realise the truth now. You know how *very* kind she was at all times to me, and how admirably she behaved from the time the King died. She was truly motherly in her kindness to us and to our children, and it always made her happy to be with us, and to see us. She is a great loss to us both, and an irreparable one to hundreds and hundreds. . . . The dear Queen has left the most affecting directions (written eight years ago) for her funeral, which she wishes should be as private as possible. She wishes her coffin to be carried by *sailors*—a most touching tribute to her husband's memory, and to the navy, to which she was so much attached."†

But there was joy as well as mourning in these days. New life sprang up as the old died out; and on May-day, 1850, a third son was born to Prince Albert at Buckingham Palace. With kindly humour the Prince announces the event to his mother, the Dowager-Duchess of Coburg: ". . . this morning about a quarter-past eight, after a restless night (being Walpurgis-night, *that* was quite appropriate) while the witches were careering on the Blocksberg (under Ernest Augustus's mild sceptre), a little boy glided into the light of day, and has been received by his sisters with *jubilates*. 'Now we are just

* *Life of the Prince Consort*, vol. ii. 38.   † *Ibid.* vol. ii. 39.

as many as the days in the week!' was the cry, and then a bit of a struggle arose as to who was to be Sunday. Out of well-bred courtesy the honour was conceded to the new-comer."* The child was christened Arthur William Patrick Albert—the first name in compliment to the Duke of Wellington, who was his godfather, and on whose birthday he was born. Two more children were yet to be born—Prince Leopold (afterwards Duke of Albany), on the 7th of April, 1853, and Princess Beatrice, four years later, on the 14th of the same month.

Now and again the published portions of the Queen's *Journal* and stray letters of the Prince Consort afford us pleasant glimpses of the last half of their wedded life, alike at Osborne, Windsor, and Buckingham Palace.

In the beautiful island we view them at one time given up to the enjoyment of the warm summer weather; the children chasing butterflies, the Queen sitting under the trees, and the Prince drinking "the Kissinger water Ragotzky."† At another time we are privileged to witness the giving over of the Swiss cottage to the Royal children—a present indeed! for the structure is what its name expresses, a veritable Swiss cottage, with kitchen, pantry, dairy, carpenter's workshop, and no end of upstairs rooms, to say nothing of the stairs and galleries on the outside. The building was erected partly for the children's amusement, and partly for instruction in little household duties and manual industries. A museum of natural history was attached, and beside the house were plots of cultivated ground —a plot for each Prince and Princess—which the youthful owners were permitted to keep in order themselves, and from which they gathered—not flowers merely—but useful stores of horticultural and botanical knowledge.‡ The Swiss cottage is situated on the estate, at about a mile from the great house.

At Windsor the happy life went on much as we have already described it. Rides and drives in the Great Park, grand banquets, and occasional conjugal *tête-à-tête* dinners, whist and patience, and, in their season, the merry gatherings around the

---

* *Life of the Prince Consort*, vol. ii. 44.   † *Ibid.* vol. ii. 48.
‡ *Ibid.* vol. iii. 12; and *The Woman at Home*, Feb. 1894.

Christmas-tree. In January, 1851, Lady Lyttleton, who for nine years had been governess to the Royal children, retired from the Queen's service. The Queen and she were much attached to one another, and the parting was deeply felt. Of her last day at the Castle she writes: "In the evening I was sent for, to my last audience in the Queen's own room, and I quite broke down, and could hardly speak or hear. I remember the Prince's face as pale as ashes, and a few words of praise and thanks from them both, but it is all misty; and I had to stop on the private staircase, and have my cry out, before I could go up again."*

BUCKINGHAM PALACE.

In February, 1854, the guests at the Castle were invited to witness a Masque devised by the Royal children, in honour of the thirteenth anniversary of the Queen's marriage. Baron and Baroness Bunsen were among the guests, and the latter has gracefully described the various *tableaux vivants* which were presented. "First appeared Princess Alice as the Spring, scattering flowers and reciting verses, which were taken from Thomson's *Seasons;* she moved gracefully and spoke in a distinct and pleasing manner with excellent modulation, and a tone of voice sweet and penetrating like that of the Queen.

* *Life of the Prince Consort*, vol. ii. 31.

Then the curtain was drawn, and the scene changed, and the Princess Royal represented Summer, with Prince Arthur stretched upon the sheaves, as if tired with the heat and harvest-work; another change, and Prince Alfred, with a crown of vine leaves and the skin of a panther, represented Autumn— looking very well. Then followed a change to a winter landscape, and the Prince of Wales represented Winter, with a cloak covered with icicles (or what seemed such), and the Princess Louise, a charming little muffled-up figure, busy keeping up a fire; the Prince reciting (as all had done) passages more or less modified from Thomson. Then followed the last change, when all the Seasons were grouped together, and far behind, on a height, appeared Princess Helena with a long veil hanging on both sides down to her feet, holding a long cross, and pronouncing a blessing upon the Queen and Prince. . . . This was the close; but, by a command of the Queen, the curtain was again withdrawn, and the whole Royal family appeared together. . . . The baby, Prince Leopold, was carried in by his nurse, and looked at us all with big eyes, stretching out his arms to be taken by the Prince Consort."*

Even at Buckingham Palace, which was never a favourite residence with the Queen, there was no lack of home delights during the period of which we write. The Royal children, if strictly brought up, were certainly not shut off from the many and varied amusements which help to make the life of the young happy. Toys, games, parties, excursions to places of interest—all these they had, and they had them to satiety. Perhaps much of the talk about strictness originated in the fact that the children were carefully brought up, for foolishly fond mothers are apt to speak in exaggerated terms of their wiser sisters, whose maternal love shrinks from spoiling their children by a short-sighted indulgence. That the Royal children were carefully brought up is well known, and the fact has been already dwelt upon in these pages. Perhaps no better illustration of the fact could be adduced than is afforded by the following story :—

* *Life of the Prince Consort*, vol. iii. 1, 2.

"One day, when the Queen was present in her carriage at a military review, the Princess Royal, then rather a wilful girl of thirteen, sitting on the front seat, seemed disposed to be rather familiar and coquettish with some young officers of the escort. Her Majesty gave several reproving looks at her, without avail. At length, in flirting her handkerchief over the side of the carriage, she dropped it—too evidently *not* accidentally. Instantly, two or three young heroes sprang from their saddles to return it to her fair hand; but the awful voice of Royalty stayed them.

"'Stop, gentlemen!' exclaimed the Queen, 'Leave it just where it lies. Now, my daughter, get down from the carriage and pick up your handkerchief.'

"There was no help for it. The Royal footman let down the steps for the little Royal lady, who proceeded to lift from the dust the pretty piece of cambric and lace. She blushed a good deal, though she tossed her head saucily, and she was doubtless angry enough. But the mortifying lesson may have nipped in the bud her first impulse towards coquetry. It was hard, but it was wholesome. How many mothers would be equal to such a piece of Spartan discipline?"*

Of the many "treats" given to the Royal children from time to time, few, doubtless, were on a larger scale than the ball at Buckingham Palace in 1845, on the occasion of Prince Arthur's birthday. Two hundred children were present, besides a judicious sprinkling of adults, whose pleasant task it was to assist in making the young folks happy. Among the grown-up guests was the then Premier, Lord Aberdeen, to whom the following graceful invitation was sent:—" Though the Queen cannot send Lord Aberdeen *a card for a child's ball*, perhaps he may not disdain coming for a short while to see a number of happy little people, including some of his grandchildren, enjoying themselves." The adults had their own turn a fortnight later, when a great ball was given at the Palace, to which nearly two thousand guests were invited.

---

* An American writer named James Parton tells this story, and affirms that it came "from one who witnessed the occurrence."

Was it when preparing for this ball that a certain carpet merchant, whose men were laying down some new carpets in the State apartments, got into the Palace in a workman's smock, and had a very unexpected interview with his Sovereign? The gentleman in question was a connoisseur of art, and had resorted to this disguise in order to get a quiet view of the Royal pictures. In the midst of his inspection the Queen, very plainly dressed, came tripping in, followed by two or three of her younger children. Approaching the supposed workman, she inquired, "Pray can you tell me when the carpet will be put down in the Privy Council chambers?"

"Really, Madam, I cannot tell, but I will inquire," said the disguised carpet merchant.

"Stay," said Her Majesty, abruptly but not unkindly, "who are you? I perceive that you are not one of the workmen."

Blushing and stammering, the carpet merchant confessed the truth, pleading his love of art as an excuse for having practised such a *ruse*. The Queen, who seemed much amused, readily forgave him, and then added, with a smile, "I knew for all your dress that you were a gentleman, because you did not 'Your Majesty' me. Pray look at the pictures as long as you will. Good morning. Come, chicks, we must go!"

But the great event connected with the Queen's various stays at Buckingham Palace during the period which we are considering was undoubtedly the marriage of the Princess Royal, which took place on the 25th of January, 1858. It was from here that the bride and bridegroom went to St. James's to be married, and in the great hall of the Palace the wedding breakfast was spread. The Queen speaks of the day as "the second most eventful in her life as regards feelings," her own wedding-day, we may presume, being the first. There was a great gathering of Royalties for the occasion, and the presents were numerous and very costly. The Queen and Prince Consort's gift to the bridegroom consisted of three fine candelabra; the bridegroom's gift to the bride was a magnificent necklace, the pearls in which, said the Queen, were among the largest she had seen. The day before the wedding the Princess gave her mother a brooch with her hair, and clasping her in her arms, said, "I hope to be worthy to be your child!" At the close of the day—her last day in the old home—her parents kissed her and gave her their blessing. The Princess was greatly overcome, and when her father embraced her, she leaned her head on his breast and burst into tears.

The events of the day itself the reader will probably prefer to have in the Queen's own words; for who can speak so feelingly of such an occasion as the mother of the bride? At the moment when the procession left the Palace on its way to the Chapel-Royal, "the sun," says Her Majesty, "was shining brightly. ... Albert and uncle, in Field-Marshal's uniform, with batons, and the two eldest boys, went first. Then the three girls in pink satin trimmed with Newport lace, Alice with a wreath, and the two others with only bouquets in their hair of cornflowers and marguerites; next the four boys in Highland dress. The Hall full. The flourish of trumpets and cheering of thousands made my heart sink within me. Vicky was in the carriage with me, sitting opposite. ... At St. James's I took her into a dressing-room prettily arranged, where were uncle, Albert, and the eight bridesmaids, who looked charming in white tulle, with wreaths and bouquets of pink roses and white heather. Went into 'The closet,' where Mama (looking so handsome in violet velvet trimmed with ermine, and white silk and violet) and the Cambridges were. All the foreign Princes and Princesses, except uncle, the Prince of Prussia, and Prince Albert of Prussia, were already in the Chapel.

"Then the procession was formed, just as at my marriage, only how small the *old* Royal family has become! Mama last before me—then Lord Palmerston, with the Sword of State—then Bertie and Alfred. I with the two little boys on either side (which they say had the most touching effect), and the three girls behind. The effect was very solemn and impressive as we passed through the rooms, down the staircase, and across a covered-in court.

"The Chapel, though too small, looked extremely imposing and well—full as it was of so many elegantly dressed ladies, uniforms, etc. The Archbishop at the altar, and on either side of it the Royal personages. Behind me Mama and the Cambridges, the girls and little boys near me, and opposite me the dear Princess [of Prussia], and the foreign Princes behind her. Bertie and Affie, not far from the Princess, a little before the others.

"The drums and trumpets played marches, and the organ played others as the procession approached and entered. There was a pause between each, but not a very long one, and the effect was thrilling and striking as you heard the music gradually coming nearer and nearer. Fritz [the bridegroom] looked pale and much agitated, but behaved with the greatest self-possession, bowing to us, and then kneeling down in a most devotional manner. Then came the bride's procession, and our darling Flower looked very touching and lovely, with such an innocent, confident, and serious expression, her veil hanging back over her shoulders, walking between her beloved father and dearest Uncle Leopold, who had been at her christening and confirmation, and was himself the widower of Princess Charlotte, heiress to the throne of this country, Albert's and my uncle, Mama's brother, and one of the wisest kings in Europe!

"My last fear of being overcome vanished on seeing Vicky's quiet, calm, and composed manner. It was beautiful to see her kneeling with Fritz, their hands joined, and the train borne by the eight young ladies, who looked like a cloud of maidens hovering round her, as they knelt near her. Dearest Albert took her by the hand to give her away—*my* beloved Albert (who, I saw, felt so strongly), which reminded me vividly of having in the same way, proudly, tenderly, confidently, most lovingly knelt by him, on this very same spot, and having our hands joined there. . . . The music was very fine, the Archbishop very nervous; Fritz spoke very plainly, Vicky too. The Archbishop omitted some of the passages.

"When the ceremony was over, we both embraced Vicky tenderly, but she shed not one tear, and then she kissed her Grandmama, and I Fritz. She then went up to her new parents, and we crossed over to the dear Prince and Princess [of Prussia], who were both much moved, Albert shaking hands with them, and I kissing both and pressing their hands, with a most happy feeling. My heart was so full. Then the bride and bridegroom left, hand in hand, followed by the supporters, the 'Wedding March,' by Mendelssohn, being played; and we all went up to the Throne Room to sign the register. Here general congratulations, shaking hands with all the relations—I with all the Prussian Princes. The young couple first signed, then the parents of both, and all the Princes and Princesses present (including Bertie, Alice, Alfred, and the Maharajah [Dhuleep Singh], who had come resplendent in pearls),—the ministers, clergy, etc. I felt so moved, so overjoyed and relieved, that I could have embraced everybody — I shook hands with Lord Clarendon and Lord Palmerston. Vicky gave very pretty lockets to her bridesmaids.

"The young couple returned to Buckingham Palace together, and we with uncle and the Prince [of Prussia], whom I asked to call me 'Du.' Tremendous crowd and cheering as we passed. On arriving at the Palace, we went with the young couple to the celebrated window [the window over the central archway leading to the courtyard of the Palace], at which they stepped out and showed themselves, we and the Prince and Princess [of Prussia] standing with them."*

The short honeymoon was spent at Windsor Castle, and then the newly wedded couple left England for the bridegroom's native land. The parting with the Princess was a terrible wrench to the Queen. "A dreadful moment," she wrote in her *Journal*, "and a dreadful day. Such sickness came over me, real heartache, when I thought of our dearest child being gone, and for so long—all, all being over! . . . It began to snow before Vicky went, and continued to do so without intermission all day. . . . At times I could be quite cheerful, but my tears began to flow afresh frequently, and I could not go near Vicky's corridor. Everything recalled the time now passed—

* The Queen's *Diary*, quoted in *Life of the Prince Consort*, vol. iv. 28.

all programmes, dinner lists, etc., lying about still, as if all were yet going on—and all, all over!" *

The Princess was now freed from parental control; and yet, if we may venture any conclusion from these parting scenes, the circumstance was not such a wonderful relief to her after all. Evidently the "strictness" of home had not been found so very irksome. A few months later, the Prince of Wales paid a visit to his sister in her new home, and while there, he, too, received his emancipation from parental authority. It came to him in the form of a letter from the Queen, which Greville describes as "one of the most admirable letters that ever were penned." She told the Prince that he might have thought the rule which his parents had adopted for his education a severe one, but that his welfare had been their only object. Knowing well to what seductions of flattery he would eventually be exposed, they had wished to prepare and strengthen his mind against them; but he was now to consider himself his own master; and, though they would always be ready to give him advice in the future, should he think fit to seek it, they would never intrude it upon him. The whole letter, which was a very long one, was in the same strain, and it made a profound impression on the Prince. His feelings were touched to the quick, and he brought the letter to Lord Wellesley in floods of tears.†

On the 27th of January, 1859, the Princess Royal's first child was born, and so, at thirty-nine years of age, the Queen was a grandmother! In the course of a letter to Lady Bloomfield, Her Majesty said: "Thank God, in spite of severe sufferings and some anxiety for our dear little grandson, whom we are very proud of, though he has conferred this somewhat ancient dignity on us at the age of thirty-nine (I think *my* dear Prince is one of the youngest grandfathers in existence), all has gone off satisfactorily, and we are extremely satisfied and pleased." ‡

* The Queen's *Diary*, quoted in *Life of the Prince Consort*, vol. iv. 29.
† Greville's *Memoirs*, part iii., vol. ii. 212, 213.
‡ *Reminiscences of Court and Diplomatic Life*, vol. ii. 79, 80.

One of the Queen's children had now become the founder of a new family, destined to mount the Imperial throne of Germany, and we can imagine with what pride and interest she watched the career of the child born to such high destiny. Meanwhile, the younger members of her family were rapidly growing up. The Prince of Wales was following his academic course at Oxford, with intention to complete it at the sister University; while Prince Alfred had just earned his rating as midshipman, in strict accordance with the prescribed apprenticeship, and had begun to serve zealously as such in the Fleet. A month or two later, by a curious coincidence, the brothers were almost at the opposite poles at nearly the same time—the Prince of Wales inaugurating that stupendous work of engineering genius, the great bridge over the St. Lawrence in Canada, and Prince Alfred laying the foundation-stone of the breakwater for the harbour of Cape Town.* The other Royal children were still under tutors and governesses at home, from the eldest, Alice, who was on the eve of her engagement to Prince Louis of Hesse, to Beatrice, the baby, then in her fourth year.

* See the toast given by the Prince Consort at the Dinner of the Trinity House, 23rd of June, 1860.—*Speeches and Addresses of the Prince Consort*, 243.

CHAPTER IX.

THE QUEEN AMONG HER OWN PEOPLE.
(1848-1860.)

IN her desire to gratify the loyal wishes of her subjects, there were few important places in the United Kingdom which Her Majesty left unvisited during the first twenty years of her reign. At many of these places we have already seen her, but others have yet to be spoken of, and among these such noteworthy towns as Liverpool and Manchester, Leeds and Birmingham, Edinburgh and Glasgow, Dublin and Belfast.

Unfortunately, the day of the Royal visit to Liverpool was misty and very wet, and the immense crowds which gathered in the streets got drenched to the skin. "It poured," says the Queen; "the roads were a sea of mud, and yet the whole way along was lined with people, and all so wet! The atmosphere was so thick that we could see a very little way before us. . . . We were obliged to spread Albert's large cloak over us to protect us from the rain and the splashing of the mud." They drove along part of the docks, and got out at the place of embarkation, which had been covered over for the occasion; and then the Royal party went on board the yacht *Fairy*, accompanied by the Mayor and other civic dignitaries. They steamed along by the docks and round the mouth of the Mersey, where they had hoped to have some fine views, but little was to be seen by reason of the mist. The Queen thought the docks magnificent, however, and was greatly struck by the enormous mass of shipping. At the Town Hall, which was finely decorated inside, Her Majesty received an address from the Mayor, whom she knighted, and another from the Corporation, to both of which she read answers; and then the Royal party proceeded to St. George's Hall, one of the finest of modern buildings, and "worthy," in the Queen's judgment, "of ancient Athens."*

From Liverpool the Royal visitors went by train to Patricroft, and walked to the Bridgewater Canal, where an elegant barge was waiting to convey them to Worsley Park, the seat of Lord Ellesmere. The boat glided along "in a noiseless and dreamlike manner," amidst the cheers of the people who lined the sides of the canal. Now and again they passed under bridges, beautifully decorated, and within sight of more than one village occupied by the pitmen employed in Lord Ellesmere's vast coal mines. In half-an-hour they were at the landing-place in Worsley Park, and in a few minutes more had reached the house, a fine Elizabethan mansion, where they were received by the noble but gouty owner. "The evening was enhanced by the presence of Mr. Nasmyth, the inventor of the steam-hammer, who had extensive works at Patricroft. He exhibited and explained the maps in which he had embodied the results of his investigations of the conformation and atmosphere of the moon"; and also exhibited some of his pictures, which were generally admired, for Mr. Nasmyth was a fine landscapist as well as star-gazer and engineer. The same evening brought the news of the successful laying of the first Submarine Telegraph—that between Dover and Calais.†

Next morning at ten o'clock the Royal party proceeded to Salford and Manchester, escorted part of the way by Yeomanry, and the remainder of the distance by a regiment of Lancers, commanded by Lord Cathcart. "The mechanics and workpeople, dressed in their best," records Her Majesty, "were ranged along the streets, with white rosettes in their buttonholes; both in Salford and Manchester a very intelligent, but painfully unhealthy-looking population they all were, men as

* The Queen's *Journal*, 9th Oct., 1851.
† *Life of the Prince Consort*, vol. ii. 67.

well as women. We went into Peel Park, before leaving Salford—the Mayor having got out and received us at the entrance—where was indeed a most extraordinary and, I suppose, totally unprecedented sight—82,000 school children, Episcopalians, Presbyterians, Catholics (these children having a small crucifix suspended round their neck), Baptists, and Jews, whose faces told their descent; with their teachers. In the middle of the Park was erected a pavilion, under which we drove (but did not get out), and where the address was read. All the children sang 'God save the Queen' extremely well together, the director being placed on a very high stand, from which he could command the whole Park."* A second visit was paid to Lancashire in June of 1857, when the Queen opened the Manchester Exhibition. The crowds on this occasion were greater than ever, and it was computed that upwards of a million persons witnessed the Royal entry into the city. To make it the more pleasant to the Queen none but kind and friendly faces were to be seen, and the enthusiasm was as great as the people were numerous. The Exhibition was opened on the 29th, and the following morning was devoted to a long examination of the contents of the building; the Royal party returning to Worsley Hall by way of Peel Park, to enable them to inspect a statue of Her Majesty which had been placed there since her first visit to Manchester.

Six years before this second visit to Lancashire, however—in fact, in the year of the first visit—an exhibition of far grander proportions had been opened by the Queen in London. We refer, of course, to the Great Exhibition of 1851—that colossal structure of glass and iron erected by Sir Joseph Paxton in Hyde Park, in which were collected from the four quarters of the earth exhibits of almost every object under the sun. This, the first of the exhibitions, owed its existence entirely to the wisdom, courage, and enterprise of the Prince Consort, who developed and carried out his idea in the face of strong opposition both at home and abroad. The result was a triumph, of which the Queen was justly proud.

* The Queen's *Journal*, 10th Oct., 1851.

> " But yesterday a naked sod,
>   The dandies sneered from Rotten Row,
> And cantered o'er it to and fro ;
>   And see, 'tis done !
>
> As though 'twere by a wizard's rod,
>   A blazing arch of lucid glass
> Leaps like a fountain from the grass
>   To meet the sun !"*

Her Majesty's account of the opening is the most vivid piece of description we have seen from her pen, and we give it to the readers almost without abridgment, merely interpolating occasional matter from other sources by way of giving completeness to the picture. The ceremony took place on the 1st of May, 1851, and the entry in the Queen's *Diary* for that date opens thus :—

" The great event has taken place—a complete and beautiful triumph—a glorious and touching sight, one which I shall ever be proud of for my beloved Albert and my country. . . . Yes ! it is a day which makes my heart swell with pride and glory and thankfulness !

" We began it with tenderest greetings for the birthday of our dear little Arthur. At breakfast there was nothing but congratulations. . . . Mama and Victor [Prince Victor of Hohenlohe Langenburg] were there, and all the children and our guests. Our humble gifts of toys were added to by a beautiful little bronze *replica* of the Amazon (Kiss's) from the Prince [of Prussia], a beautiful paper-knife from the Princess [of Prussia] and a nice little clock from Mama.

" The Park presented a wonderful spectacle, crowds streaming through it, carriages and troops passing, quite like the Coronation-day, and for me the same anxiety,—no, much greater anxiety on account of my beloved Albert. The day was bright and all bustle and excitement. . . . At half-past eleven the whole procession in State carriages was in motion. . . . The Green Park and Hyde Park were one densely crowded mass of human beings, in the highest good humour and most enthusiastic.

* Thackeray.

I never saw Hyde Park look as it did,—as far as the eye could reach. A little rain fell just as we started; but before we came near the Crystal Palace, the sun shone and gleamed upon the gigantic edifice, upon which the flags of all the nations were floating. We drove up Rotten Row, and got out at the entrance on that side.

"The glimpse of the transept through the iron gates, the waving palms, flowers, statues, myriads of people filling the galleries and seats around, with the flourish of trumpets as we entered, gave us a sensation which I can never forget, and I felt much moved. We went for a moment to a little side room, where we left our shawls, and where we found Mama and Mary [afterwards Princess of Teck], and outside which were standing the other Princes. In a few seconds we proceeded, Albert leading me, having Vicky at his hand and Bertie holding mine. The sight, as we came to the middle, where the steps and chair (which I did *not* sit on) were placed, with the beautiful crystal fountain just in front of it,—was magical,—so vast, so glorious, so touching. One felt—as so many did whom I have since spoken to—filled with devotion,—more so than by any service I have ever heard. The tremendous cheers, the joy expressed in every face, the immensity of the building, the mixture of palms, flowers, trees, statues, fountains,—the organ (with 200 instruments and 600 voices, which sounded like nothing), and my beloved husband the author of this 'Peace-festival,' which united the industry of all nations of the earth,—all this was moving indeed, and it was and is a day to live for ever. God bless my dearest Albert, God bless my dearest country, which has shown itself so great to-day! One felt so grateful to the great God, who seemed to pervade all and to bless all!"

Sentiments not dissimilar from these were expressed by Thackeray (himself a witness of the ceremony), in his stirring *May Day Ode*:—

> "I felt a thrill of love and awe,
> To mark the different garb of each,
> The changing tongue, the various speech,
> Together blent,

THE OPENING OF THE EXHIBITION OF 1851, BY THE QUEEN AND PRINCE ALBERT.

> A thrill, methinks, like his, who saw
> 'All people dwelling upon earth,
> Praising one God with solemn mirth,
>   And one consent.'
>   * * * * *
> "Behold her in her Royal place;
> A gentle lady—and the hand
> That sways the sceptre of this land,
>   How frail and weak!
> Soft is the voice, and fair the face;
> She breathes Amen to prayer and hymn,
> No wonder that her eyes are dim,
>   And pale her cheek.
>   * * * * *
> "The fountain in the basin plays,
> The chanting organ echoes clear,
> And awful chorus 'tis to hear,
>   A wondrous song!
>
> "Swell, organ, swell your trumpet blast,
> March, Queen and Royal pageant march
> By splendid aisle and springing arch
>   Of this fair hall!
> And see! above the fabric vast,
> God's boundless heaven is bending blue,
> God's peaceful sun is beaming through
>   And shining over all."

The National Anthem having been sung, Prince Albert left the Queen's side, and placing himself at the head of the Commissioners, read a long report, to which Her Majesty read a short answer. The Archbishop of Canterbury then offered up a prayer, and the *Hallelujah Chorus* was given by the choir and orchestra. In the midst of those thrilling strains, a Chinese mandarin, impressed by the solemnity of the scene, came forward and made a profound obeisance to the Queen. "This live importation from the Celestial Empire," says a contemporary newspaper, "managed to render himself extremely conspicuous, and one could not help admiring his perfect composure and nonchalance of manner. He talked with nobody, yet he seemed perfectly at home, and on the most friendly terms with all. A most amusing advantage was taken of his appearance, for, when the procession was formed, the diplomatic body had no Chinese representative, and our stray Celestial friend was quietly impounded and made to march in the rear of the Ambassadors. He submitted to this arrangement with the same calm indifference which marked the whole course of his proceedings, and bore himself with a steadiness and gravity that fully justified the course that had been adopted. His behaviour throughout was that of 'a citizen of the world' as perfect as Goldsmith's philosopher himself."

The procession just referred to was of great length, but was admirably arranged—indeed, it seems to have been the most attractive part of the ceremony. "The nave," writes the Queen, "was full, which had not been intended; but still there was no difficulty, and the whole long walk from one end to the other was made in the midst of continued and deafening cheers and waving of handkerchiefs. Every one's face was bright and smiling, many with tears in their eyes. Many Frenchmen called out ' *Vive la Reine!* ' One could, of course, see nothing but what was near in the nave, and nothing in the courts. The organs were but little heard, but the military band at one end had a very fine effect as we passed along. They played the march from *Athalie*. The beautiful Amazon, in bronze, by Kiss, looked magnificent. The old Duke and Lord Anglesey walked arm-in-arm, which was a touching sight. I saw many acquaintances among those present.

"We returned to our own place, and Albert told Lord Breadalbane to declare that the Exhibition was opened, which he did in a loud voice—' Her Majesty commands me to declare this Exhibition opened '—which was followed by a flourish of trumpets and immense cheering. All the Commissioners, the Executive Committee, etc., who worked so hard, and to whom such immense praise is due, seemed truly happy, and no one more so than Paxton, who may be justly proud; he rose from being a common gardener's boy. Everybody was astonished and delighted, Sir George Grey [Home Secretary] in tears.

"The return was equally satisfactory — the crowd most

enthusiastic, the order perfect. We reached the Palace at twenty minutes past one, and went out on the balcony, and were loudly cheered. The Prince and Princess [of Prussia] quite delighted and impressed. That *we* felt happy—thankful —I need not say; proud of all that had passed, of my darling husband's success, and of the behaviour of my good people. I was more impressed than I can say by the scene. It was one that can never be effaced from my memory, and never will be from that of any one who witnessed it.

"I must not omit to mention an interesting episode of this day—viz., the visit of the good old Duke on this his eighty-second birthday to his little godson, our dear little boy. He came to us both at five, and gave him a golden cup and some toys, which he had himself chosen, and Arthur gave him a nosegay."

It remains to be said that the Exhibition lasted nearly six months, and that it was financially—indeed, in every respect— a great success. Though over six million persons visited it, there was not one accident; and the receipts amounted to £500,000. Not the least noteworthy of the visitors was an old woman, named Mary Kerlynack, who walked all the way from Cornwall to see the great house of glass—"a most hale old woman," writes the Queen, "who was near crying at my looking at her." The knighting of Paxton and two other gentlemen, who had laboured indefatigably in the work, came in as an appropriate finish on the closing day.

In June and August, 1853, the Queen paid several visits to the camp at Chobham to witness some experiments in field operations, which were being carried on for the improvement of the army. On the 21st of June there was a sham fight—"a well-contested, though bloodless, battle, over ground broken by hollows, streams, marshes, and woods"—which was watched, not by the Queen and Prince alone, but by a hundred thousand of her subjects, to say nothing of the King of Hanover and Duke of Coburg. A day or two later the Prince himself took part in the operations, camping out at night like the rest of the army, and submitting to all the discomforts of the situation with cheerful grace. The camp broke up on the 20th of August, and not long after the troops were sent abroad to engage in operations against a real foe, the Crimean War having just broken out.

Eight or nine days before the breaking up of the camp, there was also a review of the Fleet at Spithead, in which forty ships of war took part, thirty-seven of which were steam vessels. The weather was favourable, and the spectacle all—yet shall we say, "all"?—that could be desired. Perhaps there are more desirable things than reviews of fleets and armies; for what, after all, are these great naval and military shows but reminders of that awful reality—War? War, the desolator who has filled the world with carnage times out of number, who has destroyed fruitful lands, and brought hunger and sorrow to the homes of millions of the human race. In the light of such gruesome facts, we confess that we find it difficult to eulogise even so harmless a spectacle as a Naval Review.

Eight months later, many of these same vessels were on their way to the Baltic, laden with troops for the seat of war. Their departure is said to have been a very impressive sight. Off the Isle of Wight the Royal yacht *Fairy*, in which were the Queen and Prince, took her place at the head of the squadron, and led the way for several miles. Then she stopped, and the fleet defiled past, saluting as it went, the Admiral's ship, the *Duke of Wellington*, bringing up the rear. "Her Majesty," says a *Times* chronicler of that day, "stood waving her handkerchief towards the mighty ship as she departed, and for a long time after the whole fleet had gone the Royal yacht remained motionless, as if the illustrious occupants desired to linger over a spectacle calculated to impress them so profoundly."*

In June, 1858, the Queen and Prince Consort were the guests of Lord Leigh at Stoneleigh Abbey, a noble mansion with terrace garden sloping down to the Avon. A large crowd gathered in the Home Park, close up to the balustrade of the garden, and here, at midnight, they suddenly started singing "God Save the Queen"—an act of spontaneous loyalty as impressive as it was unexpected. Next day (the 15th of June)

* *Life of the Prince Consort*, vol. iii. 7.

the Queen drove through Birmingham, which was decked out in its best to receive her. The day was broiling hot and the air stifling, but the smoke for which the city is so unpleasantly notorious had entirely cleared away. Banners and flags fluttered from all the windows, and the streets were crossed and inter-crossed with festoons of flowers, which produced a singularly beautiful effect. The crowds were as dense as bees in a hive, and the cheering was tremendous. Her Majesty heard one excited spectator call out: "Quite a pattern lady!" and another: "What a darling!" expressions which seem to have diverted her not a little. An interesting feature of the visit was the drive through Aston Park, which, with the Hall, was about to be converted into a people's pleasure-grounds and museum, the property having been secured by the working-men themselves out of their hard-earned wages. Several of these rough mechanics were presented to the Queen, to one or two of whom she said a few words: and when the presentation was over, Her Majesty stepped out on a balcony overlooking the grounds, and the park was proclaimed open.

The Royal party stayed a second night at Stoneleigh, and then went on through Leamington, to the Castle of the Warwicks. Here they lunched, and then proceeded to Warwick station, which was reached just as a thunderstorm began to break. "We had barely got into the railway carriage," writes the Queen, "before the rain came down with fearful violence. . . . We got to Buckingham Palace a little before eight. So hot, it had been 90° in the shade, and people half-smothered." A few months later Leeds was taken on the way to Scotland, and the Queen opened the new Town Hall. Repetition would be tedious, and we need only say that the reception here, as at Birmingham and other places, was extremely loyal.

We now come to Scotland. Of the Queen's life at Balmoral between the years 1848 and 1861 we have already spoken, as well as of the four great expeditions from Balmoral, but during this period there were also visits to other parts of Scotland, and notably to Aberdeen, Edinburgh, and Glasgow.

The first-named place was taken on the way to Balmoral in September, 1848, and during the few hours spent there, the Prince was presented with the freedom of the city, and found time to visit the universities, the museum, and the great granite quarries in the neighbourhood. The Queen was loyally welcomed, but nothing occurred that calls for special mention, and we pass quickly on to Edinburgh.

Of the visits to "Modern Athens" (for there were two) the earliest was in August, 1850, when Her Majesty stayed at Holyrood for the first time. "Not since Queen Mary quitted that scene of sad remembrances had the halls of the old Palace been trodden by queenly footsteps. What wonder if the hearts of the assembled thousands beat quicker, and their cheers rang with a deeper tone at the spectacle of their Queen taking up her abode in the only palace now left in their land, and one which is to them a cherished memorial of their national story!" The Queen herself was too much excited by the associations of the spot to care for rest after the fatigues of the day. Scarcely pausing to look at the rooms provided for their reception, the Royal guests hurried to see the more striking objects of the Palace. "We wandered out," says Her Majesty, "with the two girls and Miss Hildyard, to look at the old ruined Abbey which adjoins the Palace, and which you see from our windows. It is beautiful inside. One of the aisles is still roofed in, but the other is not. It was originally an Abbey, and the very old tombstones are those of friars. It was afterwards the Chapel Royal, and Queen Mary, my unfortunate ancestress, was married to Lord Darnley at this very altar, of which you see the remains. . . . When we returned, we saw the rooms where Queen Mary lived, her bed, the dressing-room into which the murderers entered who killed Rizzio, and the spot where he fell, where, as the old housekeeper said to me, 'if the lady would stand on that side,' I would see that the boards were discoloured by the blood." Next morning the Queen walked to the top of Arthur's Seat, and enjoyed the fine view from the top, which comprehends not only the whole city, but the bay, the island of Inchkeith, and the far-distant Bass

Rock. The same day the Prince laid the foundation-stone of the National Gallery of Scotland, and made one of his most successful speeches. Some idea of the interest felt on this occasion may be gathered from the fact that 70,000 tickets were disposed of; after the ceremony the Royal visitors drove through the finest part of the city, inspecting its monuments and public buildings.

The second important visit to Edinburgh was in August, 1860, when the Queen reviewed the Volunteers in Holyrood Park. The gathering was a truly national one, and a force of some 22,000 men saluted their Sovereign under the windows of Holyrood Palace. The Queen came upon the ground in an open carriage-and-four, in which, besides Her Majesty, were the Duchess of Kent, Princess Alice, and Prince Arthur. The Prince Consort rode on the right side of the carriage, and the Duke of Buccleuch on the left. As the Queen passed along the saluting lines, the cheering of the assembled spectators was deafening. "The effect," wrote a spectator, "was not less than sublime. Peal after peal broke forth in thunder, carried away by the strong wind, to be again and again renewed." The march past lasted an hour and ten minutes; and was a splendid and inspiriting sight. "Very good—very fine men," was the Queen's comment; "Lord Breadalbane, riding at the head of his own body of five hundred Highlanders, looked magnificent, and was loudly cheered. The only drawback was the dust, which came at times in such clouds as to prevent the men from seeing anything, and yet they marched so well." Directly the review was over, the Volunteers, who had hitherto been debarred from cheering by the British rule of military discipline, advanced in a line to the Royal carriage, and made up for lost time by such bursts of acclamation as even the Queen herself had seldom listened to. Again and again the cheers were renewed; while caps were thrown into the air, or stuck upon rifles and waved to and fro. As the Royal party drove away, the men fairly broke ranks and followed the carriage, huzzaing and shouting in the most picturesque disorder!*

* *Life of the Prince Consort*, vol. v. 29.

Of the two visits to Glasgow it is only necessary to speak of the first, and then we may cross with the Royal yacht to Ireland. The second of the two visits—namely, that of 1859, when the Queen went to open the Glasgow Waterworks— was a failure owing to the heavy rain. On the first occasion, which was ten years earlier, the reception was brilliant, and the Prince describes it as "a veritable triumphal procession through five to six hundred thousand human beings."* The landing-place was tastefully decorated, and as the Queen with her two eldest children stepped into their carriage, Mr. Alison (the historian of Europe), rode up and took his place on one side, while the Commander of the Forces in Scotland, General Riddell, stationed himself on the other. After driving through the main streets of the town, admiring the fine stone buildings for which the city is noted, the Royal visitors were shown over the old Cathedral by Principal Macfarlane. Before entering the edifice the aged Principal directed the Queen's attention to a factory chimney of enormous height, at that time the tallest in existence. Probably the Americans are now able to show something taller. Her Majesty seems to have been chiefly interested in the crypt of the Cathedral, the beautiful architecture of which is still in a high state of preservation. "It is in this crypt," she writes, "that the famous scene in *Rob Roy* is laid, where Rob Roy gives Frank Osbaldistone warning that he is in danger."† On leaving the Cathedral the Royal party inspected the fine equestrian statue of the Duke of Wellington, which stands in front of the Exchange, and the visit was then brought to a close.

We come now to Ireland. The Queen first touched Irish ground at Cove, in County Cork, on the 3rd of August, 1849. The name of the place was changed to Queenstown to commemorate the event, and the fact is interestingly set forth in the Royal *Journal.* "To give the people the satisfaction of calling the place Queenstown, in honour of its being the first spot on which I set foot upon Irish ground, I stepped

* *Life of the Prince Consort*, vol. ii. 36. † *Leaves*, 275.

on shore amidst the roar of cannon (for the artillery were placed so close as quite to shake the temporary room which we entered), and the enthusiastic shouts of the people."*
The Royal party re-embarked almost immediately, and proceeded to Cork, where they were received with all that effusiveness of welcome (too often so deceptive) for which the Irish character is remarkable. "I cannot describe our route," says the Queen, "but it will suffice to say that it took two hours; that we drove through the principal streets, twice through some of them; that they were densely crowded, decorated with flowers and triumphal arches; that the heat and dust were great; that we passed by the new College which is building—one of the four which are ordered by Act of Parliament; that our reception was most enthusiastic; and that everything went off to perfection, and was very well arranged. Cork is not at all like an English town, and looks rather foreign. The crowd is a noisy, excitable, but very good-humoured one, running and pushing about, and laughing, talking, and shrieking. The beauty of the women is very remarkable, and struck us much; such beautiful dark eyes and hair, and such fine teeth; almost every third woman was pretty, and some remarkably so. They wear no bonnets, and generally long blue cloaks; the men are very poorly, often raggedly, dressed, and many wear blue coats and short breeches with blue stockings."†

When the illustrious visitors had re-embarked, the Royal yacht proceeded to Kingstown harbour, outside of which they were met by other vessels, the *Sphinx*, and *Stromboli*, the *Trident*, and the *Dragon*, and with this large squadron they steamed into the harbour. Here thousands upon thousands of spectators were assembled—cheering, we need not say, and that very heartily. The effect is said to have been extremely fine, for the sun was just setting, and his ruddy glow was reflected upon everything — ships, harbour, buildings, and country. Her Majesty did not disembark till the following morning at ten o'clock, when an immense multitude was

* *Leaves*, 249.   † *Ibid.* 251.

waiting to receive her. As she stepped on shore, the ships saluted, the bands struck up, the vast crowd broke into bursts of welcome, and hats and handkerchiefs were waved excitedly. The fears which had been gravely entertained in some quarters that Her Majesty's reception would be disappointing and cold were at once and for ever dispelled. The capital was quickly reached, and the Queen received the keys from the Mayor. There were no gates to the city, so temporary ones had been erected under an arch, and here this ancient formality was gone through. The Queen then drove through the city, the streets of which were gay with flowers and flags and bunting, and alive with human faces. "At the last triumphal arch," says Her Majesty, "a poor little dove was let down into my lap, with an olive branch round its neck, alive and very tame."* This pretty symbol was hardly needed, for the voice of Ireland had been already heard in the acclamations of the multitude. "Och! Queen, dear!" cried one old lady, as the Royal carriage, with one or two of the young Princes in it, rolled past her, "make one of thim Prince Pathrick, and all Oireland will die for ye!" The old lady's wish was gratified, for the Prince that was born at Buckingham Palace in the following year was called Arthur William *Patrick* Albert, and a letter from his father to Baron Stockmar contains the interesting statement, "Patrick is in remembrance of our recent visit to Ireland."†

To tell of all the places visited on this occasion would require far more space than we have at our disposal. Whatever was worth seeing in the city Her Majesty saw. The Bank, the Model School, College Green, Stephen's Green, the Four Courts, the Cathedral, Kilmainham Hospital, Maynooth and Trinity Colleges—these perhaps were the chief places; but as the Queen spent nearly a week in Dublin it will be readily understood that she saw far more than these. At Trinity College Her Majesty was shown some interesting ancient manuscripts and relics, including St. Columba's Book (in which she inscribed her name), and the original harp of King O'Brian, supposed to be the one from which the Irish arms are taken. On one of

* *Leaves*, 256.   † *Life of the Prince Consort*, vol. ii. 44.

the days there was a grand review in Phœnix Park, when six thousand one hundred and sixty men, including the Constabulary, passed before the Queen. Lady Bloomfield tells us that there must have been at least 150,000 people out, and that Her Majesty was immensely cheered.* At Carton, a little distance out of Dublin, the Royal guests witnessed some dancing, the country people going through their jigs with great cheerfulness and zest. The Irish jig is " quite different from the Scotch reel," writes Her Majesty ; "not so animated, and the steps different, but very droll. The people were poorly dressed in thick coats, and the women in shawls. There was one man who was a regular specimen of an Irishman, with his hat on one ear. Others in blue coats, with short breeches and blue stockings. There were three old and tattered pipers playing. The Irish pipe is very different from the Scotch ; it is weak, and they don't blow into it, but merely have small bellows which they move with the arm." †

From Dublin the Royal party proceeded to Belfast, where the reception, though necessarily on a smaller scale, was not less hearty than at the capital city. There was the usual display of flowers, hangings, and triumphal arches, and the galleries which had been erected along the line of the procession were crowded with spectators. The favourite motto written up on most of the arches was, "Cead mile failte," a piece of pure Irish, meaning, "A hundred thousand welcomes." The Queen remarks in her *Diary* that the Irish language "is very like Gaelic ; it is in fact *the* language, and has existed in books from the earliest period, whereas Gaelic has only been *written* since half-a-century, though it was always *spoken*." Her Majesty frequently heard the people call out "Cead mile failte !" and she met with the expression in every shape and form.‡ At one place in the town the visitors were shown the whole process of the manufacture of linen, from the steeping and spinning of the flax to its manufacture into cambric and other kinds of cloth. They also

* *Reminiscences of Court and Diplomatic Life*, vol. i. 300.
† *Leaves*, 261, 262. ‡ *Ibid.* 266, 267.

went over the Botanic Gardens, and stopped to admire the College, then a new building. The following day they left for Scotland.

On the 27th of August, 1853, Her Majesty again crossed to Ireland, on this occasion to visit the Dublin Art and Industrial Exhibition, which had been opened a week or two before. It had been established upon the model of the Great Exhibition of 1851, and naturally both the Queen and Prince felt a warm interest in its success. "The Court went by railway to Holyhead. They were detained there by a violent storm until the morning of the 29th; but the delay was turned to account by the Prince in inspecting, along with Mr. Rendel, the engineer, the gigantic works then in progress for converting this port into a harbour of refuge, and in visiting the Stack Lighthouse with some of the Trinity Brethren, whom he found at Holyhead on their tour of lighthouse inspection. By eight o'clock next morning Kingstown Harbour was reached, and the Royal guests, as they made their way to the Viceregal Lodge through what now seemed the familiar streets of Dublin, were greeted with an enthusiasm almost beyond that which had welcomed them four years before. 'The morning,' the Queen notes, 'was fine and bright, and the scene gay and animated.' A State visit was paid to the Exhibition next day. Its general arrangement brought up agreeable recollections of its great prototype of 1851. 'Everything was well conducted,' says the same record, 'and the people most kind.' Through 'deplorable rain' the Queen and Prince paid a visit the same day to Mr. Dargan, at whose sole expense the Exhibition building had been constructed. His demeanour is noted as 'touchingly modest and simple. I would have made him a baronet, but he was anxious it should not be done.' The morning of each day was devoted to the Exhibition, and every visit showed it to be even more complete and more interesting than had been anticipated. The products of Irish industry were found to be most attractive—their poplins, lace, and pottery in particular. 'By the novel process of hatching salmon, exhibited here for the first time,' the Queen writes, 'Albert was especially interested, as he is by every new and useful discovery.' The greater inclination of the people to apply themselves to industry is strongly dwelt upon in Her Majesty's *Journal*. 'For this,' it says, 'the Exhibition will be of immense use. It has raised the feeling of the people, showing them that they can succeed. Mr. Dargan's own history they are likewise inclined to study and reflect upon.'"*

This very auspicious visit was brought to a close on the 3rd of September, on which day the Queen wrote in her *Journal*: "A beautiful morning, and this the very day we are going away, which we felt quite sorry to do, having spent such a pleasant, gay, and interesting time in Ireland. . . . At half-past five we started for Kingstown. We drove gently, though not at a foot's pace, through Dublin, which was unusually crowded (no soldiers lining the streets), to the station, where again there were great crowds. In eight minutes we were at Kingstown, where again the crowds were immense, and most enthusiastic. The evening was beautiful, and the sight a very fine one—all the ships and yachts decked out and firing salutes, and thousands on the quay cheering. As night closed in a magnificent aurora borealis lighted up the northern sky, while from the land fireworks were let off until a late hour. It was a gay, fine evening, and the hum and singing and noise made by the people made one fancy one's-self in a foreign port in the South."†

* *Life of the Prince Consort*, vol. ii. 85. † *Ibid.*

CHAPTER X.

ROYALTY ABROAD, AND AN EMPEROR'S VISITS.
(1848–1860.)

NOW that Her Majesty had two such paradises as Osborne and Balmoral to fly to whenever she was free from the irksome but unavoidable restraints of London Court life, it is not surprising that she seldom went abroad. Between the years 1848 and 1860 the Queen and Prince visited the Continent only five or six times, and these visits, with the exception of the last (in 1860), were all extremely short. They may be taken in their order.

From the 10th to the 14th of August, 1852, the Queen was a second time the guest of her much-loved uncle, the King of the Belgians. The Royal visitors stayed, as before, at Laeken, but of the life there we have no record in the published pages of the Royal *Journal;* nor are we much better informed with regard to the few hours spent at Antwerp. We know that the Royal party entered the city in a hurricane of rain and wind, and we know that they visited the Cathedral and Museum; but that is all. Before steaming out of the Schelde, however, a visit (of which we must say a few words) was paid to the old-world town of Terneusen, on the Wester Schelde, situated in Holland. Of this quaint little place and its people, the Queen has written very pleasantly and instructively.* She has described the narrow, cleanly-kept town, with its houses that seem to have been newly washed, and its

---
* *Leaves*, 315.

primitive carriages without springs; the dress of the women, so neat and ancient-looking, the colours of their handkerchiefs, their bright jackets, and their ample woollen petticoats, with waistbands high up, almost under the arms. She has spoken admiringly of their little white caps and golden pins, and the peculiar arrangement of their hair—in a curl on the forehead. The sight of these things carried back Her Majesty's thoughts to other days—the times of James and Charles I., when the style of dress was not dissimilar. The costumes of the men did not escape her quick observation either. With the exception of some ugly imitations of our modern dress, they, too, were very characteristic. The low and very small-brimmed hat, the full leathern trousers, with the belt and large silver buttons and clasps reminded her of the German peasants; while a solidity and respectability about the people generally showed at once that they were Protestants. "We drove to one of the farms, a rich one, in the neighbourhood," writes Her Majesty. "The pilot went in to ask the owners if we might look at their farm, and immediately they came out and welcomed us most kindly. They were fine and striking specimens of the Dutch peasantry. The man, Peter Feiter, was a tall, very dark, and handsome slim young man, dressed in the strict costume of the country, and the woman, his mother, was a very fine, tall hearty old woman, the picture of cleanliness. Albert said she reminded him of the Tyrolese women. They took us into their house, which was beautifully clean and charmingly arranged—all the walls covered with Dutch painted tiles. In the parlour everything was decked out. There were the dishes, the china, a handsome mahogany press, a large book, with massive clasps, containing (as Lady Gainsborough thought, who looked into it) the pedigree of the family. They insisted on our sitting down and tasting some fresh milk. The old lady brought out a number of smart glasses for the purpose, and, like the Scotch, seemed not satisfied that we did not take it all. Then they showed us their cowsheds, which in the summer they fill with their corn, and afterwards a pretty garden."*

* *Life of the Prince Consort*, vol. ii. 77.

The Queen's next visit abroad was to Napoleon the Third at the French capital, in 1855; but as, in the interval, the Emperor was the guest of Her Majesty in England, it may be well to speak of this visit first. In a previous chapter we have seen the representatives of the two other great European Powers at the English Court—namely, the Emperor of Russia and the King of Prussia, and it is only fitting that some particulars should be given of the visit, or visits, of the Emperor of France. True, we have already seen a French King at Windsor Castle—Louis Philippe; but that is the more reason why some space should be given to his supplanter, Louis Napoleon. Poor Philippe! the next time he came to England it was as a fugitive, for the Revolution of 1848 had driven him from the throne, and he was glad enough to find an asylum in England. The Revolution, and the troubles which it brought in its train, gave the opportunity which Louis Napoleon had been waiting for all his life, and on the night of the 1st of December, 1851, he struck his tremendous *coup d'état* by which his name will be ever remembered. Paris woke on the following morning with fifty thousand drawn daggers at its throat, and the nephew of Buonaparte, having brought all France to his feet by his adroitness, mounted the throne over the dead bodies of thousands of his victims.

This, then, was the man who was the guest of our gentle Queen in the April of 1855, and again in 1857. The Queen's excitement on the occasion of his first visit seems to have been as great, or greater, than that of any of her subjects. Perhaps Her Majesty was thinking more of the uncle than the nephew, of the great Napoleon rather than of "Napoleon the Little," —as Victor Hugo mercilessly named him. "At ten minutes to five," writes the Queen from Windsor Castle on the 17th of April, "news arrived that the Emperor had reached London. I hurried to be ready, and went over to the other side of the Castle, where we waited in one of the tapestry-rooms, near the guard-room. It seemed very long. At length, at a quarter to seven, we heard that the train had left Paddington. The expectation and agitation grew more intense. The evening was fine and bright. At length the crowd of anxious spectators lining the road seemed to move, then came a groom, then we heard a gun, and we moved towards the staircase. Another groom came. Then we saw the advanced guard of the escort, then the cheers of the crowd burst forth. The outriders appeared, the doors opened, I stepped out, the children and the Princes close behind me, the band struck up '*Partant pour la Syrie*,' the trumpets sounded, and the open carriage, with the Emperor and Empress, Albert sitting opposite to them, drove up, and they got out. I cannot say what indescribable emotions filled me—how much all seemed like a wonderful dream. These great meetings of sovereigns, surrounded by very exciting accompaniments, are always very agitating. I advanced and embraced the Emperor, who received two salutes on either cheek from me, having first kissed my hand. I next embraced the very gentle, graceful, and evidently very nervous Empress."*

To tell of even a fifth part of all that went on during the Emperor's three days in England—of the ball in his honour in the Waterloo Room at the Castle, of his investiture with the Order of the Garter by the Queen, of his reception of an address from the Corporation of London at Windsor, of the grand dinner given to him afterwards at the Guildhall, of his visits in State to the Opera and the Crystal Palace—to treat of all these things would require several pages, and we have not so much space at our disposal. A few anecdotes, however, gleaned from the Royal *Journal*, may not be unacceptable. Among other curious facts about himself, the Emperor told the Queen that he first saw her eighteen years before, when she went in State to prorogue Parliament, and that the sight of one so young in that position had impressed him deeply. He also mentioned that he was a special constable on the 10th of April, 1848, when the Chartist disturbances in London began to wear a serious aspect, and had wondered whether she had known it. At the Opera, the Emperor told her that when, after the Royal marriage in 1840, she went in State to Covent Garden, he had with great difficulty obtained a box, for which he had had

* *Life of the Prince Consort*, vol. iii. 41.

to pay £40, "which struck me, nevertheless," said he, "as a little too much." On the occasion of their visit to the Crystal Palace, it came to the Queen's knowledge that the day was the Emperor's forty-seventh birthday; "and though not fêted or taken notice of publicly," says Her Majesty, "we felt we could not do otherwise than take private notice of it. Consequently, when we went along the corridor to meet him, I wished him

NAPOLEON III.

joy. He seemed for a moment not to know to what I alluded, then smiled, and kissed my hand, and thanked me, and I gave him a pencil case. . . . The Emperor was also very much pleased at (Prince) Arthur's giving him two violets—the flower of the Buonapartes."* On the day that the Emperor was invested with the Order of the Garter there was a meeting of the Privy Council at Windsor, which, being prolonged for

* *Life of the Prince Consort,* vol. iii. 41-43.

an unusual time, gave occasion to an amusing incident. The luncheon-time had been fixed for two o'clock, and the Council met an hour before noon. Both the Emperor and Prince Albert were present, but the Queen remained in a neighbouring apartment with the Empress. An hour passed away—two hours—three, but the Council showed no signs of breaking up. Her Majesty began to grow restless, for the hands were travelling swiftly round the clock, and the investiture of the Garter had been fixed for the same afternoon. At last, at her suggestion, the Empress went and told Lord Cowley how late it was. The desired end was not achieved, however, and still no one appeared. "Then," writes Her Majesty, "the Empress advised me to go to them—'*Je n'ose entrer, mais votre Majesté le peur ; cela vous regarde*' ('I dare not go in, but your Majesty may ; it is your affair'). So I went through the Emperor's room (the Council-room adjoined his bedroom) and knocked, and at last stepped in and asked what we should do. The Emperor and Albert got up, and said they would come. However, they did not," and luncheon was presently served without them.*

Before taking leave of his entertainers, the Emperor inscribed his name in the Queen's album ; and on giving it back to her, said : "I have tried to write what I feel." The writing was : "*Je porte à votre Majesté les sentiments qu'on éprouve pour une reine et pour une sœur, dévouement respectueux, tendre amitié*" ("I tender to your Majesty the feelings which one entertains for a queen and a sister, respectful devotion, tender friendship "). In the Prince of Wales's autograph book he wrote some German lines (not his own), of which we have attempted a translation :—

> Youth, of pure soul, ingenuous, innocent,
> Weigh and reflect ; nor let thine object be
> Mere praise. And whether plaudits greet
> Or calumnies assail thee, waver not.
> The path of truth is narrow, and the way
> Of duty lies 'twixt chasms. Heedful walk,
> For minstrel praises oft deceitful are.

* *Life of the Prince Consort*, vol. iii. 42.

Very good counsel, but think of Napoleon the Third commending it!

The return visit was paid in August of the same year, and extended a little over a week. The reception of the Queen and Prince in Paris was a grand affair—worthy of the First Empire. Night had come on, but the capital was brilliantly illuminated. Banners, flags, arches, flowers, and inscriptions everywhere met the eye, and the broad streets were thronged with people. The whole way from the station to the Palace of St. Cloud was lined with troops—National Guards, troops of the line and *Chasseurs d'Afrique;* and as the Royal cortège passed along, shouts of "*Vive la Reine d'Angleterre!*" "*Vive l'Empereur!*" and "*Vive le Prince Albert!*" broke from thousands and tens of thousands of lips. "In all this blaze of light from lamps and torches," writes the Queen, "amidst the roar of cannon, and bands and drums and cheers, we reached the Palace. The Empress (the Emperor had travelled with his guests all the way from Boulogne), with Princess Mathilda and the ladies, received us at the door, and took us up a beautiful staircase, lined with the splendid *Cent-Gardes,* who are magnificent men, very like our Life Guards. . . . We went through the rooms at once to our own, which are charming. . . . I felt quite bewildered, but enchanted; . . . everything is so beautiful!"*

The next day being Sunday, there was morning service (in English) in one of the rooms of the Palace, the chaplain of the Embassy officiating; and in the afternoon came a drive with the Emperor and Empress to the *Bois de Boulogne,* and thence, at the Queen's desire, to the pretty suburb of Neuilly, a quarter where many of the professional classes engaged in Paris have their homes. The following day sight-seeing began in earnest, the *Exposition des Beaux Arts,* the *Palais de l'Elysée,* the *Palais de Justice, Nôtre Dame,* and the *Hotel de Ville,* being the most notable places visited. At the *Elysée,* now the residence of the President of the Republic, what interesting thoughts must have been awakened in the Queen's mind!

* *Life of the Prince Consort,* vol. iii. 54.

Here had lived successively Madame de Pompadour, Murat, Napoleon I., the King of Holland, and much later, the King of Holland's son, Her Majesty's imperial host, who had plotted the *coup d'état* within its walls! Later in the day, the Emperor took his guests to the *Sainte Chapelle* and the *Palais de Justice;* and in crossing the *Pont au Change*, he pointed out the *Conciergerie*. "That is where I was imprisoned!" said he. "Strange contrast," remarks the Queen, "to be driving with us as Emperor through the streets of the city in triumph!"

To tell of all the places visited during this eventful week, or of the ceremonies and receptions in the Queen's honour, is manifestly impossible. Of course the *Trianon* palaces, the *Grand* and the *Petit*, associated with Marie Antoinette, were not forgotten; and the *Exposition* was re-visited two or three times. There was a stay of some hours at the Tuileries, where the Queen received the Préfet and the Municipalité, who had come to invite her to a ball at the Hôtel de Ville. The Préfet wished to read an Address, but the Emperor considerately stopped him. Her Majesty told the Préfet that she would go to the ball with pleasure, and that she had been deeply moved by her reception in France, which could never be forgotten. "Then," writes the Queen in her *Journal*, "the Préfet asked whether they might call the new street leading to the Hôtel de Ville after me, on which I said—'I shall feel greatly flattered by your doing so—' then, turning towards the Emperor—'if the Emperor allows it;' on which he cordially gave his consent." *

On the Friday there was a grand review in the *Champs de Mars*, and a short visit to the *Ecole Militaire* (military school); after which they drove straight to the *Hôtel des Invalides*, under the dome of which Napoleon the Great was lying. This (though wanting all the glitter and display of much that had gone before) was perhaps the most impressive incident of the week. "It was nearly seven when we arrived," the Queen notes; ". . . the Governor, Count d'Ornans, was terribly put out at not having been *prévense*. However, it all did very well. There

* *Life of the Prince Consort*, vol. iii. 56.

were four torches which lit us along, and added to the solemnity of the scene, which was striking in every way. The Church is fine and lofty. We went to look from above into the open vault, the effect of which the Emperor does not like, as he says it looks like 'a great basin.' 'At the first glance,' he said, 'one asks one's-self what is in the Emperor's tomb; one expects to see water in it.'" The Emperor led the Queen into an adjoining chapel—the chapel of St. Jerome—where the remains of "the little Corsican" were at that time deposited; "and there I stood," says Her Majesty, "at the arm of Napoleon III., his nephew, before the coffin of England's bitterest foe; I, the granddaughter of that King who hated him most, and who most vigorously opposed him, and this very nephew, who bears his name, being my nearest and dearest ally! The organ of the church was playing, 'God save the Queen' at the time, and this solemn scene took place by torchlight, and during a thunderstorm. Strange and wonderful indeed. It seems as if, in this tribute of respect to a departed foe, old enmities and rivalries were wiped out, and the seal of Heaven placed upon that bond of unity, which is now happily established between two great and powerful nations. May Heaven bless and prosper it!"*

On Monday, the 27th, the visit came to a close, and the Queen, who had immensely enjoyed everything, parted from her hosts with a heavy heart. It was past twelve o'clock at night when she took a final farewell of the Emperor on board her own yacht. "You will come back again!" he said; and, of course, the Queen expressed a hope that he would come to England. "I embraced him twice," writes Her Majesty, "and he shook hands very warmly with Albert and the children. We followed him to the ladder, and here I again pressed his hand, saying, 'Once more, *Adieu, Sire!*' We looked over the side of the ship and watched him getting into the barge. The Emperor called out, '*Adieu, Madame, au revoir;*' to which I replied, '*Je l'espère bien.*'" †

The hope expressed by the Queen that Louis Napoleon would

* *Life of the Prince Consort*, vol. iii. 57.   † *Ibid.* vol. iii. 59.

repeat his visit to England, was fulfilled in the summer of 1857, when the Emperor and Empress were her guests at Osborne. The visit was of an altogether quiet and informal character. They came over in the *Reine Hortense*, and the Queen and Prince Albert hurried down to the private landing-stage on the beach to receive them. The Imperial visitors remained about four days, and the Queen described their stay as very *gamüthlich*—*i.e.*, tranquilly pleasant. "Good Osborne in no way changed its unpretending privacy and simplicity," she wrote to the King of the Belgians, "and with the exception of a little dance in a tent on Sunday (which was very successful) and additional carriages and ponies, our usual life remained unchanged. Albert truly observed, that the first evening, when the gentlemen came out of the dining-room, he had to rub his eyes, as one says, to feel quite sure that he was not dreaming when he saw the Emperor and Empress standing there." * Biographers have to deal with facts, and we must confess that this allusion to a Sunday dance rather spoils the anecdotes on pages 79 and 80.

The Imperial party returned to France on the 10th of August; and nine days later the Queen also crossed again. Her intentions seem to have been kept secret, and the good people of Cherbourg were not a little startled when, on the evening of the 19th, the Royal yacht steamed into the harbour.

Their surprise gave place to a kind of delirious joy when it was ascertained that the Queen and Prince and six of the Royal children were on board. Very little time elapsed before the *Préfet Maritime* and other military officials were on board paying their respects to the Sovereign of Great Britain, and next morning all the fortresses saluted. Then the Admiral arrived in great state; and the Royal party were conducted on shore. The reception was half private, no troops being drawn up, but all the generals and officers of various grades were there. Conspicuous among them was General Borel de Bretizel, a Companion of the Bath, whom the Queen recognised as an old acquaintance, having seen him at her fancy ball in 1845.

* *Life of the Prince Consort*, vol. iv. 17.

Her Majesty tells us that the sight of the vast docks and "basins" in course of erection at Cherbourg made her "very unhappy," for she realised the uses to which they might be turned in the event of a war with France. The works were defended by a triple line of forts and rock-built batteries, and a magnificent breakwater, treble the size of the breakwater at Plymouth. It was a real relief to her to look away from these warlike preparations to the picturesque little town and its humble inhabitants. She describes the former as a foreign-looking place, with narrow, badly-paved streets; and the latter as very friendly and noisy. The women wore dazzling white caps and full woollen petticoats and aprons (generally of a dark blue or violet colour) and gaudy handkerchiefs. After luncheon the Royal party were driven through the town in a regular French *poste*—*i.e.*, a carriage without springs, the horses harnessed with ropes, and driven by one postillion on the wheel horse. By this time the streets were much fuller, and some flags had been hung out. The people were still very friendly, and cried out, "*Vive la Reine d'Angleterre!*" while the post-boys made a terrible noise, cracking and flourishing their whips.

"We drove to Bricquebec," writes the Queen, "twenty-two kilometres from Cherbourg; and by Octeville, a very small village, along a beautiful hilly, richly wooded country, with cornfields, but very small ones, and literally not one village, only detached cottages and farms, some close to the road. Everything most picturesque and primitive—all the women in white caps, often with children in their arms, but many weighed down with the weight of corn which they carried on their backs; many sitting and resting on the door-sill, knitting; children running about, lattices open, showing in some cottages nice pewter-pots and platters, loaves, and here and there a ruddy, healthy *paysanne*, with her snow-white cap, looking at the strangely filled carriages passing before her. The horses and carts most picturesque, with sheepskins over them. The road, quite straight, turning to neither right nor left after leaving Octeville, up and down the long steep hills, so that a sort of drag had to be constantly let down on both sides to keep back the wheel. Intensely hot and dusty, but too delightfully interesting for one to feel tired. We could hardly believe we were really driving in this quiet way in France. Half of the way the country was very like Devonshire. Beautiful beech and elm trees, and everything very green, and thoroughly rustic and unsophisticated. . . . It grew later and later, and it seemed as though we should never reach our destination. At length, at the bottom of a hill, surmounted by the high old tower of the Château, appeared the little town of Bricquebec. Most picturesque, the outskirts with good houses, well-dressed peasant women and fat babies at doors and windows. Then came a narrow street with shops, two old figures of saints in a conspicuous place, and people working and knitting at doors; picturesque groups without end. We stopped at an old narrow gateway, and walked into the yard of the old Château, part of which is now a very humble country inn called *Le Vieux Château;* and close to the gateway rises the very high old château. Got out, had very tired horses to feed, walked about, and finally climbed portion of the castle, and went into the only portion of the interior which remains entire. The château is of the date of the eleventh century, and very curious. The somewhat tipsy mayor of the town conducted us over it; and then, as our horses had to rest, we walked a little about the outskirts, and began to be surrounded by the *gamins, moutards,* and little beggar boys of the village; by the time we returned to the inn the inhabitants of the village came up and surrounded us, chatting away and staring at and rather mobbing us. The horses, to our despair, not yet being rested, we decided to wait in a room upstairs—a small one with two beds—where we sat with the children and ladies, Vicky and I sketching the picturesque women and children standing below, in agony how and when we were to get back. It was near seven before we got into our carriage. . . .

"The drive back was charming, sun setting, air deliciously fresh, and horses getting along very well. Many people coming home or at their supper. At last we stopped to light our lanterns at Montinvart, a third part of the way. Most amusing to see people running out with candles, which they held up trying to get a sight of us. Great crowd at Octeville, when we stopped to adjust harness, and many gathering round and trying to see '*qui est donc la Reine?*' [which is the Queen?] Cherbourg very full, but very dark; streets only lit by a lantern here and there slung across. Drove on to Port, and then pushed with great difficulty into barge, through a loudly-talking crowd; and left General Bouverie with a lantern in his hand on the steps. People cheering."*

So much for the Cherbourg visit of 1857: that of the following year was a far more important affair. It was a visit of State to the Emperor, and the Royal yacht *Victoria and Albert* was escorted across the Channel by no less than eleven ships, of which six were first-class war vessels. The evening was closing in, dull and grey, when this imposing squadron steamed into the harbour, where nine French line-of-battle ships, and numberless small vessels, all tastefully decorated, were waiting to receive them. "As the Royal yacht turned round between the marine forts which mark the western entrance, Admiral Hamelin, in the *Bretagne*, 120, fired a single gun. There was a moment's pause, and then the salute began, not in a close, irregular, and dropping cannonade, which so distinguishes a similar honour from the English navy, but gun after gun, running along each tier like a train of fire, till the very frame of the listener seemed shaken, as if even the air smote him in its reverberation. Hardly had this great cannonade commenced, when all the ugly forts which dominate every part of the harbour, threatening with a thousand ominous, fearful-looking embrasures each ship that passes, took up the same song, only firing their massive guns in volleys of eight at once, and as fast as they could be reloaded and discharged. The ring of fire seemed not only to embrace the town, but to extend far into the country, up among little ravines, where no one ever dreamt that guns lay lurking, at the top of picturesque eminences, where one fancied only villas and rural cottages could exist; around thick clumps of

* *Life of the Prince Consort*, vol. iv. 21.

trees and flanking yellow cornfields came the same dreadful uproar, till it seemed as if all France, even from her hills and mountain tops, were doing honour to the advent of the Queen of England."*

These salutes over, the *Minister de la Marine*, Admiral Hamelin, came on board the Royal yacht with greetings from the Emperor, and about an hour later Napoleon III. himself appeared, accompanied by the Empress. The Imperial party put off from shore in a splendid barge, white, with a green velvet canopy surmounted by a golden eagle, and were received on deck by the Queen. Her Majesty embraced them both, and then spent an hour with them in conversation, after which they returned to shore. Next morning, while Her Majesty was dressing, she was honoured with another tremendous salute, three times repeated, which set all the doors and windows shaking. Among the new arrivals in the harbour was a vessel chartered by Members of the House of Commons, with one hundred of their number on board. More deafening salutes were fired at intervals (as many as three thousand discharges were counted in twenty minutes), and the firing was kept up, from fort to fort, till the Queen landed. She was received on shore by the Emperor and Empress. The former handed her out of the Royal barge, and when she had stepped into the Imperial carriage she was driven to the Préfecture, where the French Court was temporarily located. "Here we talked for a little," notes the Queen, "and then breakfasted, or rather lunched, in one of the small salons with the Emperor and Empress, George [Duke of Cambridge], Ernest [Prince Leiningen], and Bertie—a regular luncheon finishing with coffee. Both were amiable, but the Emperor rather *boutonné* and silent, and not ready to talk."† A kind of reception in miniature followed, and then the Queen drove out and was shown over some of the fortifications.

The great event of the day, however—indeed, of the visit as a whole—was the dinner in the evening, on board the French

---

* *The Times*, 5th August, 1858, quoted in *Life of the Prince Consort*, vol. iv. 46. † *Life of the Prince Consort*, vol. iv. 47.

flag-ship *Bretagne*, when some sixty persons, in addition to the Emperor and Empress and their Royal guests, sat down together at one long table, under the deck awning of the vessel. There was but one thing to mar the joy proper to such an occasion, and that was the fact that some speech-making had to follow. The relations between England and France were rather strained about this time, and both the Queen and Prince Consort knew very well that the two chief speeches of the evening (the Emperor's and the Prince's) would be flashed all over Europe within the next twenty-four hours, and that they would be narrowly examined for latent meanings by a host of friendly and unfriendly diplomatists and journalists. The Queen frankly acknowledges that both she and the Prince were not a little nervous in view of the task which the latter had to face. How the ordeal came off Her Majesty has herself told us, and we cannot but admire the wifely tenderness and solicitude which are so conspicuous in the narrative. "The Emperor unbent," says the Queen, "and talked in his usual frank way to me during dinner. But he was not in good spirits, and seemed sensitive about all that has been said of him in England and elsewhere. At length, dinner over, came the terrible moment of the speeches. The Emperor made an admirable one, in a powerful voice, proposing my health and those of Albert and the Royal Family. Then, after the band had played, came the dreadful moment for my dear husband, which was terrible to me, and which I should never wish to go through again. He did it very well, though he hesitated once. I sat shaking, with my eyes riveted to the table. However, the speech did very well. This over, we got up, and the Emperor, in the cabin, shook Albert by the hand, and we all talked of the terrible emotion we had undergone, the Emperor himself having 'changed colour,' and the Empress having also been very nervous. I shook so I could not drink my cup of coffee."* That evening there was a grand display of fireworks in the harbour, the final rush of bombs and rockets alone costing 25,000 francs. A moment of comparative darkness followed this discharge, and

* *Life of the Prince Consort*, vol. iv. 47.

then, as by the touch of a magician's wand, the yards, masts, and bulwarks of the ships were suddenly illuminated by blue lights, while showers of rockets shot into the air. In the midst of these brilliant coruscations the Queen returned to the Royal yacht, and shortly afterwards the Emperor and Empress returned to shore. A memorable day, even in the Queen's history, had come to a close; and next morning, under more heavy salutes, the Royal squadron steamed out of Cherbourg Harbour, and the Court returned to Osborne.

A week later, the Queen and Prince were in Germany, on a visit to their recently married daughter, the Princess Victoria. They travelled overland from Antwerp, staying a night at Düsseldorf, and proceeding *viâ* Hamm, in Westphalia, and Hanover. At the latter town they were met by the King and Queen of Hanover, with whom they proceeded at once to Herrenhausen, the country palace of the King, a place naturally full of interest for Her Majesty, because of its associations with her family history. But they remained only an hour or two, and then resumed their journey, making brief halts at Wolfenbüttel and Oschersleben. At eight in the evening Magdeburg was reached, when the travellers were welcomed by their son-in-law, Prince Frederick William, who, says the Queen, was "*rayonnant*" (radiant). He gave them the joyful news that the Princess was waiting for them at Wildpark, a few stations off. "It became gradually dark," notes the Queen, "and the time seemed very long as we approached nearer what we had come for. One more stoppage at Brandenburg, and we arrived at the Wildpark station. There on the platform stood our darling child, with a nosegay in her hand. She stepped in, and long and warm was the embrace, as she clasped me in her arms. So much to say, and to tell, and to ask, yet so unaltered, looking well—quite the old Vicky still! It was a happy moment, for which I thank God!"*

In five or six minutes more Potsdam station was reached, and the Royal party alighted, and drove at once to Babelsberg, the residence of Prince Frederick, which was beautifully lit up for

---

* *Life of the Prince Consort*, vol. iv. 49.

the occasion. The next day was passed quietly at the Castle, which, though not large as Royal residences go, is admirable as a piece of architecture. "Everything there," says the Queen, "is very small, a Gothic *bijou*, full of furniture and flowers (creepers), which they arrange very prettily round screens and lamps and pictures. There are many irregular turrets and towers and steps. . . . My sitting-room commands splendid views of the lake, the bridge, Glieniche, etc., and looks on one of the lovely terraces. . . . There are charming walks under trees, and fountains on all the terraces. . . . Vicky came and sat with me. I felt as if she were my own again."* What with sight-seeing in the town, drives into the country, a steamboat excursion on the Hafelsee, a fête on Hafel Island, and other delightful dissipations, a fortnight soon slipped away, and on the 28th of August the visit was brought to a close. The parting was very painful. "Our tears flowed fast," wrote the Queen, "and so did Vicky's, but our last words were '*Auf baldiges Wiedersehn!*' (To a speedy meeting again!)"†

The next meeting was three years later, in September, 1860, and the *rendezvous* was Coburg, the birthplace and early home of the Prince Consort. "I felt so agitated," writes the Queen, "as we approached nearer and nearer, and Albert recognised each spot. At last we caught the first glimpse of the Festung, then of the town, with the cheerful and lovely country round, the fine evening lighting it all up so beautifully." The visit was as quiet and private as possible, owing to recent deaths in the ducal family. The Princess Victoria was among the guests at the Palace, and her meeting with her parents was no less warm than at Wildpark station, three years before. "We remained together for some little time," says Her Majesty, "and then our darling grandchild was brought. Such a little love! He came walking in at Mrs. Hobbs's (his nurse's) hand, in a little white dress with black bows, and was so good. He is a fine, fat child, with a beautiful white soft skin, very fine shoulders and limbs, and a very dear face, like Vicky and Fritz, and also Louise of Baden. He has Fritz's eyes and Vicky's

* *Life of the Prince Consort*, vol. iv. 49. † *Ibid.* vol. iv. 52.

mouth, and very fair curly hair. We felt so happy to see him at last!" It is interesting to remember that the young gentleman here so feelingly described is the present Emperor of Germany. A day or two after the Queen's arrival, the Royal guests attended service in the Schloss-Kirche (the church of the Palace), where a sermon, on the death of the Prince Consort's mother, was preached by Dr. Meyer. "What he said did not move me greatly," observes the Royal diarist, "it was too general, too much a mere eulogy"—a remark which throws an interesting side-light on the Queen's character. During one of her quiet country drives in the Duchy, Her Majesty alighted at a very pretty farm, belonging to the family of Erfa, where the peasants in their picturesque dresses, the carts with oxen, and other peaceful objects, gave her much pleasure. "We met a child carrying a basket full of plums (*Zwetschen*)," writes the Queen, "who refused money for two we took. The trees are laden with them, yet we cannot get them to grow in England. . . . We walked through the wood and little village to Ketschendorf (the Duke of Coburg's family villa). We went all over the dear old house, where everything has remained as in our beloved grandmother's time—all the pictures of the family, and drawings by her grandchildren, including one by me! I think so much of dear Mama when I visit all these lovely places."*

Two days after this pleasant drive and walk the Prince Consort had a very narrow escape. He was driving alone, in an open carriage with four horses, about three miles from the Palace, when the horses took fright, became uncontrollable, and bolted. To avoid concussion with the wooden barrier of a railway crossing, towards which the frightened animals were dashing at full gallop, the Prince leapt out, and was thrown violently to the ground. Fortunately he was not even stunned, and beyond the shock to his system, and a few cuts and bruises, no harm was done. The coachman, however, who had stuck to his box, was seriously hurt, and one of the horses was killed. "Oh God! what did I not feel!" wrote the Queen, when it

* *Life of the Prince Consort*, vol. v. 34.

was all over, and the physician in attendance had assured her that there was no serious injury, and that the features, though badly scratched, would not suffer; "I could only, and do only, allow the feelings of gratitude, not those of horror at what might have happened, to fill my mind." A few days later she gave practical expression to these sentiments in a touching letter to Sir Charles Phipps, the administrator of her Privy Purse, in the course of which she said: "The Queen feels so deeply impressed with gratitude to her Heavenly Father in having guided her beloved husband to do what was the only right thing, and in having watched over and protected him at this hour of peril, that she cannot rest without doing something to mark permanently her feelings. In times of old a church or a monument would probably have been erected on the spot. What the Queen wishes to do is to be able to benefit her fellow-creatures, and her desire would be to found, or add to some charity at Coburg (her dear husband's home), by adding a wing either to some school or hospital (of both of which they are much in want), which might bear the Queen's name. £1000, or even £2000, given either at once, or in instalments yearly, would not, in the Queen's opinion, be too much. She will not rest satisfied till she has done this. She has been thinking of it continually, day and night."* This noble desire was realised by "the establishment in the Duchy of the trust known as the 'Victoria Stift' (Victoria Foundation). A sum of 12,000 florins (about £1000) was invested in the names of the burgomaster and chief clergyman of Coburg, the interest from which was devoted to the apprenticing to industrial occupations of deserving young men and women in the humbler walks of life, and to the purchase of tools, etc., in furtherance of that beneficial object.

When their stay in Coburg began to draw to a close, the Queen and Prince Albert paid a farewell visit to Rosenau, the house in which the Prince was born, and Her Majesty made a successful sketch of the place. "A nice old woman, in her Sunday dress, coming past, we stopped her," says the Queen,

* *Life of the Prince Consort*, vol. v. 37.

"and she stood with her basket on her back while I made a sketch of her. When finished I showed it to her, and she was delighted; she called her grandson to look at it, and then shook hands with me. They are so good, so simple, so unaffected, these people. . . . A funny, rather tipsy old man, in Sunday dress, with silver buttons in his plush waistcoat, came up to the carriage, and was not pleased at being sent off. ' *Sie thun mir Nichts, ich thue Ihnen Nichts*' (You don't meddle with me, I don't meddle with you) was his observation when the footman sent him away."*

The last day arrived, and at ten in the morning, says the Royal *Journal*, " with heavy hearts we left dearest Coburg, where we had been very, very happy. . . . We looked at it from the train as long as we could, till the last glimpse was gone. We returned by precisely the same way as we had come, but I felt no pleasure in gazing at the pretty scenery, my heart being so sad. That fortnight, with its joys and sorrows, and its fearful episode of my dearest Albert's accident, will be for ever deeply engraven on my heart."†

Well, indeed, for us that the future is hidden from our eyes! What would Her Majesty have felt, could she have known that before the next year had run its course, her idolised husband would be taken from her indeed?

* *Life of the Prince Consort*, vol. v. 36. † *Ibid.* vol. v. 36.

CHAPTER XI.

THE YEAR OF THE GREAT SORROW.
(1861.)

IN the present chapter we propose to consider the events of a single year—the year 1861. The death of the Duchess of Kent in the spring of the year, and of the Prince Consort at the close, mark it off with painful distinctness from the rest of the Queen's life.

In the November of the previous year the oldest of the Queen's unmarried daughters (Princess Alice) had become engaged to Prince Louis of Hesse, nephew of the then reigning Grand Duke. How much was to happen before the Royal lovers could consummate their happiness by marriage! The circumstances of the betrothal, which happened when the Court was at Windsor, are interestingly told in the Queen's *Diary*. "After dinner, whilst talking to the gentlemen, I perceived Alice and Louis talking before the fire-place more earnestly than usual, and when I passed to go to the other room, both came up to me, and Alice in much agitation said he had proposed to her, and he begged for my blessing. I could only squeeze his hand and say, 'Certainly,' and that we would see him in our room later. Got through the evening working as well as we could. Alice came to our room . . . agitated but quiet. Albert sent for Louis to his room; he went first to him, and then called Alice and me in. . . . Louis has a warm, noble heart. We embraced our dear Alice, and praised her much to him. He pressed and kissed my hand, and I embraced him. After talking a little, we parted; a most touching, and to me most sacred, moment."*

It was about this time that the health of the Duchess of Kent began to break up, and the Princess, during the first happy weeks of her engagement, spent the greater part of her evenings with her grandmother at Frogmore. The Duchess's health would no longer allow of her dining at Windsor Castle, so her granddaughter read or played to her, and thus beguiled the tedium of her enforced imprisonment. Unconsciously, the Princess was training for a more difficult task, and one that would call forth all the fortitude and tenderness of her beautiful character.

In March of the following year the Duchess died. The Queen, who loved her so deeply, and with so much cause, was with her the whole of the night before she died, lying most of the time on a sofa at the foot of the bed, but never closing her eyes in sleep. Familiar night-sounds—the crowing of a cock, or dogs barking at a distance—fell upon her ears from time to time, and at every quarter the repeater watch in tortoiseshell case, which had belonged to her father, and which she had not heard for twenty-three years, would strike with memory-awakening sound. The breathing from the sick-bed grew heavier and heavier as those quarters struck; and the Queen marked the changes, and knew—alas! too well—what the laboured breathing meant. The life which had given her life was fast ebbing away; the mother, who had watched over her so devotedly through all the happy days of her infancy and girlhood, was about to yield up her spirit—to pass away into the Silent Land. About eight in the morning the Prince Consort took the Queen from the room for a short time; "but," says Her Majesty, "I could not remain. When I returned, the window was wide open and both doors. I sat on a footstool, holding her dear hand. . . . Meanwhile the dear face grew paler, . . . the features longer, sharper. The breathing became easier; I fell on my knees, holding the beloved hand, which

* *Princess Alice*, 16, 17.

was still warm and soft, though heavier, in mine. I felt the end was fast approaching, as Clark went out to call Albert and Alice—I, only, left gazing on that beloved face, and feeling as if my heart would break. . . . It was a solemn, sacred, never-to-be-forgotten scene. Fainter and fainter grew the breathing. At last it ceased; but there was no change of countenance, nothing; the eyes closed, as they had been for the last half-hour. . . . The clock struck half-past nine at the very moment. Convulsed with sobs, I fell upon the hand, and covered it with kisses. Albert lifted me up, and took me into the next room, himself entirely melted into tears, which is unusual for him, deep as his feelings are, and clasped me in his arms. I asked if all was over: he said, 'Yes!'"* Yes—all was over. Death had done its work in that Palace chamber. The tender intercourse of forty years had been broken, and Mother and Daughter would know each other no more until the resurrection morning.

The funeral, by the Duchess's express desire, was a very quiet one, and as soon after it as possible the Prince Consort got the Queen away to Osborne. Writing to Stockmar soon after their arrival at their seaside home, he said: "Our leave-taking of Windsor and Frogmore was a very painful one; still, the Queen's mind will find more rest here. She is greatly upset, and feels her whole childhood rush back once more upon her memory with the most vivid force; and with those recollections comes back the thought of many a sad hour. . . . By business I am well-nigh overwhelmed, as I do my utmost to save Victoria all trouble, while at the same time I am Mama's sole executor."†

It would be impossible to speak in terms too high of the Prince Consort's devotion to Her Majesty during this time of sorrow. To say that he did his utmost to save her "all trouble" is, of course, a fact, but the statement does not express half enough. The Prince had not only the complicated affairs of the late Duchess to engross him, but the retirement of the Queen during the period of Court mourning threw upon him

* *Life of the Prince Consort*, vol. v. 54. † *Ibid.* 57.

the discharge of many heavy duties, which were rendered more heavy by the temporary absence of the Keeper of the Privy Purse, Sir Charles Phipps, whose wife had had a nervous seizure the day after the Duchess's death. In addition to all this there were his own proper duties to engage him, such as attending at levees, laying foundation stones, opening new public buildings, and last, though by no means least, preparing for a new Exhibition—the International of 1862. In spite of this enormous pressure of work, however, his home affections remained unblunted; and he was ever able to find room in his thoughts—not for his wife only, but—for all his children, whether they were under his immediate eye at home, or away in foreign and it might be distant countries. "We have good news of Alfred from Montserrat, St. Christopher, and Nevis," he writes in one letter; "the Prince of Wales is back at Madingley, and is now pursuing his studies in constitutional law at Cambridge. Yesterday [the 14th of April] we celebrated little Beatrice's fourth birthday. The old woman in the children's Swiss Cottage celebrated her eighty-fourth, which greatly interested the little one."* The Queen's birthday was very quietly kept that year, but, of course, it was not overlooked. The Prince's gifts were a sculptured group by Engel, a picture of the *König See* (a lake in Upper Bavaria), and a number of little things—all unspeakably precious to Her Majesty now, as being the last of such presents which he ever gave her.

More domestic trouble came with the illness of Prince Leopold, the Queen's youngest son, who caught the measles from Prince Louis of Hesse, at that time on a visit to Osborne. He got over it eventually, but his recovery was slow, and when the Court left the Isle of Wight for London he was still too ill to be moved. On the 5th of June the Royal Horticultural Gardens were opened to the public by the Prince Consort. It was the last public ceremonial in London in which he took part, and many persons who were present on the occasion remarked the pallid and somewhat worn looks of the Prince. The same evening he presided at a meeting of the Society of

* *Life of the Prince Consort*, vol. v. 58.

THE YEAR OF THE GREAT SORROW. 233

Arts, and spoke hopefully of the prospects of the forthcoming Exhibition. Towards the end of the month there were Royal visitors at Buckingham Palace—first, King Leopold, and then the Queen's son-in-law and daughter, the Crown Prince and Princess of Prussia, with their children. They brought sunshine with them, though the Queen's grief for the loss of her mother was still fresh. Writing to the King of the Belgians, she said, "This happy family meeting with our children and grandchildren, while our dear Alice's bridegroom is still here, makes one long and pine for *her*, who would have been so happy and so proud."*

On the 4th of July the Court returned to Osborne, and remained there till the 19th of August, when the Queen and Prince Consort set out on their third visit to Ireland. Writing to Baron Stockmar during the interval, the Prince says: "The Prince of Wales is serving in the camp at the Curragh of Kildare; perhaps he may be present at the reviews and manœuvres on the Rhine in autumn. . . . Alfred comes for four weeks in the middle of next month on leave from America; Leopold has been much better of late, but is to pass the winter in Nice or Cannes. We are perplexed about the formation of the requisite suite for him. . . . We have had no lack of visitors here; first, Augustus and Clementine, then the Montpensiers, and we are now expecting Max and Charlotte of Austria, the Princess Charles of Hesse (Louis's mother), Fritz of Baden, and, last of all, the King of Sweden. Fritz and Vicky leave us on the 14th of August. We ourselves go on the 19th to Ireland, and thence on to Balmoral. I have been far from well of late." The expected visitors came and went; and then, on the 16th of August, Her Majesty and Prince Consort, together with the Princess Alice, set out for Frogmore, where the mausoleum had been prepared to receive the body of the late Duchess. The 17th was the anniversary of her birthday. The coffin had been placed in a splendid granite sarcophagus; and on and before this the Royal mourners placed the wreaths which they had brought. "Our excursion to Frogmore was

* *Life of the Prince Consort*, vol. v. 63.

sad," the Prince afterwards wrote, "but it did us good. The mausoleum has become very beautiful, and just what it should be, appropriate, pleasing, solemn—not doleful or repellent."*

Of the trip to Ireland we need not say a great deal. The first week was spent at the Viceregal Lodge, with the exception of one day at Curragh, where the Prince of Wales was fulfilling his army duties in camp. At this place there was a review of the troops—or, rather, some manœuvres which the Royal party watched from a distance, and which went off very well. When it was over the Queen and Prince Consort, with their whole party, took lunch in the Prince of Wales's "hut," a rather comfortable kind of hut, by the way, for it contained a "nice little bedroom, sitting-room, drawing-room, and a good-sized dining-room." Some of the officers were also invited to join the party—among the rest Colonel Percy, under whom His Royal Highness had been specially placed. "I spoke to him," says the Queen, "and thanked him for treating Bertie as he did, just like any other officer, for I know he keeps him up to his work in a way, as, General Bruce told us, no one else has done; and yet Bertie likes him very much."†

Next day was the Prince Consort's birthday. "Alas! there is so much so different this year," wrote the Queen; "nothing festive, and we on a journey and separated from many of our children, and my spirits bad. But I wished him joy, warmly, tenderly. Beloved Mama! how she loved and admired him!"‡ Among Her Majesty's presents to the Prince were a picture by Portaels and a pair of Lancaster breech-loading rifles; the Princess Royal and Princess Alice gave him some drawings executed by themselves. At dinner that evening—an oppressive, sultry evening, with not a breath of air stirring—he sat next to the Queen, and his health was drunk at dessert. It was his last birthday on earth.

From Dublin the Royal party went on to the Lakes of Killarney, to see which was one of the chief objects of their visit to Ireland. Fortunately, the weather was favourable most of the time. There is a simple, unpretentious account of the

* *Life of the Prince Consort*, vol. v. 64. † *Ibid.* 65. ‡ *Ibid.*

visit in the Royal *Journal*, from which we again take leave to
quote. " We rowed first round Innisfallen Island and some way
up the Lower Lake. The view was magnificent. We had a
slight shower, which alarmed us all, from the mist which over-
hung the mountains; but it suddenly cleared away and became
very hot and fine. At a quarter to one we landed at the foot of
the beautiful hill of Glena, where on a small sloping lawn there
is a very pretty little cottage. We walked about, though it was
overpoweringly hot, to see some of the splendid views. The
trees are beautiful—oak, birch, arbutus, holly, yew—all growing
down to the water's edge, intermixed with heather. The hills,
rising abruptly from the lake, are completely wooded, which
gives them a different character from those in Scotland, though
they often reminded me of the dear Highlands. . . . We
lunched, and afterwards re-embarked, and then took that most
beautiful row up the rapid, under the Old Weir Bridge, through
the channel which connects the two lakes, and which is very
intricate and narrow. Close to our right as we were going, we
stopped under the splendid hill of the Eagle's Nest to hear the
echo of a bugle, the sound of which, though blown near by, was
not heard. We had to get out near the Weir Bridge to let the
empty boats be pulled up by the men. The sun had come out and
lit up the really magnificent scenery splendidly; but it was most
oppressively hot. We wound along till we entered the Upper
Lake, which opened upon us with all its high hills—the highest,
The Reeks, 3400 feet—and its islands and points covered with
splendid trees—such arbutus (quite large trees) with yews,
making a beautiful background. We turned into a small bay
or creek, where we got out and walked a short way in the shade,
and up to where a tent was placed, just opposite a waterfall
called Derryconochy, a lovely spot, but terribly infested by
midges. In this tent was tea, ice, cakes, and everything most
tastefully arranged. We just took some tea, which was very
refreshing in the great heat of this relaxing climate. The vegetation is quite that of a jungle—ferns of all kinds and shrubs
and trees—all springing up luxuriantly."* Next morning, the

* *Leaves*, 310-312.

Royal party went for a delightful drive, through the village and round the Tore Mountain, as far as the celebrated Tore Waterfall; and in the afternoon there was a long row on the Muckross Lake. "At Mr. and Mrs. Herbert's request," writes the Queen, "I christened one of the points which runs into the lake with a bottle of wine, Albert holding my arm when we came close by, so that it was most successfully smashed."* The evening closed in clear and beautiful; "and the effect of the numbers of boats full of people, many with little flags, rowing about in every direction and cheering and shouting, lit up by the evening light, was charming. At Darby's Garden the shore was densely crowded, and many of the women in their blue cloaks waded into the river, holding their clothes up to their knees." † The following day the Royal party returned to Dublin, where they made no halt, but passed on to Kingstown, and at once embarked on the *Victoria and Albert.*

Weighing anchor at four next morning they reached Holyhead by nine, where there was a stay of twelve hours, to enable the Prince to pay a flying visit to Carnarvon and Beddgellert. He was accompanied by Prince Alfred, Lord Granville, and Sir Charles Phipps, but the Queen remained on board the yacht. Leaving Holyhead at nine the same evening, and travelling all night, they reached Balmoral the following afternoon—delighted, we need scarcely add, to be once again in their dear Highland home.

The holiday in Scotland this year was a memorable one, not merely because it was the last which the Queen and Prince were destined to spend together, but also because of *the way it was spent.* During the seven weeks of their stay, they not only went for numberless walks, rides, and drives in the neighbourhood of the Castle, but no less than three "great expeditions," as the Queen terms them, were undertaken, besides a shorter one to Loch Avon.

The first of these expeditions was to Invermark and Fettercairn, and occupied two days. The Royal party put up at a small inn at Fettercairn, the "Ramsay Arms," where the

* *Leaves,* 314. † *Ibid.* 315.

accommodation, though clean, was anything but regal. "We dined at eight," writes the Queen, "a very nice, clean, good dinner. Grant and Brown waited. They were rather nervous, but General Grey and Lady Churchill carved, and they had only to change the plates, which Brown soon got into the way of doing. A little girl of the house came in to help—but Grant turned her round to prevent her looking at us! The landlord and landlady knew who we were, but no one else except the coachman, and they kept the secret admirably." A commercial traveller arrived at the inn the same night, and wanted to go into the dining-room, which was the commercials' recognised sanctum, and there was not a little difficulty in impressing upon him that he *must not* enter. He joined Grant and Brown at their tea, and demanded somewhat resentfully: "What's the matter here." Whereupon Grant replied: "It's a wedding party from Aberdeen," which indeed was no great exaggeration of the truth.* "The evening being bright and moonlight and very still," observes the Queen, "we all went out, and walked through the whole village, where not a creature moved; through the principal little square, in the middle of which was a sort of pillar or Town Cross on steps, and Louis (Prince Louis of Hesse) read, by the light of the moon, a proclamation for collections of charities which was stuck on it. We walked on along a lane a short way, hearing nothing whatever—not a leaf moving—but the distant barking of a dog. Suddenly we heard a drum and fife! We were greatly alarmed, fearing we had been recognised; but Louis and General Grey, who went back, saw nothing whatever. Still, as we walked slowly back, we heard the noise from time to time, and when we reached the inn-door we stopped, and saw six men march up with fifes and a drum (not a creature taking any notice of them), go down the street, and back again. Grant and Brown were out; but had no idea what it could be. Albert asked the little maid, and the answer was, 'It's just a band,' and that it walked about in this way twice a-week. How odd! It went on playing some time after we got home. We sat till half-

* Prince Louis of Hesse and the Princess Alice were of the party.

past ten working, and Albert reading, and then retired to rest."*

Among the many beautiful spots visited on the following day was Glen Tavar, part of Lord Huntly's forest, a richly-wooded and very lovely glen, between high hills. "Here a wretched idiot girl was by herself," writes the Queen, "as tall as Lady Churchill; but a good deal bent, and dressed like a child, with a pinafore and short-cut hair. She sat on the ground with her hands round her knees, rocking herself to and fro and laughing; she then got up and walked towards us. General Grey put himself before me, and she went up to him, and began taking hold of his coat, and putting her hands into his pockets. . . . An old man walked up hastily soon after, and on Lady Churchill asking him if he knew the poor girl, he said: 'Yes, she belongs to me, she has a weakness in her mind;' and led her off hurriedly."† Coming down a peat road to the Bridge of Muick, the Prince dropped behind with Grant, in order to look at the Choils which he intended as a deer-forest for the Prince of Wales, and to give directions as to the planting in Glen Muick. While so engaged he said to his servant: "You and I may be dead and gone before that;" a remark which was painfully verified as regards himself.‡ At the bridge, "we found," writes Her Majesty, "my dearest Mother's sociable, a fine large one, which she has left to Albert, waiting to take us back. It made me very sad, and filled my eyes with tears. Oh, in the midst of cheerfulness, I feel so sad! But being out a great deal here, and seeing new and fine scenery, does me good."§ The excursion was now practically at an end, and at seven o'clock that evening Balmoral was reached. During the two days, they had travelled in all eighty-two miles.

The second great expedition that year was to Glen Fishie and Blair-Athol, the Royal party spending a night at the inn of Dalwhinnie. Unfortunately, there was hardly anything to eat or drink—"only tea, and two miserable starved Highland chickens, without any potatoes! No pudding, and no *fun*." The five servants whom the Queen brought with her had to

* *Leaves*, 209, 211. † *Ibid.* 214, 215. ‡ *Ibid.* 215. § *Ibid.* 216.

subsist on the remnants of the two starved chickens! At Kingussie the people were very inquisitive, hovering about the carriages, and chattering as though they half-guessed the secret, and the curiosity of one old gentleman, with a high wide-awake hat, made a particular impression on the Queen. But all this only added to the pleasure of the expedition, and no one was more ready than Her Majesty to enter into and enjoy the fun.

The last expedition from Balmoral was on the 16th of October, and will ever have an unspeakably sad interest for the Queen. Little did she think on that happy day how soon she was to lose the beloved partner of her life! They went by an entirely new route, past Lochs Callater and Cauter to Ca-Ness, returning by Garb Chory, the Glas Meall, and Shean Spittal. The Queen got one of her gillies, Duncan, to make a list of the places visited, which she has inserted in her *Leaves*. "This," she writes, "gave one a very good idea of the geography of the country, which delighted dear Albert, as this expedition was quite in a different direction from any that we had ever made before. But my head is so very ungeographical, that I cannot describe it. We came down by the Mouth Eigie, a steep hill covered with grass—down part of which I rode, walking where it was steepest; but it was so wet and slippery that I had two falls. . . . We went back on our side of the river; and if we had been a little earlier Albert might have got a stag—but it was too late. The moon rose and shone most beautifully, and we returned at twenty minutes to seven o'clock, much pleased and interested with this delightful expedition. Alas! I fear our *last* great one!" How prophetic was the fear!

In a little more than a week the Court was back again at Windsor, and for some days the Prince appeared to be in fair health, and applied himself with his accustomed energy to the work he had to do. His solicitude was for his wife and children, whom to see well and happy was his constant wish and prayer. "I must announce to you our safe return to old Windsor," he wrote to Stockmar on the 28th of October, "where we are once more settled. The first day the Queen's wounds were opened afresh, and she suffered greatly, as it is the first time she has lived here without finding Mama at Frogmore. The void struck home to the heart; but now habit, with its healing power, grows daily stronger."* Then there was their delicate child, Prince Leopold, to engage his thoughts, and on the 4th of November the young Prince was sent off to Cannes under the care of Sir Edward and Lady Bowater. In London, too, Prince Albert's presence was frequently required, for alterations were in progress in the Chapel of Buckingham Palace, and the building for the 1862 Exhibition was in a forward state. Marlborough House, also, was being got ready for the Prince of Wales, who was now nearly at an age to undertake the responsibilities of an establishment of his own. On the ninth was His Royal Highness's twentieth birthday, and a number of distinguished guests were at the Castle to celebrate the occasion. "I pray God," wrote his Royal Mother, "to assist our efforts to make him turn out well. . . . The bells rang in the afternoon, and I felt so sad! I missed beloved Mama so much! Last year she was still here. . . . It was the first birthday fête spent here without her, and the difference was most painfully felt. All our people, in and out of the house, came to dinner. Bertie led me in, by Albert's wish, and I sat between him and Albert. The band played for the first time since our sad loss." † Then, about a fortnight later, came the birthday of the Princess Royal, to whom the Prince Consort sent a loving and paternal letter, full of practical wisdom. At the close of the letter he referred to the recent deaths by typhoid fever of the King of Portugal and his brother Ferdinand, and admonished the Princess to be careful of her own health. "Without the basis of health it is impossible to rear anything stable. The frightful event in Portugal stands in strong outline before our eyes. Therefore, see that you spare yourself now, so that at some future time you may be able to do more." ‡ The advice which he gave to others his own noble self-forgetfulness made him neglect for himself. Already

* *Life of the Prince Consort*, vol. v. 69.   † *Ibid.* 70.   ‡ *Ibid.* 70.

he had begun to suffer from insomnia, the result of overwork, and on the 23rd of November the Queen notes in her *Diary* that this sleeplessness makes him "weak and tired." That same day he went out shooting with the Queen's nephew, Prince Ernest Leiningen, but it was for the last time. Next day he wrote in his own *Diary:* "Am full of rheumatic pains, and feel thoroughly unwell. Have scarcely closed my eyes at night for the last fortnight." As days went on these unfavourable symptoms increased, and Her Majesty became really anxious. On the 1st of December, Sunday, he rose at his usual early hour, and walked for half-an-hour on the Lower Garden terrace. Then he accompanied the Queen to chapel, but looking wretchedly ill. He was advised by Dr. Jenner to sit during the service, but would not do so, and knelt and stood with the rest. Next day he was unable to take his place at dinner as usual, nor could he be prevailed upon to eat anything in his own room. Her Majesty was now thoroughly alarmed, and, by the suggestion of Lord Palmerston, a second physician was called in. This was Sir James Clark. Sir James spoke reassuringly; said there was no cause for alarm; and the anxious Wife took heart again. But still the patient's appetite did not return, and his nights were as restless as ever. "He would take nothing," writes the Queen, "hardly any broth, no rusk or bread—nothing. My anxiety is great when he, to whom I confide all, is in such a listless state, and hardly smiles! Sir James arrived, and was grieved to see no more improvement, but not discouraged. Albert rested in the bedroom, and liked being read to, but no book suited him, neither *Silas Marner* nor *The Warden*."*

On the 4th of December, Dr. Jenner sat up all night with the patient, and next day the Prince seemed to be really better. This apparent improvement continued throughout the day, and the Queen wrote in her *Journal* with thankful, almost joyous heart: "I found my Albert most dear and affectionate, and quite himself, when I went in with little Beatrice, whom he kissed. He quite laughed at some of her new French verses, which

* *Life of the Prince Consort*, vol. v. 75.

I made her repeat—then he held her little hand in his for some time, and she stood looking at him." Next day there was a relapse. When the Queen entered his sitting-room he was looking weak and exhausted, and complained that he was no better. Her Majesty told him that his illness was due to worry and overwork, and he answered: "It is too much. You must speak to the Ministers." "Then," writes the Queen, "he said that, when he lay awake there, he heard the little birds, and thought of those he had heard at Rosenau in his childhood. I felt quite upset. When the doctors came in, I saw that they thought him less well, and more feverish, and I went to my room, and felt as if my heart would break."*

All doubt as to the nature of the illness was now at an end. Unmistakable signs of gastric or low fever had shown themselves; and it became the doctors' painful duty to break the intelligence to Her Majesty. "The fever must have its course," they said, "namely, a month, dated from the beginning," which in their opinion was the 22nd of November, on which day the Prince had inspected the new Military College at Sandhurst, in wretched weather. "My heart was ready to burst," wrote the poor Wife, "but I cheered up, remembering how many people have fever," and then she touchingly adds, "Good Alice was very courageous, and tried to comfort me." Of the devotion and fortitude of the Princess throughout her father's illness, it is indeed impossible to speak too highly. A member of the Queen's Household, who had every opportunity of observing her, records that "she saw from the first that both her father's and mother's firmness depended on her firmness, and she set herself to the duty. He loved to speak openly of his condition, and had many wishes to express. He loved to hear hymns and prayers. He could not speak to the Queen of himself, for she could not bear to listen, and shut her eyes to the danger. His daughter saw that she must act differently, and she never let her voice falter, or shed a single tear in his presence. She sat by him, listened to all he said, repeated hymns, and then, when she could bear it no longer, would walk

* *Life of the Prince Consort*, vol. v. 75.

calmly to the door, and rush away to her room, returning with the same calm and pale face, without any appearance of the agitation she had gone through." *

More than once after that, however, there was a return of favourable signs, and on the 8th of December the Prince, at his own desire, was moved into one of the larger rooms of the Palace. His bed was drawn up close to the window, that he might look out upon the beautiful prospect and see the white clouds sailing past. It was Sunday, and the morning was mild and bright for the time of the year. "When I returned from breakfast," notes the Queen, "I found him lying on the bed in the Blue Room, and much pleased. The sun was shining brightly, the room was fine, large, and cheerful, and he said, 'It is so fine!' For the first time since his illness he asked for some music, and said, 'I should like to hear a fine chorale played at a distance.' We had a piano brought into the next room, and Alice played '*Ein' feste Burg ist unser Gott*' ['*A strong tower is our God*'], and another; and he listened, looking upward with such a sweet expression, and with tears in his eyes." † "After she had played some time," writes the Court lady, from whom we have before quoted, "she looked round and saw him lying back, his hands folded as if in prayer, and his eyes shut. He lay so long without moving that she thought he had fallen asleep. Presently he looked up, and smiled. She said, 'Were you asleep, dear papa?' 'Oh, no,' he answered, 'only I have such sweet thoughts.'" ‡ That morning Canon Kingsley preached at the Castle, "but," says Her Majesty pathetically, "I heard nothing." This was the Prince's last Sunday on earth.

His condition had now become so serious that it was thought well the public should know of it; and the papers next morning contained references to the illness, "which," said they, "is likely to continue for some time." Other physicians were now called in, for the Prince had been delirious once or twice, and the Queen's fears had naturally increased. Sir Henry Holland and Dr. Watson were the two selected, and the Prince himself

* *Life of Queen Victoria*, 131.   † *Ibid.* 76.   ‡ *Ibid.* 131.

was well satisfied with the choice, declaring that Dr. Watson was "quite the right man." "He (the Prince) was so kind," wrote the Queen on that day, "calling me '*gutes Weifchen*' ('good little wife'), and liking me to hold his dear hand. Oh, it is an anxious, anxious time, but God will help us through it. . . . The doctors were satisfied."*

On the 12th of December there was another relapse, and next morning the Prince's breathing had become quicker and more difficult. The symptom was serious, and Dr. Jenner felt that he must now prepare the Queen for the worst. There could be little doubt that the end was approaching.

Nevertheless, the Prince appeared once more to rally. He might yet throw off the fever. Mr. Brown, a medical practitioner of Windsor, who knew the Prince's constitution, even declared that "there was ground to hope that the crisis was over." This favourable opinion was expressed at about six o'clock in the morning, on Saturday, the 14th of December, and an hour later, Her Majesty went to the Prince's room, according to her usual wont, to sit and talk with him. "It was a bright morning," she records, "the sun just rising and shining brightly. The room had the sad look of night-watching, the candles burnt down to their sockets, the doctors looking anxious. I went in, and never can I forget how beautiful my darling looked, lying there with his face lit up by the rising sun, his eyes unusually bright, gazing, as it were, on unseen objects, and not taking notice of me."

Meanwhile, the Prince of Wales, summoned by telegram, had arrived at the Castle, and Sir Henry Holland acquainted him with his father's critical condition. Later in the day, the Queen inquired of the physicians whether she might go out for a breath of air, and received the ominous answer, "Yes, just close by, for a quarter-of-an-hour;" so she went out on the Castle terrace with the Princess Alice. The military band was playing at a distance, and the sound was too much for Her Majesty's over-wrought nerves. She burst into tears, and came home again. Immediately on entering, she inquired, tremu-

* *Life of the Prince Consort*, vol. v. 76.

lously, of Dr. Watson, if the Prince were better. "We are very much frightened," was the reply, "but we don't, and won't, give up hope." "Every hour, every minute was a gain," writes the anguished wife, "and Sir James Clark was very hopeful—he had seen much worse cases. But the breathing was the alarming thing, it was so rapid. There was what they call a dusky hue about his face and hands, which I knew was not good. I made some observation about it to Dr. Jenner, and was alarmed by seeing he seemed to notice it. Albert folded his arms, and began arranging his hair, just as he used to do when well, and he was dressing. These were said to be bad signs. Strange! as though he were preparing for another and greater journey." *

The distress of Her Majesty at this time was painful to witness. She remained at the bedside, save only when compelled to go to an adjoining room to give way to the grief that overmastered her. Towards evening, as she was sitting beside his bed, the Prince said to her, "*Gutes Frauchen*" ("good little wife"), and kissed her; and then he gave a sort of weary sigh, as though he felt that he were leaving her, and pillowed his head upon her shoulder. His children now came in one after another and kissed his hand, but he was dozing and did not recognise them. A little later he asked for Sir Charles Phipps, who came in and also kissed his hand; and then General Grey and Sir Thomas Biddulph did the same. The strong men broke down under their emotion; but the Queen, with that extraordinary self-command which women often show when a crisis moment actually arrives, now controlled her feelings, and to all outward appearances was perfectly calm.

Once again that evening Her Majesty retired to the adjoining room; but it was only for a few moments. Hearing the Prince's breathing becoming worse, she hastened back to the sick chamber. He was in a violent perspiration, which the doctors were inclined to look upon as a favourable sign. They were mistaken. Going close up to his pillow, the Queen stooped down and whispered in the Prince's ear, "*Es ist*

* *Life of the Prince Consort*, vol. v. 77.

kleines Frauchen!" ("'Tis your dear little wife"); and he kissed her.

Only once after that did she leave him for a few moments. Night had come on, darkness brooded over the Castle, and the hour of ten had been told out by the Castle clock, when she was recalled to the sick bed for the last time. Too well she knew what the summons meant. The moment to part was at hand—the Prince was dying. Had she failed to realise the fact when the message to return was conveyed to her, she could not fail to realise it as she entered the room. Her children, her nephew, the physicians, the Dean of Windsor—all, in short, who were there present, were kneeling around the bed. Then the Queen knelt, too, and took in her own the Prince's left hand, which was already cold. He was breathing gently now, and as the solemn moments passed, and the hour hand of the Castle clock moved nearer to the third quarter, the breathing grew fainter and fainter. As the quarter chimed, a beautiful serenity settled upon his face, he drew two or three long but gentle breaths, his heart's feeble beating ceased, and in that hushed and awful moment, the weary spirit quitted its earthly prison-house, and went forth upon its homeward way. . . . The Prince was dead.

* * * * *

Yes, the Prince was dead. He who had been the Queen's constant companion for nearly a quarter of a century, who had loved and cherished her with a singleness of devotion such as few princes have ever shown, who had been her guide and counsellor in all times of difficulty, and her stay and comfort in sorrow and in weakness—had been called away in the midst of his labours and usefulness, and had entered a purer world than ours. All was now light and happiness for him.

> "Envy and calumny and hate and pain
> And that unrest which men miscall delight,
> Could touch him not, and torture not again."

But the Queen! Ah! she must wait. Her time was not yet. Twenty-two years of blissful wedded life had run their

PHOTOGRAPHED FROM THE STATUE IN WINDSOR CASTLE.

Inscription:
"HE POINTS TO HEAVEN AND LEADS THE WAY."

course, and now she had a new, a strange future to face. Her Majesty was a widow! a widowed Queen! "There is no one to call me Victoria now!" was her desolate cry in the first days of her sorrow; and what an awful *loneliness* of grief those words express! There was need that a poet should address to her the inspiring lines :—

> "Break not, O woman's heart, but still endure;
> Break not, for thou art Royal, but endure,
> Remembering all the beauty of that star
> Which shone so close beside thee that ye made
> One light together, but has passed and leaves
> The crown a lonely splendour.
>   May all love,
> His love unseen but felt, o'ershadow thee,
> The love of all thy sons encompass thee,
> The love of all thy daughters cherish thee,
> The love of all thy people comfort thee,
> Till God's love set thee at his side again!"

It only remains to be said that the funeral took place on the morning of Monday, the 23rd of December, 1861, when the Prince's remains were temporarily deposited in the Royal vault of St. George's Chapel. The Prince of Wales was the chief mourner, and during the earlier part of the service, he was observed to speak a few soothing words to his little brother, Prince Arthur, who at first was inconsolable. At a later moment, when the precious dust had been committed to the grave, and the mourners came forward to take a last look at the coffin, the elder brother's own fortitude forsook him. He stood for a moment with his hands clasped, looking down into the vault, and then, hiding his face, burst into tears.

The Queen, of course, was not present; but she sent a bouquet of violets with a white camellia in the centre, which was placed, with other bouquets from Osborne, on the coffin. The day was a day of mourning throughout the country; business was suspended, shops and public buildings were draped in black, and everywhere the sympathy expressed for the widowed Queen was genuine and deep. Her Majesty had lost an ideal husband and the country one of its ablest, kindliest, and most single-minded men. His life had been a life of great and varied usefulness, and it is no exaggeration to say that his death was a national misfortune.

It is now thirty-five years since he went from us, but he is not forgotten. His deeds have lived after him, and *will* live; and the poet was speaking well within the truth, who described him as a man—

> " Dear to Science, dear to Art,
> Dear to his land and ours, a Prince indeed,
> Beyond all titles, and a household name,
> Hereafter, thro' all times, Albert the Good."

CHAPTER XII.

SHADE AND SHINE TO THE JUBILEE.
(1861-1887.)

THE sad, sad Christmas season passed away, the spring came and passed away, too, and then, in the early summer, the sorrowing Queen revisited Balmoral. It was the first time she had seen the spot since the Prince's death, nor had she previously visited her Highland home at this season of the year. The graceful birch-trees were in tender leaf, the yellow blossoms had not yet fallen from the broom, and the pink bells of the heather were beginning to open. How *he* would have admired it all!

One of Her Majesty's first acts on reaching the Castle was to visit a poor woman on the estate, who, like herself, had been widowed during the past few months. "We both cried," said the simple cottager to one who saw her not long since; "the Queen cried and I cried." Yet when she noticed Her Majesty's grief, she controlled herself and asked pardon for crying. "But oh!" added the old lady, "she was so thankful to cry with some one who knew exactly how she felt. And afterwards she said, 'You saw your husband's death coming; but I—I did not see mine. It was so sudden!'"*

The Queen was much helped during the early years of her widowhood by the sympathy of Dr. Macleod, whose Christian counsel and cheery words of comfort did much to soften and mitigate the sorrow. On one occasion (11th of May, 1862) after attending service in the Presbyterian Kirk where the doctor

* *The Queen at Balmoral*, 97, 98.

preached, she noted in her *Journal:* "The sermon was admirable, all upon affliction, God's love, our Saviour's sufferings, which God would not spare Him; the blessedness of suffering in bringing us nearer to our eternal home, where we should all be together, and where our dear ones were gone on before us. He . . . prayed most touchingly for me. The children and I were much affected on coming upstairs." *

It was the Princess Alice, however, who was the Queen's great stay and comfort in the hour of her deepest sorrow. During her father's illness the Princess had changed from a gay, bright girl into a thoughtful woman, and now her one object seemed to be to help and support her Mother. Whatever was necessary to be done in those first dark days, she did it; and for six months the Princess was the chief means of communication between the Sovereign and her Ministers.† Her marriage, which was solemnised at Osborne in July, 1862, was a very quiet affair. The Duke of Saxe-Coburg-Gotha, in the place of her father, led the bride to the altar; and the Queen retired to her own room directly the ceremony was over. On the 9th of July the newly wedded couple left England for their German home, accompanied by the sincerely felt good wishes of the English people. They knew what a treasure the Queen was losing, and, in their measure, also felt her loss. A graceful sonnet in *Punch* contained the following lines, which admirably expressed the popular sentiment:—

> . . . "Thou, in affection wise
> And strong, wert strength to Her who even but now
> In the soft accents of thy bridal vow
> Heard music of her own heart's memories.
> Too full of love to own a thought of pride
> Is now thy gentle bosom; so 'tis best:
> Yet noble is thy choice, O English bride!
> And England hails the bridegroom and the guest
> A friend—a friend well loved by him who died.
> He blessed your troth: your wedlock shall be blessed."

---

* *More Leaves from the Journal of a Life in the Highlands,* 210.

† Memorandum by the Grand Duchess of Baden in the *Princess Alice* Memorial Volume, 18, 19.

We should much like to quote from some of the Princess's tender and comforting letters to her Mother written from Auerbach and Darmstadt after the marriage, but our space is limited. A single passage must suffice. "Take courage, dear Mama," she wrote on the 16th of August, 1862, "and feel strong in the thought that you require all your moral and physical strength to continue the journey which brings you daily nearer to *Home* and to *Him!* I know how weary you feel, how you long to rest your head on his dear shoulder, to have him to soothe your aching heart. You will find this rest again, and how blessed will it not be! Bear patiently and courageously your heavy burden, and it will lighten imperceptibly as you near him, and God's love and mercy will support you. Oh, could my feeble words bring you the least comfort! They come from a trusting, true and loving heart, if from nought else."* Who could doubt it?

Among the many touching tributes of sympathy which came to the Queen from time to time was one from the widows of England, who sent Her Majesty a Bible—the Book which had been their own solace in times of kindred sorrow. The gift was presented through the Duchess of Sutherland, and the Queen replied:—

"WINDSOR CASTLE, 19*th December*, 1862.

"MY DEAREST DUCHESS,—I am deeply touched by the gift of a Bible 'from many widows,' and by the very kind and affectionate address which accompanied it, and which you read to me. Pray express to all these kind *sister widows* the deep and heartfelt gratitude of their widowed Queen, who can never feel grateful enough for the universal sympathy she has received, and continues to receive, from her loyal and devoted subjects. But what she values far more is their appreciation of her adored and perfect husband, to whom she and the country owe everything. To her the only sort of consolation she experiences is in the *constant* sense of his unseen presence and the blessed thought of that *Eternal Union* hereafter, which will make the

* *Princess Alice*, 36.

(*From a Drawing by* Percy Wadham.)

bitter anguish of the present appear as nought. That our Heavenly Father may impart to 'many widows' those sources of consolation and support, is their broken-hearted Queen's earnest prayer. The Bible itself is very handsome, as well as the reading-desk, and both with the address and signatures will ever be kept by the Queen and her children as a mark of the living, tender sympathy of her subjects.—Believe me ever, Dearest Duchess, yours most affectionately, VICTORIA." *

Though Her Majesty's great grief was by no means healed, yet a pause was given to sorrow early in the following year, when the Prince of Wales was married at Windsor. His engagement to the beautiful Princess Alexandra of Denmark had taken place nearly three months before his father's death, and the Prince Consort had noted in his *Diary* on the 30th of September: "We hear nothing but excellent accounts of the Princess Alexandra"; to which he had added the not less satisfactory item: "The young people seem to have taken a warm liking for each other."†

The Princess's reception in England was one continued ovation, and when, on the 7th of March, she passed through London on her way to Windsor the crowds and the cheering were alike immense. "The sea-king's daughter from over the sea" had won her way to the hearts of thousands by the mere charm of her presence; and those who saw her make her entrance into London on that memorable March morning will not soon forget the sight. Three days after, the marriage took place in St. George's Chapel, Windsor. A more gorgeous spectacle could hardly be imagined. The Knights of St. George in their stalls—the gathering of illustrous men and fair women —the sheen and glitter of uniforms and stars, of satins and silks, of jewels countless and invaluable—the clash of kettle-drums and the loud pealing of the organ—all these things contributed to make an impression not easily effaced from the mind. "The bride," says an eye-witness, "looked lovely; she did not raise her eyes once going in, and but little when coming

* *My Reminiscences*, vol. i. 150, 151.
† *Life of the Prince Consort*, vol. v. 67.

THE MARRIAGE OF THE PRINCE OF WALES TO PRINCESS ALEXANDRA OF DENMARK.

out of the chapel when on her husband's arm."* She wore a dress of white satin and Honiton lace, with a silver moiré train, and her jewels consisted of a necklace, earrings and brooch of pearls and diamonds, the gift of the bridegroom; a splendid *riviére* of diamonds, given by the Corporation of London, and valued at £10,000; two opal and diamond bracelets, one of which was the gift of the Queen; and a third bracelet of diamonds only, presented by the ladies of Leeds. Her Majesty, in widow's weeds, sat apart from the brilliant company in the Royal closet of the Chapel, from which she watched the ceremonial, but took no part in it. It was noticed that she was much affected, and the English Princesses also were seen to weep behind their bouquets. It opened up their grief afresh to see their brother waiting *alone* before the altar for his bride.

A few months after the wedding, the Queen indulged her sad heart by re-visiting the birthplace of the Prince Consort. She had made a short visit to Coburg in the previous year, when she had seen and conversed with the aged Baron Stockmar, who had soothed her with his talk about his noble pupil, "the dear good Prince," cut off in the midst of his years and usefulness. *Now*, the Baron himself was dead, and the widowed Queen paid a visit of sympathy to the widowed Baroness. While staying at Rosenau on this second occasion, she received visits from the King of Prussia and the Emperor of Austria, and also from the Princesses Victoria and Alice and their husbands. The Princess Alice had now a little daughter—a fat, good-humoured baby with pink cheeks—who had been named Victoria Alberta, after her grandparents.†

Twice this year the Queen went to Balmoral—in May and September. In the former month she drove to Craig Lowrigan to see the cairn which had been erected on the summit to the Prince Consort's memory. Her Majesty describes the cairn as "a fine sharp pyramid, admirably constructed out of granite without any mortar."‡

The pyramid is forty feet square at the base, and thirty-five

---

* Lord Ronald Gower—see *My Reminiscences*, vol. i. 161.
† *Princess Alice*, 44-52.   ‡ *More Leaves*, 5.

feet high, and can be seen from a great distance. The initials of the Queen and her children are cut on one side of it; and on another side—that which fronts the valley—is the following inscription:—

To the Beloved Memory

OF

ALBERT, THE GREAT AND GOOD,

PRINCE CONSORT,

RAISED BY HIS BROKEN-HEARTED WIDOW,

VICTORIA R.,

AUGUST 21, 1862.

"He being made perfect, in a short time fulfilled a long time,
For his soul pleased the Lord;
Therefore hastened He to take him
Away from among the wicked."
—*Wisdom of Solomon*, vol. iv. 13, 14.

During the autumn stay at Balmoral the Queen paid a melancholy visit to Blair Athole, the scene of so much past happiness. The Duke was suffering from cancer in the throat, but he was able to receive Her Majesty, and having kissed her hand, he gave her a white rose, the old tribute of the Lords of Athole to their Sovereign.* On her departure he insisted on accompanying her to the station, where he walked about, giving directions. "I embraced the dear Duchess," writes Her Majesty, "and gave the Duke my hand, saying, 'Dear Duke, God bless you!' He had asked permission that his men, the same who had gone with us through the Glen on that happy day two years ago, might give me a cheer, and he led them on himself. Oh! it was so dreadfully sad!"†

Three weeks later, on the 7th of October, the Queen met with an alarming accident. She was returning from Alt-na-Giuthasach with the Princesses Alice and Helena, when the carriage was overturned in the moorland, and Her Majesty was thrown on her face. The Princess Alice was the first to be

* *More Leaves*, 6.   † *Ibid.* 7.

R

extricated, and she behaved with her usual calmness and discretion, holding a lamp while Brown rendered assistance to her sister, whose dress had got entangled with the vehicle, and who was in great alarm. The Queen herself was the worst sufferer, her face being a good deal bruised and swollen, and her right thumb badly sprained. As no water was to be had, the bruises and injured hand had to be bathed with claret; and until assistance arrived, which was not for half-an-hour, the Royal excursionists were reduced to the extremity of sitting on the inverted carriage wrapped up in plaids.*

On the 13th of the same month the Queen went from Balmoral to unveil a statue of the Prince Consort at Aberdeen. It was her first appearance in public since the Prince's death, and the procession through the crowded but silent streets was a mournful sight. Heads were bared respectfully, but there were no cheers; and, as though to add a finish to the desolate picture, a heavy cheerless rain was falling the whole time. "I got out trembling," writes Her Majesty, "and when I had arrived, there was no one to direct me and to say, as formerly, what was to be done. Oh! it was and is too painful, too dreadful! I received (only handed) the Provost's address, and knighted him (the first since all ended) with General Grey's sword. Then we all stepped on to the uncovered and wet platform directly opposite the statue, which certainly is low, and rather small for out of doors, but fine and like. Principal Campbell's prayer was very long—which was trying in the rain—but part of it (since I have read it) is really very good. I felt very nervous when the statue was uncovered, but much regretted that when they presented arms there was no salute with the drums, bugles, or the pipes, for the bands below were forbidden to play. I retired almost immediately."†

On returning to Windsor for the Christmas season, the Queen and those of her family who were with her, visited the recently erected mausoleum at Frogmore, where the Prince Consort's remains were now lying. More than £200,000 from Her Majesty's private purse had been expended on this superb tomb,

* *More Leaves*, 10–14. † *Ibid.* 16, 17.

which, indeed, is as much like an elaborately decorated chapel as a sepulchre. The year before, Dr. Macleod had entered the mausoleum in company with the Queen. "She had the key," he wrote, "and opened it herself, undoing the bolts, and alone we entered and stood in silence beside Marochetti's beautiful statue of the Prince. I was very much overcome. She was calm and quiet." *

About this time the Prince and Princess of Wales resided occasionally at Frogmore, and the chief domestic event of the following year (1864) was the birth there of their first child, Prince Albert Victor. He was baptised at Buckingham Palace on the first anniversary of his parents' marriage, the Queen and old King Leopold being present among the sponsors.

The next year Her Majesty again went to Coburg, on this occasion to unveil a statue of the Prince Consort in the square of the little town where he was born. Her second son, Prince Alfred, had been formally acknowledged heir to his childless uncle, the Duke of Saxe-Coburg, two days before she set out. Four of her children accompanied her, and the Royal party arrived at Rosenau, the family villa of the Duke, on the 11th of August, and remained there till the ceremony was over. The unveiling took place on the Prince Consort's birthday, and was perhaps the most interesting of all the inaugurations of monuments to his memory. The gilt-bronze statue is ten feet high, and represents the Prince with his hand on a plan of the Great Exhibition. Luther's hymn, *Ein feste Burg ist unser Gott* ('A strong tower is our God') was sung at the beginning of the ceremony, and when the Queen had unveiled the statue, she handed a bouquet to the Duke, who laid it on the pedestal. The Princesses then came forward and also deposited flowers, after which other ladies did the same, and so the fragrant offerings rose higher and higher till they reached to the feet of the statue.

Much of the autumn of the same year was spent at Balmoral, the Queen finding a melancholy pleasure in retracing the old rides and drives which she had taken with the Prince in the

* Tytler's *Life of the Queen*, vol. ii. 208.

happy days that could never return. She also spent a few days
with the now widowed Duchess of Athole at Dunkeld, whose
"snug little cottage," as Her Majesty calls it, was situated just
outside the town, in the midst of fine and extensive grounds.
On one of these days she walked with the Duchess in the grounds,
and along by the River Tay as far as the American garden, and
then round by a terrace overlooking the park. It was in this
park that the tents had been pitched twenty-three years before,
when the Duke (then Lord Glenlyon) had given a grand *déjeûner*
to the young Queen and her husband, in honour of their first
visit to the Highlands. The following year (1866) when Her
Majesty was again the guest of the Duchess at Dunkeld, she
went on one specially pleasant expedition as far as Loch Tummel,
passing Taymouth (Lord Breadalbane's seat), a dear and familiar
spot. "We got out," writes the Queen, "and looked down
from a height upon the house below, the mist having cleared
away sufficiently to show us everything; and here, unknown,
quite in private, I gazed, not without deep inward emotion, on
the scene of our reception, twenty-four years ago, by dear Lord
Breadalbane in a princely style, not to be equalled for grandeur
and poetic effect ! Albert and I were only twenty-three, young
and happy. How many are gone who were with us then !"*
At Loch Tummel the excursionists alighted and took tea;
"but," says Her Majesty, "the fire would not burn, and the
kettle would not boil. At length Brown ran off to a cottage,
and returned after some little while with a can full of hot water,
but it was no longer boiling when it arrived, and the tea was
not good." † At Ballinluig, which they passed through on the
way back, "the good people had put two lighted candles in each
window" (their idea of illuminations in honour of a Royal
visit), and they pressed round the carriage, offering to bring
"Athole brose"—whatever that may be. The travellers did
not get back to Dunkeld till nearly nine o'clock, "but,"
says Her Majesty, "it was a very interesting day." ‡

On the 6th of October the Queen returned to Balmoral, and
ten days later went to Aberdeen to open the new waterworks,

* *More Leaves*, 53.   † *Ibid.* 56, 57.   ‡ *Ibid.* 58.

THE QUEEN AND HER CHILDREN.

(The respective groups in the above picture are from photographs by Messrs. Bassano, W. & D. Downey, Elliott & Fry, and Walery Ltd.)

which were to convey to the city 6,000,000 gallons of water daily, and which had been built at a cost of £130,000. The Lord Provost read an address, and "then," says Her Majesty, "I had to read my answer, which made me very nervous; but I got through it well, though it was the first time I had read anything since my darling husband was taken from me."* The ceremony was over in less than a quarter of an hour, and when the Queen drove away she was heartily cheered.

Earlier in the same year Her Majesty's third daughter, the Princess Helena, had been married to Prince Christian of Schleswig-Holstein, a man of real worth of character; the ceremony taking place in the private chapel at Windsor. Four of the Queen's children were now happily married, and as the years rolled round the others also found wives or husbands. In March, 1871, the Princess Louise was united to the Marquis of Lorne, the only instance of a *subject* of the Queen marrying into the Royal Family. The first of the bridal party to enter St. George's Chapel on the wedding morning was the bridegroom, attended by Lord Ronald Gower and Earl Percy. The Princess of Wales and other members of the Royal Family were ranged in a row before the altar rails, while the Prince of Wales awaited the entrance of the Queen and bride at the door of the chapel. When the eight bridesmaids, heralds of the bride, had made their appearance, there was a pause of several seconds; then an alarm of trumpets and a roll of drums announced the approach of Her Majesty and the Princess, and the whole procession moved on to the altar. The Queen, who appeared to be in excellent health, was warmly received, and repeatedly bowed her acknowledgments. As she ascended the *haut pas*, the noble bridegroom made a profound obeisance, and the wedding-service proceeded. The officiating clergy were the Bishops of London, Winchester, Oxford and Worcester, assisted by some lesser dignitaries of the Church. The service over, Her Majesty extended her hand to her new son-in-law, who bowed again and kissed it; and then, with the Princess on

* *More Leaves*, 67.

his arm and followed by the Queen, he proceeded down the long passage of the choir and nave, and so to his carriage.

The next of the Royal weddings was on the 23rd of January, 1874, and took place out of England. We refer, of course, to the marriage of the Duke of Edinburgh with the Grand Duchess Marie of Russia, only daughter of the Czar. This partook more of the nature of a pageant even than the marriage of the Prince of Wales, for it was celebrated at St. Petersburg, where there is greater scope for splendid ceremonial than in this country. The bridegroom being a Protestant, and the bride a member of the Greek Church, there were two distinct marriage services— one at the Imperial Chapel of the Winter Palace, and the other at the Alexander Hall. The first, which was the Greek ceremony, was itself a sort of dual service, consisting of a betrothal ceremony and the marriage service proper. The latter began with a series of interrogations, something like those in the English Church, followed by prayers; "and the most picturesque portion of the ceremony was the placing of two massive golden crowns on the heads of the bride and bridegroom, which were subsequently held above them by the groomsmen, Prince Arthur and the Grand Duke Vladimir. After this they partook of the 'common cup,' each drinking thrice from a goblet of wine, in memory of the marriage at Cana of Galilee, while the service concluded with an act which renders the marriage indissoluble. Joining hands under the priest's stole, the bridal pair followed the Archbishop three times round the altar, in commemoration of the Trinity, the circles being also made in allusion to the eternity of marriage. The procession was then re-formed, and proceeded to the Alexander Hall, for the ceremony according to the Anglican rite," which was performed by Dean Stanley. The bride wore a mantle of crimson velvet trimmed with ermine, and a glittering coronet; the bridegroom, the uniform of the British Navy.* The Queen was represented at both ceremonies by the Prince and Princess of Wales.

To tell of the marriages of the three other Royal children—

* *The Graphic*, 20th March, 1879.

namely Princes Arthur and Leopold and the Princess Beatrice
—would be taking us too far at present, and there are some
events of a sadder kind, of which as yet we have said nothing,
which must lead up to them.

One of the earliest of these was the death of Her Majesty's
uncle, the King of the Belgians—her friend from her cradle.
He died on the 9th of December, 1865, at Laeken, in his
seventy-fifth year, the last of a family of nine sons and
daughters. "How much for you, for us, for all, goes with
him to the grave!" wrote the Princess Alice to her Mother;
"one tie more of those dear old times is rent! I do feel for
you so much, for dear Uncle was indeed a father to you. Now
you are head of all the family—it seems incredible, and that
dear Papa should not be by your side. The regret for dear
Uncle Leopold is universal—he stood so high in the eyes of all
parties; his life was a history in itself—and now that book is
closed."*

Three months later (February, 1866), the Queen opened
Parliament in person, for the first time since the death of the
Prince Consort. There was much to emphasise the change
in her condition—no flourish of trumpets—no cheers—and a
vacant seat beside the throne. Her Majesty did not wear the
robes of state, as on former occasions—they were merely laid
upon the throne, and her speech was read (not, as hitherto, by
herself, but) by the Lord Chancellor. In the following year,
when she again came forth from her seclusion to open Parliament,
there were the same saddening omissions and alterations
in the State ceremonial. A month or two later she laid the
foundation-stone of the Albert Hall. The Prince of Wales and
Duke of Edinburgh received her; and the former made a
speech, to which Her Majesty replied, though in a voice that
was hardly audible. At the beginning of the ceremony they
presented her with a bouquet, which she took, and then kissed
them both.

Of course, there were the regular flittings to Windsor,
Osborne, and Balmoral during this period—indeed, the greater

* *Princess Alice*, 112.

part of each year was spent at these places—and what with the constant presence of her unmarried children, and occasional visits from the married ones, and the incessant coming and going of distinguished visitors, it can hardly be said that the Queen's life was dull or lonely. No one, it is true, could ever take the place of the dead Prince; but such compensations as are granted to the most favoured in like circumstances Her Majesty did not lack. The love of sons and daughters, the sympathy of her subjects, the means of gratifying every passing desire, however great or however trivial—all these she had; and thus, though a full cup of sorrow had been hers, her cup of blessings was full also.

To tell of all the pleasant times spent at Balmoral alone, during the years which we are now considering, would run away with what little space we have remaining, and if we are to speak of them at all it must be in the fewest possible words. The volume entitled, *More Leaves from the Journal of a Life in the Highlands*, which, like the *Leaves*, is simply a collection of extracts from the Queen's *Diary*, contains many appreciative descriptions of Highland customs, as well as accounts of visits to places not mentioned in the earlier volume. Thus, in one place we have particulars of a torchlight procession on Hallowe'en. Her Majesty had been out driving, and was met on her return by two gillies bearing torches. "Louise got out and took one," notes the Queen, "walking by the side of the carriage, and looking like one of the witches in 'Macbeth.' As we approached Balmoral, the keepers and their wives and children, the gillies, and other people met us, all with torches, Brown also carrying one. We got out at the house, where Leopold joined us, and a torch was given to him. We walked round the whole house, preceded by Ross playing the pipes, going down the steps of the terrace. . . . After this a bonfire was made of all the torches, close to the house, and they danced reels whilst Ross played the pipes."*

In another place we have a bright account of a house-warming in one of the Royal hunting lodges—the Glas-Alt Shiel—

* *More Leaves*, 69, 70.

where, to the strains of the bagpipe, five animated reels were danced in the Queen's presence, and then the inevitable "whisky-toddy" was handed round. Afterwards, Grant made a little speech, in which references to the wild country, and his Royal mistress, and "living for ever" were finely confused, and the speech was followed by cheers, led on by the pipes, and, in due course, more of the "toddy"! But even this homely celebration had its mournful side for the Queen. "Sad thoughts filled my heart," she wrote, "both before dinner and when I was alone and retired to rest. I thought of the happy past and my darling husband whom I fancied I must see, and who always wished to build here, in this favourite wild spot, quite in amidst the hills."*

Anon we get a really entertaining account of "juicing the sheep," to see which process the Queen drove over specially to a neighbouring farm. The practice, says Her Majesty, is "pursued all over the Highlands before the sheep are sent down to the low country for the winter. It is done to preserve the wool. Not far from the burnside, where there are a few hillocks, was a pen, in which the sheep were placed, and then, just outside it, a large sort of trough filled with liquid tobacco and soap, and into this the sheep were dipped one after the other; one man . . . took the sheep one by one out of the pen, and turned them on their backs; and then . . . [assisted by the farmer], he dipped them well in, after which they were let into another pen into which this trough opened, and here they had to remain to dry. To the left, a little lower down, was a cauldron boiling over a fire, and containing the tobacco with water and soap; this was then emptied into a tub, from which it was transferred into the trough. A very rosy-faced lassie, with a plaid over her head, was superintending this part of the work, and helped to fetch the water from the burn, while children and many collie dogs were grouped about, and several men and shepherds were helping. It was a very curious and picturesque sight."†

Elsewhere, Her Majesty describes a Highland "Kirstnin'" or christening in the cottage of her wood forester, and remarks

* *More Leaves*, 107, 108. † *Ibid.* 109, 110.

that she thought the service "appropriate, touching, and impressive." She gave a silver mug to the father, and a kiss to the baby, and then joined with the rest in drinking the health of the little one and its mother.* The *Journal* also contains an account of a sheep-shearing, and the sad, simple story of the drowning of a cottager's child in the Dee. The little body was found, and taken home, and laid upon the kitchen table, with a white sheet over it, and then Her Majesty went with Princess Beatrice to see the poor mother. "She cried a little at first," writes the sympathising Queen, "when I took her hand and said how much I felt for her, and how dreadful it was. She checked herself, and said, with that quiet resignation and trust which it is so edifying to witness, and which you see so strongly here, 'We must try to bear it; we must trust to the Almighty.'"†

The death of Grant's mother and of Brown's father are also dwelt upon; and the service in the little farmhouse before the burial of the latter, as well as the solemn procession to the grave, are feelingly described. Here is an extract: "Mr. Campbell, the minister of Crathie, stood in the passage at the door, every one else standing close outside. As soon as he began his prayer, poor dear old Mrs. Brown got up and came and stood near me— able to hear, though, alas! not to see—and leant on a chair during the very impressive prayers, which Mr. Campbell gave admirably. When it was over, Brown came and begged her to sit down while they took the coffin away, the brothers bearing it. Every one went out and followed, and we also hurried out and just saw them place the coffin in the hearse, and then we moved on to a hillock, whence we saw the sad procession wending its way down. . . . It fortunately ceased raining just then. I went back to the house and tried to soothe and comfort dear old Mrs. Brown, and gave her a mourning brooch with a little bit of her husband's hair which had been cut off yesterday, and I shall give a locket to each of the sons."‡

Then we read of visits to Floors and the Scotch Border country—to Glenfiddich and to Invertrossachs—to Holyrood,

* *More Leaves*, 111, 112.   † *Ibid.* 156-163.   ‡ *Ibid.* 320, 321.

Edinburgh, and Dunrobin—to Inverlochee and Inveraray—to Loch Maree, Broxmouth and Edinburgh.

At Kelso, in August, 1867, the Sovereign was welcomed by large and enthusiastic crowds, and the little town made a wonderful show with its triumphal arches and mottoes, its flags and flowers. The volunteers were out, and bands were playing, and, to crown all, fifty beautiful young ladies dressed in virgin white strewed blossoms as the Royal carriage passed. On this occasion Her Majesty was the guest of the Duke of Buccleuch, whose mansion, built by Sir John Vanbrugh in 1718, is situated in the midst of a fine park, in which are grand old beeches, sycamores and oaks. "It was the first time," notes the Queen, "I had gone in this way on a visit (like as in former times), and I thought so much of all dearest Albert would have done and said, and how he would have wandered about everywhere, admired everything, looked at everything—and now! Oh! must it ever, ever be so?"* From Kelso the Royal party drove on to Melrose Abbey and Abbotsford, the well-known residence of Sir Walter Scott. They were taken over the part of the mansion in which the great novelist had lived, and were shown "all his rooms—his drawing-room with the same furniture and carpet, the library where we saw his MS. of 'Ivanhoe,' and several others of his novels and poems in a beautiful handwriting with hardly any erasures, and other relics which Sir Walter had himself collected." Then his study, a small, dark room, with a little turret in which is a bust in bronze of Sir Walter, done from a cast after death. "In the study," continues the Royal diarist, "we saw his *Journal*, in which Mr. Hope Scott asked me to write my name (which I felt it to be a presumption in me to do), as also the others. We went through some passages into two or three rooms where were collected fine specimens of old armour, etc., and where in a glass case are Sir Walter's last clothes. We ended by going into the dining-room," † in which the great romancer died.

At Glenfiddich, the Duke of Richmond's shooting-lodge, where the Queen paid an informal visit in September, 1867,

* *More Leaves*, 75.   † *Ibid.* 81, 82.

the ladies of the Royal party found themselves in sad straits in consequence of the non-arrival of the luggage. In fact, they had to go to dinner in their riding-skirts, and Her Majesty, having no cap, had to make shift with a black lace veil belonging to one of her maids, which was arranged on her head as a coiffure! Midnight came, but no luggage, and at one o'clock Brown came in to say that nothing had been seen or heard of it and to urge that his Royal Mistress should retire to rest. "My maids had unfortunately not thought of bringing anything with them," notes the Queen, "and I disliked the idea of going to bed without any of the necessary toilette. However, some arrangements were made which were very uncomfortable; and after two I got into bed, but had very little sleep at first: finally fatigue got the better of discomfort, and after three I fell asleep."* That same year, on the twenty-eighth anniversary of her engagement day, the Queen unveiled a statue of the Prince Consort at Balmoral—Her Majesty's gift to her tenantry. A detachment of the 93rd Highlanders was drawn up just behind the statue, and as the covering fell off, they presented arms and the pipes played cheerful music—cheerful for bagpipes.

The ten days at the Invertrossachs in September, 1869, seem to have been greatly enjoyed; and of course when the Royal party found themselves at Kirkton of Balquhidder, they went to the old kirkyard to look at the tomb of the famous outlaw, Rob Roy MacGregor.† At Ferguson's Inn, close by the Brig of Turk, the landlady was brought out to be shown to the Queen. She was an immensely fat woman, well dressed and quite rich, but so attached to her little tumbledown cottage of an inn that she would not leave it. "She seemed delighted to see me," writes the Queen, "shaking hands with me and patting me!"‡ Her Majesty did a good deal of sketching in the Invertrossachs, and perhaps to this period belongs the story of her encounter with a certain shepherd boy, who addressed her in terms not often used by a subject to a sovereign. "Get out of the road, lady, and let the sheep gang by," he shouted, and although the

* *More Leaves*, 94, 95. † *Ibid.* 130. ‡ *Ibid.* 140.

order was obeyed, **the sheep were** timid and would not advance. "I say, gang back, will you! and let the sheep pass," cried the boy again; whereupon one of Her Majesty's attendants asked with some severity: "Do **you** know, boy, **to** whom you are speaking?" "I dinna know, and I dinna care," said the youthful shepherd; "that's the sheep's road and she has no business to stand there." "But that's the Queen," said the gentleman. "The Queen! Is it the Queen?" cried the lad, momentarily abashed; but quickly recovering himself he inquired: "Well, but why don't she put on clothes so that folks would know her?"

The visit to Dunrobin, the seat of the Duke **of** Sutherland, was in September, 1872, and extended over five or six **days.** The engine of the Royal train was driven all the way from Inverness by the Duke himself, but the Queen did not know of this till they stopped at Bonar Bridge station, when the Duke came **to** the carriage door **and** introduced himself. Here, writes the Queen, "there was a most excited station-master, who would not **leave the crowd of** poor country people in quiet, but told **them to** cheer and 'cheer again,' 'another cheer,' etc., without ceasing."* At Golspie station the Royal party alighted, and were received by the Duchess—a guard of honour of the Sutherland Volunteers, in their red jackets and tartan kilts, being drawn up on the platform. The little town, which consists merely of one long street, was prettily decorated with heather and flowers, and there were many triumphal arches with English and Gaelic inscriptions. On one of the arches was the winning little couplet :—

> "Better lo'ed you canna' be;
> Will you no come back again?"

In less than ten minutes **the** Royal party were at Dunrobin Castle—an imposing structure, with high roof and turrets, something between a Scotch castle and a French *château*—and here they were received by the Marchioness of Westminster. The next morning, the Queen and Princess Beatrice went for a stroll

* *More Leaves*, 182.

through the beautiful gardens, and so on in the direction of the sea, the Duchess chaperoning them round. "We walked along here" (*i.e.*, by the sea), says Her Majesty, "and then up and into the pretty byre for Ayrshire cows, and a little farther on to the dairy, a very nice, cool, round one. The Duchess told Brown to open the sitting-room, and we found it occupied by a policeman in bed, which we were not at all prepared for, and which caused much amusement." *

During her stay at Dunrobin, the Queen laid the first stone of a memorial to the late Duchess, raised by the clansmen and servants on the estate, by whom she was greatly beloved. On reaching the spot, a short prayer was offered up by the minister of the place, who afterwards presented an address to Her Majesty, which, however, he did not read. The Queen then answered extempore, "It gives me great pleasure to testify on this occasion my love and esteem for the dear Duchess, my valued friend, with whose children I am happy to be now staying, and I wish also to express my warm thanks for the loyal and hearty welcome I have met with in Sutherland." † These few words are interesting as affording the only instance that we have met with of an extemporaneous speech by the Queen. Her Majesty confesses that she was very nervous at the time, but adds that the words were spoken without hesitation.

It was in the summer of this year, while the Court was at Balmoral, that Dr. Macleod, whose helpful sympathy in the early years of the Queen's widowhood we have already dwelt upon, died at Glasgow. The news was brought to Her Majesty as she was going to rest one Sunday night, and it greatly affected her. Next evening, she wrote in her *Diary*, "After breakfast, when I thought of my dear friend, Dr. Macleod, and all he had been to me—how in 1862-63-64 he had cheered and comforted and encouraged me—how he had ever sympathised with me, and how much I always looked forward to the few occasions I had of seeing him when we went to Balmoral, and that this too, like so many other comforts and

* *More Leaves*, 186, 187.   † *Ibid.* 195.

helps, was for ever gone—I burst out crying!"* "No one,"
she says elsewhere, "ever felt so convinced, and so anxious as
he to convince others that God was a loving Father, who
wished all to come to Him, and to preach of a living personal
Saviour, One who loved us as a brother and a friend, to whom
all could and should come with trust and confidence. No
one ever raised and strengthened one's faith more than Dr.
Macleod."† Pious souls, who feel (and, we think, rightly)
that works *alone* are not sufficient to salvation, are rather fond
of raising the question, "Is the Queen a Christian?" Surely
there is enough in the words just quoted to set that question
for ever at rest!

Before finally parting company with the Royal *Journal*, we
shall have to say a few words about the Queen's visits to
Inverlochy, Inveraray, and one or two other places in Scotland,
but as they will take us almost into the 'Eighties, it may be
well first to devote a page or two to matters more exclusively
English. It is true that we are seeking to *group* facts rather
than to treat them in strict order of time, yet we do not wish
to destroy all sense of chronological sequence.

Towards the close of the year 1871, the Queen and her people
were united in a common anxiety on account of the alarming
illness of the Prince of Wales. When the Prince had returned
from Germany in the previous autumn, it was seen that he had
lost a good deal of his buoyancy of spirit; and it was said that
he had exerted himself too much. "But," says Dr. Russell,
"it was not generally known that, attended by only three
gentlemen, he had made an excursion *incognito* to the battle-
fields of Sedan and Metz before he went to Frankfort, and that
he had, owing to curious mischances of which the story is too
long to tell now, been subjected to great inconvenience, and
had to sleep, after a long and trying day, in the pestilential air
of a town in the centre of a battlefield, which had been for
many months filled with wounded men."‡ It was probably at
this time that the fever germs got into his system. Be that as

* *More Leaves*, 227, 228. † *Ibid.* 231.
‡ *Harper's Magazine*, April, 1885, 773.

it may, the physicians, who were summoned to Sandringham at the first symptoms of indisposition, were not long in coming to the conclusion that the Prince was in the incipient stage of typhoid fever, and their conclusion was unfortunately but too correct. Day by day the fever gathered strength, and each bulletin that was issued was more alarming than the last. "Morning after morning crowds, ever shifting, ever pouring from the parks and streets, and drifting away in sadness, were collected before the gates at Marlborough House, and at the various places in London where the bulletins from Sandringham were posted up, and every word in the measured sentences were noted, weighed, and discussed with an interest, in the depths of which all differences of party feeling and policy lay buried. In the sympathy for the Princess, in the popular regard for the Prince, Radical, Whig, and Tory, stood on common ground."* A poet has beautifully said :—

> "In the drear November gloom
> And the long December night,
> There were omens of affright,
> And prophecies of doom;
> And the golden lamp of life burned spectral dim,
> Till love could hardly mark
> The little sapphire spark,
> That only made the dark
> More dark and grim.
>
> There not around alone
> Watch'd sister, brother, wife,
> And she who gave him life,
> White as if wrought in stone;
> Unheard, invisible, by the bed of death
> Stood eager millions by;
> And as the hour drew nigh,
> Dreading to see him die,
> Held their breath."†

By Saturday, the 9th of December, the terrible crisis was

* *Harper's Magazine,* April, 1885, 772.
† Palgrave's *Visions of England,* 170.

over, and the Princess was able next day to write a hurried line to the Vicar of Sandringham, which, even at this distance of time, we confess we cannot read without emotion. The letter ran :—" My husband being, thank God, somewhat better, I am coming to church. I must leave, I fear, before the service is concluded, that I may watch by his bedside. Can you not say a few words in prayer in the early part of the service that I may join with you in prayer for my husband, before I return to him ?" Despite the better news, however, many people shook their heads, and the ominous remark was often heard, " His father died on the 14th; wait and see!" But when the dreaded 14th had come and gone, and the Prince continued to improve, the hopes of all grew stronger, and it was felt that he would recover. Who knows but that he would have been taken on that sad anniversary day, but for a nation's prayers?

> ". . . If reason said;
> 'Gainst Nature's laws and death
> ' Prayer is but idle breath,'
> Yet faith was undismayed,
> Around with the deeper insight of the heart;
> Nor can the wisest say
> What other laws may sway
> The world's apparent way,
> Known but in part."*

The day of Public Thanksgiving for the recovery of the Prince (27th February, 1872), will long be remembered in this country. Countless thousands lined the route of the procession from Buckingham Palace to St. Paul's, and in the cathedral itself, where a special thanksgiving service was held, some 13,000 persons were assembled. The enthusiasm, both coming and going, was intense; and the Queen is said to have looked happier on that day than she had been known to look for years. The *London Gazette* of the 1st of March contained a letter of grateful thanks from the Sovereign to her people, which had been sent to Mr. Gladstone for publication. In the course of

* *Visions of England*, 171.

the letter she said:—"Words are too weak for the Queen to say how deeply touched and gratified she has been by the immense enthusiasm and affection exhibited towards her dear son and herself, from the highest down to the lowest, on the long progress through the capital, and she would earnestly wish to convey her warmest and most heartfelt thanks to the whole nation for the demonstration of loyalty. . . . The remembrance of this day, and of the remarkable order maintained throughout, will for ever be affectionately remembered by the Queen and her family."

The day before the publication of this letter—in fact, only two days after the procession to St. Paul's, there was a scare throughout London. The report came that an attempt had been made upon the Queen's life. It turned out than an Irish youth, named O'Connor, had climbed over some railings as Her Majesty was returning from a drive in the Park, and had rushed up to the Royal carriage in a threatening manner—a pistol in one hand and a paper in the other. He was promptly seized by the ubiquitous John Brown, and handed over to the civil authorities, the Queen sitting unmoved the whole time. When the pistol came to be examined, it was found to be an old flint-lock, unloaded, and without hammer or flint. The paper was a petition for the Fenians, drawn up by the lad himself—a weak, foolish production, of no political significance whatever. In fact, it was presently ascertained that the culprit was a poor, half-witted creature, without accomplices or abettors; and at the earliest possible moment, he was put under the restraint which his mental condition required. Brown was rewarded for his pluck and presence of mind by a pension of £25 per annum.

The only other attack which has been made upon Her Majesty (and the last we trust that it will ever be necessary to record) took place at Windsor, ten years later. The Queen was entering her carriage at the railway station on the 2nd of March, when a man stepped out from the crowd, and fired a pistol. Both Her Majesty and the Princess Beatrice had a narrow escape, for the ball passed just between them. The man was instantly arrested, and having been unmercifully belaboured about the head and shoulders by a demonstrative Eton boy, who made wreck of a new umbrella during this ebullition of loyalty, was led away to prison. As in each of the former cases the culprit turned out to be a person of weak intellect; but love of notoriety does not seem to have prompted his act. After a short and impartial trial, he was found not guilty, on the ground of insanity, and was ordered to be detained in safe keeping during Her Majesty's pleasure. His name was Roderick Maclean, and he was a person of respectable connections, who had fallen into want.

To tell of all the public functions of one kind and another in which the Queen was engaged during the years which our chapter covers would of course be impossible, or, at least, would reduce us to the necessity of placing before the reader a mere catalogue of events—a dry skeleton with no graces of flesh and blood to relieve it. We might tell of the opening of Victoria Park by Her Majesty in April, 1873, and of the Review of the Troops returned from the Ashantee War, in the following March, when the Queen decorated Sir Garnet Wolseley with the Order of St. Michael and St. George, and Lord Gifford with the Victoria Cross; we might dwell upon the illness of Prince Leopold with typhoid fever a year later, an illness from which he recovered, though his life was at one time despaired of; of the extended tour of the Prince of Wales in India (a kind of triumphal procession through that rich and princely land) in 1876; of the morning State concert at the Albert Hall in the February of that year, when Her Majesty for the first time since the death of the Prince Consort was seen in a place of public amusement; of the opening of a new wing of the London Hospital by the Queen on the 7th of the following month, on which occasion a little sick girl made plaintive request to one of the nurses, "Please do let me see the Queen; I shall be quite better if I see the Queen," and the wish was granted; of the unveiling of the Albert Memorial at Kensington, that splendid token of a nation's gratitude and a Sovereign's love; of Her Majesty's visit to Coburg a few weeks later, when she made a sad pilgrimage to

THE ALBERT MEMORIAL, ERECTED IN HYDE PARK, LONDON.

the grave of her half-sister, Princess Hohenlohe, the "Feodora" of her childhood days; of her proclamation as Empress of India a day or two after her return; of her visit to Lord Beaconsfield at Hughenden Manor in December, 1876, when she and the Princess Beatrice planted trees on the lawn in front of the house; of her procession to Westminster in the following February, when she again opened Parliament in person; of the marriage of one of her grandchildren, the Princess Charlotte of Prussia, early in 1878; of the death in Paris and burial in St. George's Chapel, Windsor, in June of that year, of Her Majesty's cousin, the blind and exiled King of Hanover; of the Naval Review off Spithead in August. And so we might proceed, step by step, to the death of the beloved Princess Alice in December, 1878, exactly seventeen years from the death of the Prince Consort. Here indeed we may fitly pause, for such an event cannot be passed over with quite the same brevity as the others.

The Princess had been at Osborne with all her family in the early part of the year, as full of activity and gentle goodness as ever, and in excellent health. On the 8th of November her eldest child was suddenly attacked with diphtheria, and the devoted mother telegraphed to the Queen from Darmstadt: "Victoria has diphtheria since this morning. The fever is high. I am so anxious."* Then her other little ones were attacked—first, her "precious Aliky," as she called him, then the Princesses "May" and Irène—then her eldest boy, Prince Ernest, and last of all, on the 14th of the month, her husband, the Grand Duke. All recovered but one, the little Princess May, her "sunshine" as the Grand Duchess lovingly spoke of her. She died on the 16th of November, and the grief-stricken mother telegraphed to the Queen: "Our sweet little one is taken. Broke it to my poor Louis this morning; he is better. . . . In great anguish." †
The Queen wrote at once—a letter, we may be sure, that was full of tenderly-worded sympathy, and the Princess in acknowledging it, thus alludes to her loss: "Our sweet May waits for us up there, and is not going through our agony, thank God! Her bright, happy, sunshiny existence has been a bright spot in

* *Princess Alice*, 368. † *Ibid.* 370.

our lives—but oh! how short! I don't touch on the anguish that fills me, but God in His mercy helps me, and it must be borne."* "May" was her brother Ernest's favourite sister, and on the 22nd of November, not knowing she was dead, the young Prince sent her a present of a book, which the poor mother had to make pretence of having delivered. "It made me almost sick to smile at the dear boy," she wrote, "but he must be spared yet awhile what to him will be such a sorrow." † On the 7th of December the Princess was herself taken ill. The day before, she had written out some instructions for a new tutor about the educating of her eldest son. She wished him to be a "truly good man," she said, "in every sense of the word— upright, truthful, courageous, unselfish, ready to help others, modest and retiring"; ‡ and desired his tutor to encourage in him the fear of God and submission to His will.

The condition of the Princess grew rapidly worse, and on the morning of the 13th, the physicians informed her husband that their efforts to save the beloved life were in vain. To enter minutely into the circumstances of the solemn closing scene is not our purpose. At half-past eight the following morning the gentle Princess died peacefully, "murmuring to herself, like a child going to sleep, 'From Friday to Saturday—four weeks— May—dear Papa——!'"

The grief felt in this country at her loss, can only be compared to that which was felt at the death of her father. Her tender love, her simple trust, her self-forgetfulness, her life of active but unobtrusive benevolence, were known to all, and many were the touching tributes to her worth which found their way into the English and German newspapers. A memorial poem in *Truth*, in which she was described as a favourite sister, a darling daughter, a doting mother and a perfect wife, also dwelt feelingly upon her public life as Princess.

"'She being dead yet speaketh'—all may hear
  The message left us by her lovely life
In deeds that live, in actions that endear,
  As Princess, sister, daughter, mother, wife!

* *Princess Alice*, 372.   † *Ibid.* 372.   ‡ *Ibid.* 374.

> "The fierce, rude light that beats upon a throne
>   For which so many royal heads are hid,
>   Served but to make her worth more widely known,
>   To glorify the acts of grace she did.

* * * * *

> "Then let not grief persuade us she is dead;
>   She has but left us for a fairer shore;
>   And though her spirit heav'nward may have fled,
>   Her influence remains for evermore."

The Queen's memorial to the dead Princess was a handsome cross, in Aberdeenshire granite, about twelve feet high, which now stands in the park at Balmoral, to the west of the Castle and not far from the Dee. It bears the inscription :—

To the Dear Memory

OF

ALICE, GRAND DUCHESS OF HESSE,

PRINCESS OF GREAT BRITAIN AND IRELAND,

BORN APRIL 25, 1843; DIED DEC. 14, 1878,

THIS IS ERECTED

BY HER SORROWING MOTHER

QUEEN VICTORIA.

"Her name shall live, though now she is no more."

In March of the following year the Princess's "soldier-brother," the Duke of Connaught, was married to the Princess Louise Margaret, daughter of Prince Ferdinand Charles of Prussia. The Duke was—as, indeed, he still is—the favourite of the Royal Princes, and the English people were glad of the choice which he had made. The ceremony took place at St. George's Chapel, Windsor, on the 13th of the month, and passed off with great éclat and success. The Queen and upwards of thirty Princes and Princesses were present, besides a brilliant assemblage of Ambassadors, Foreign Ministers, Cabinet Ministers, British noblemen and distinguished commoners, to say nothing of a Maharajah (Dhuleep Singh) and a Maharanee. " Ladies in exquisite toilettes filled the stalls appropriated to the Knights of the Garter, where the brasses of more than one ancestor of the bride, Margraves of Brandenburg and Kings of Prussia, are to be found. The eye was almost wearied with the blaze of diamonds in necklaces, in tiaras, and in Orders. The oriental splendour of the Maharajah, and the costume of the Turkish Ambassador, who sat near the spot where is the brass of Abdul Medjid, a past Knight of the Garter, formed a picturesque exception to the Court and military uniforms."*

It was a pretty sight to see the youthful daughters of Princess Christian and the Duchess of Teck looking down from the cabinet above, from which the Queen sixteen years before had witnessed the marriage of the Prince of Wales. The dress in which the bride was married was of heavy white satin, trimmed in the front with Brussels point lace, which had been made especially for Her Royal Highness. This lace was twenty-three inches wide, and its design contained the coat-of-arms of the Duke and Duchess. Round the skirt of the dress ran a pleating of satin and garlands of myrtles (emblematic of the wedding state in Germany) and orange blossoms. The train was six yards in length. The bridegroom was dressed in the dark uniform of the Rifle Brigade, over which were suspended the collars of his various Orders. The Queen wore a black silk dress and a white tulle veil surmounted by a diadem of diamonds, while other diamonds and precious stones sparkled about her person. Chief among these was the celebrated Koh-i-noor, which Her Majesty wore as a brooch, and from which depended a miniature of the Princess Alice. The Archbishop of Canterbury performed the marriage ceremony, and when it was over, and the bride rose from her knees before the altar, the Queen came forward and kissed her affectionately. Then the happy pair entered their carriage, and amid the pealing

* *The Graphic Wedding Numbers*, 20th March, 1879.

of bells, the waving of handkerchiefs, and the hearty cheering of the assembled crowds, drove back to the Castle.

A few months after the wedding there was a "Home-coming" at Balmoral, to welcome the Duke and Duchess, but we must reserve for a time our remarks on this subject, as there are other Highland matters which must engage us first. The Queen's visits to Inverlochy, Inveraray, etc., belong to an earlier date, and now is the time to mention them, if they are to be mentioned at all. The visit to Inverlochy Castle, the seat of Lord Abinger, was in September, 1873, and lasted about a week. There is a very full account of it in the Queen's *Journal*. The country of the Camerons of Lochiel interested Her Majesty greatly, and one most enjoyable afternoon was spent on Loch Arkaig, a lovely piece of water embosomed among thickly-wooded hills. "I feel a sort of reverence," wrote the Queen, "in going over these scenes in this most beautiful country, which I am proud to call my own, where there was such devoted loyalty to the family of my ancestors—for Stuart blood is in my veins, and I am *now* their representative, and the people are as devoted and loyal to me as they were to that unhappy race."* On alighting from the little screw steamer the Royal party drove through the Dark Mile, a beautiful road so called from the number of trees which overshadow it on the one side, and of beetling rocks which darken it on the other. They saw here a cave in which Prince Charles Edward was once hidden for a week.

Another day there was a visit to the Pass of Glencoe, and to Ossian's Cave, which overlooks the celebrated glen; and near the cave they sat down, and the Queen began sketching. But there were interruptions. "Here, in this complete solitude," writes her Majesty, "we were spied upon by impudently inquisitive reporters, who followed us everywhere; but one in particular (who writes for some of the Scotch papers) lay down and watched with a telescope and dodged me and Beatrice and Jane Churchill, who were walking about, and was most impertinent when Brown went to tell him to move, which Jane herself had thought of doing."† In fact, words rose so high

* *More Leaves*, 255. † *Ibid.* 262, 263.

that they almost came to blows, and the "impertinent individual," as Her Majesty calls the reporter, flatly told the indignant Brown that he had as much title to remain where he was as the Queen of Great Britain herself, with more in a similar strain, till his brethren of the quill came up, and advised him to retire.

On leaving Inverlochy Castle the Royal party drove to Banavie, where they stepped on board a vessel which had been chartered for their use, and steamed along the Caledonian Canal, through Lochs Lochy, Oich, and Ness, as far as Dochgarroch, where they landed. Here carriages were waiting for them, and they drove to Inverness, the streets of which were lined with Volunteers, and bright with decorations and arches. Thence they proceeded by train to Ballater, where an open landau and four was in readiness to convey them to Balmoral.

The visit to Inveraray, the seat of the Duke of Argyll, father-in-law of the Princess Louise, lasted, like the visit to Inverlochy, about a week. It was made in the autumn of 1875. The Royal party arrived at Inveraray Castle about one o'clock in the afternoon, on the 22nd of September, and were received by the Duke and Duchess in true Highland state. "After lunch," says the Queen, "we went into the large drawing-room, next door to where we had lunched in 1847, when Louise was only two years old. And now I return, alas! without my beloved husband, to find Lorne my son-in-law."* During Her Majesty's stay at Inveraray there was a ball of the Campbells, at which between eight and nine hundred people were present. On this occasion the Princess Louise danced a reel with Brown, and the Princess Beatrice another with one of the Duke's foresters. During a part of the festivities a Gaelic song was sung by some of the people. Next day the Princess Louise introduced a Miss M'Gibbon to the Queen, a "good old lady," says Her Majesty, "who was too ill to come out and see me. She patted Louise on the shoulder, and said: 'We are so fond of the Princess; she is a great pet.' Louise said, 'Lorne was her great pet,' and she answered, 'Yes, he is; and so you are a double pet.'"†

* *More Leaves*, 291. † *Ibid.* 301.

The poor old lady died not long after perpetrating this lamentable joke.

The principal events in the Queen's Scottish life in the year 1876 were the unveiling of a statue of the Prince Consort at Edinburgh (a most successful ceremony), and the presentation of colours by Her Majesty to the *Royal Scots*, in an open space outside Ballater. Of the latter event the Queen writes: "Nothing could be finer. A great many people were there, it is said between two and three thousand; but none of the spectators were in uniform. . . . [After the Royal salute], came the trooping of the colours, with all its peculiar and interesting customs, marching and counter-marching, the band playing the fine old marches of the 'Garb of old Gaul' and 'Dumbarton Drums,' also the march from the 'Fille du Régiment,' which was evidently played as a compliment to me, whom they considered as 'born in the regiment,' my father having commanded it at the time I was born. Then came the piling of the drums and the prayer by Mr. Middleton, minister of Ballater, after which the new colours were given to me. I handed them to the two sub-lieutenants who were kneeling, and then I said the following words:—

"'In entrusting these colours to your charge, it gives me much pleasure to remind you that I have been associated with your regiment from my earliest infancy, as my dear father was your Colonel. He was proud of his profession, and I was always told to consider myself a soldier's child. I rejoice in having a son who has devoted his life to the army, and who, I am confident, will ever prove worthy of the name of a British soldier. I now present these colours to you, convinced that you will always uphold the glory and reputation of my First Regiment of Foot—the Royal Scots.'

"Colonel M'Guire then spoke a few words in reply, and brought the old colours to me, and begged me to accept them. In doing so, I said I should take them to Windsor, and place them there in recollection of the regiment and their Colonel. Then they marched past well (they were fine men), and after the Royal salute gave three cheers for me. The 79th kept the ground, and took charge of the old colours. We left at once." *

It was while in her beloved Highlands in the summer of 1879 that the awful tidings reached Her Majesty of the death of the Prince Imperial, the widowed Empress Eugénie's only son. "At twenty minutes to eleven," writes the Queen on the 19th of June, "Brown knocked and came in, and said there was bad news; and when I, in alarm, asked what, he replied, 'The young French Prince is killed;' and when I could not take it in, and asked several times what it meant, Beatrice, who then came in with the telegram in her hand, said, 'Oh! the Prince Imperial is killed!' I feel a sort of thrill of horror now while I write the words." † Confirmation of the terrible news arrived in due course from Natal, telling how the Prince, while out on a reconnaissance from Colonel Wood's camp, had been set upon by a number of Zulus, and assegaied before he could get back into his saddle. "Poor, poor dear Empress!" wrote the horror-stricken Queen, "her only—only child—her all gone!" ‡ and she at once brought her stay at Balmoral to a close, and hurried back to London.

In the autumn, when the Court again went North, the Duke and Duchess of Connaught came on a visit to Balmoral, and, needless to say, they were both warmly welcomed by the Queen. Her Majesty met them at a little distance from the Castle, and gave her daughter-in-law a nosegay of heather. Near Balmoral bridge an arch had been erected of moss and heather, on one side of which was wrought in flowers: " Welcome to Balmoral—Ceud mille Failte," and on the other the initials, A. W. and L. M. Three days afterwards they all went off to the Duke of Connaught's cairn, accompanied by the keepers and servants and their families. "When we had got to the top," writes the Queen, "and had our glasses filled, and were standing close to the cairn, Dr. Profeit, with a few appropriate words complimentary to Arthur, and with many good wishes for both, proposed their health, which was drunk with three times three. Then Arthur, with great readiness,

* *More Leaves*, 331-333.   † *Ibid*. 381.   ‡ *Ibid*. 382.

returned thanks in a little speech. My health followed, also with loud cheering. . . . Fern (who with the other dogs was there) resented the cheering, and barked very much. We all placed a stone on the cairn, on which was inscribed:—

ARTHUR, DUKE OF CONNAUGHT AND STRATHEARN,
MARRIED TO PRINCESS LOUISE MARGARET OF PRUSSIA,
13TH MARCH, 1879.

After a few minutes we left. . . ."*

When in London the following year the Queen called to see the Duchess of Westminster (née Lady Constance Gower), who was confined to her house through ill-health—the beginning of an illness which terminated fatally. The Duchess's brother, Lord Ronald Gower, thus refers to the event:—" Her Majesty drove to Grosvenor House after being at the garden party this afternoon (13th of July) at Marlborough House. It was seven when the Queen drove into the courtyard of Grosvenor House. Princess Beatrice came also, but only the Queen and Lilah Ormonde went upstairs to my sister's room. Nothing could equal the Queen's most touching and affecting kindness—her dear eyes full of tears, and her look full of infinite compassion. Constance met her outside the sitting-room, where I left them alone together. How gladly would one lay down one's life for such a Queen and friend!" †

But it is in the cottages of the poor, rather than in the mansions of the great and wealthy, that the sympathy of the Queen is specially to be noted. It moves us more to see Her Majesty in widow Grant's humble dwelling, holding the dying woman's hand, than at the Duchess's side in the sick-room of Grosvenor House. Among the poor of Windsor, Osborne, and Balmoral the name of the Queen is a synonym for all that is generous and kind and sympathetic, and this has been the case for years. The stories of her active benevolence which are current in those places would fill a good-sized volume, and still there would be more to tell! At one time we find her in the cottage of a gamekeeper, who has met with an accident that afterwards

* *More Leaves*, 392, 393. † *My Reminiscences*, vol. ii. 342.

THE QUEEN IN A COTTAGE HOME.

proves fatal. Directly she hears of the man's condition she sends off one of her physicians to his aid, and then follows herself in a carriage laden with articles that might be useful. When the man dies, she drives over on the day of the funeral to speak a word of comfort to his bereaved sisters. At another time we find her at Monaltrie, Crathie, visiting a sorrowing couple, whose two sons have been drowned in the Dee. She leaves £10 with the afflicted parents, and when the father dies, rather suddenly, some years later, she calls again, and again leaves a substantial gift. She is very simply dressed on this occasion—in a long black cloak and an old-fashioned black hat, so that the heart-broken widow may be under no restraint in her presence. At another time—a day of wind and sleet—when she is driving past a certain cottage in her carriage, she notices that some thatch has been blown away from the roof. The horses are pulled up at her command, and the Sovereign enters the humble dwelling. She finds a woman in bed, and on the coverlet of the bed are two or three basins placed there to catch the copious drippings from the roof. Her Majesty leaves soon after, with an assurance that all shall be put right; and in due course workmen arrive at the cottage, and everything is made comfortable for the needy inmate.

Here is another story. At some time during the period of which we are writing, though of the exact year we have no record, there lived in the neighbourhood of Balmoral an old man and his wife who had notice to quit their home. Being greatly attached to the place, they refused to go, whereupon they were forcibly ejected, and their furniture cast out into the road. The Queen happened to see them in this outcast condition, and ordered inquiries to be made. On learning that misfortune and not idleness had been the cause of their destitution, and that they were really deserving people, she provided them with a house on the Balmoral estate. The old man, it appears, had a somewhat tragic history behind him, and the Duke of Albany, Prince Leopold, would sometimes get him to talk over his adventures, which, we may be sure, he was not unwilling to do.

Speaking of the Prince, we may as well embrace this opportunity of alluding to his marriage. His bride was the Princess Helen of Waldeck, but it is said that he had previously made an unsuccessful proposal for the hand of an English heiress, a young lady of spirit, who afterwards married his college chum, Lord Brooke. The Princess's parents, as well as her brother-in-law and sister, the King and Queen of the Netherlands, were present at the Royal wedding, which was celebrated at St. George's Chapel, Windsor, on the 27th of April, 1882. Claremont was assigned to the Scholar-Prince and his young wife as their future residence.

The only important public function at which the Queen was present, in the interval between the marriage of the Duke of Albany and the Princess Beatrice, if we except a Review of the Troops returned from Egypt in St. James's Park, was the opening of the Royal Courts of Justice on the 9th of December, 1882. "Punctuality is the motto of British Royalty, and punctually at 10.55 the Queen left Windsor in the train which was to reach London at half-past eleven. A field-marshal's escort of the Blues, on their coal-black horses, was in attendance at the station, and on the platform were the Duke of Westminster, Master of the Horse; the Duchess of Bedford, Mistress of the Robes; the Lord Chamberlain, the Earl of Kenmare; and Earl Sydney, the Lord Steward. Five Royal carriages, with the well-known dun horses, and postillions and outriders in scarlet and white, were waiting, and in the first of these the Queen took her seat, accompanied by the Princess Christian and the Princess Beatrice. Through Hyde Park, down Constitution Hill, past St. James's Palace (where the Duchess of Cambridge was at the window), through Pall Mall and the Strand, the carriages drove rapidly—the crowds growing denser and the cheering louder as they advanced. For the latter part of the way the road was kept by a thin red line of Guardsmen in addition to the police; while at Waterloo Place and Trafalgar Square, and where the two great lines of traffic from north and south converge upon the Strand in Wellington Street—the point of greatest pressure along the

T

route—detachments of the Household Cavalry were drawn up, and effectually, though in Wellington Street not without difficulty, prevented the cordon from being broken. The crowds on the pavements and at the windows, the always bright and often tasteful profusion of decorations, the gleam of steel as the troops along the line presented arms, and the heartiness of the popular welcome were evidently much enjoyed by the Queen, who repeatedly bowed in acknowledgment.

"The reception at the doorway was so quickly over that it seemed to the spectators scarcely a moment before the procession was again moving towards the dais, while an invisible band played the march from *Athalie*, and the whole great assemblage rose in homage. In front of the procession came the architects and builders, the Law Officers of the Crown, the Judges, the Lord Chancellor, the First Commissioner of Works, and the Chancellor of the Exchequer, and then the Queen, attended right and left by the Lord Chamberlain and the Lord High Steward, and followed by the Home Secretary, the members of the Royal Family and of the Royal Household. The Princes, who had arrived before the Queen, and for whom a reception-room had been set apart, wore their Benchers' gowns over military uniforms, and the Princesses simple morning dresses. Arrived at the dais, the Home Secretary led the Queen to her Chair of State, while the Princes and Princesses ranged themselves behind, and the Judges sat in two half circles on either side. The key, a massive work in polished steel, with the monogram R.C.J. (Royal Courts of Justice) and the Royal standard on a shield, was now handed to Her Majesty by the Commissioner of Works, and by her intrusted to the Home Secretary, while she read in clear and distinct tones, amidst a death-like silence, the speech delivering it into the charge of the Lord Chancellor. This done, she took the key once more, and gave it to Lord Selborne, who received it kneeling, and then delivered an address in reply. The Archbishop of York, the only prelate present who wore episcopal lawn and scarlet hood, now offered up a prayer; and Sir W. Harcourt then announced that he had received Her Majesty's commission to declare the building open, a fanfare of trumpets accompanying the announcement." * Some further forms and ceremonial, but only of minor importance, followed, and then Her Majesty bowed to the spectators, and withdrew.

We now return to Balmoral. Incidental reference was made a page or two back to a review of the troops engaged in the Egyptian campaign of 1882, and we may remind the reader that one of the Queen's sons took an active part in that campaign—we refer to the Duke of Connaught. He sailed with the troops for Alexandria in August of the year named, and Her Majesty's anxiety (augmented by the recollection of the death of the Prince Imperial) may be easily imagined. On the 11th of September, while the Court was in Scotland, she received a telegram in cipher, marked *very secret*, which said that it was "determined to attack the enemy with a very large force on Wednesday." "How anxious this made us," writes the Queen, "God only knows." On the day before the battle Her Majesty wrote: "I prayed earnestly for my darling child, and longed for the morrow to arrive. Read Körner's beautiful *Gebet vor der Schlacht:* '*Vater, ich rufe Dich*' [Prayer before the Battle: 'Father, I call on Thee']. My beloved husband used to sing it often. My thoughts were entirely fixed on Egypt and the coming battle." † The following day the battle of Tel-el-Kebir was fought, and in due course came a telegram with the welcome news: "A great victory; Duke safe and well," which the Queen at once communicated to the anxious Duchess. Later, came a longer telegram, equally satisfactory, and concluding with the stimulating words: "Duke of Connaught is well, and behaved admirably, leading his brigade to the attack," an item of news which gave a delightful piquancy to the Royal ladies' already overflowing joy.

About an hour later, the Duke and Duchess of Albany (Prince Leopold and his young wife) arrived at Ballater, and this being their "Home-coming," they were welcomed in the festive manner usual at Balmoral on such occasions. The pipers preceded the carriage, playing the "Highland Laddie,"

* *The Graphic*, 9th December, 1882. † *More Leaves*, 396, 397.

Brown and all the Queen's kilted men walked alongside, and behind came the tenants of the three estates (Balmoral, Birkhall, and Mains) and the rest of the servants. After the healths had been drunk, and a Highland cheer given for the Duke and Duchess of Albany, Her Majesty asked the Duke to propose "The Victorious Army in Egypt," coupling with it the name of his soldier-brother, and the toast was received with great heartiness. Then "The Duchess of Connaught" was given; and after that the health of "The Little Princess," their daughter, who was witnessing the proceedings in high good-humour from the nurse's arms. They then returned to the Castle, and the day which had begun in so much anxiety ended with jubilates.

Such is life! Sorrow and joy, shade and shine, thorn and flower, singularly interwoven: of which things the Queen has had her share. Would you wish for a more striking illustration of the truth? Here it is. We have been speaking of the happy Home-coming of the Duke of Albany—alas! we have now to record his death. Readers of this biography will have noticed that Prince Leopold was, from the first, the sickly one of the Royal Family. Four times had he been given back to them from the very brink of the grave. His fifth illness proved fatal.

In March, 1884, the Prince went to Cannes to avoid the inclement east winds, leaving his wife and little daughter behind him at Claremont. Two or three weeks went by, and he appeared to be deriving considerable benefit from the change, when he had the misfortune to fall and injure his knee. This was on the 27th of March. The knee that was hurt had been the source of some trouble on other occasions, but no serious consequences were anticipated, and the Prince wrote to the Duchess on the same day, making light of the accident. The following night he was seized with an apoplectic fit, and before four o'clock in the morning he expired in the arms of his equerry, Captain Perceval. Long disciplined in sorrow, the Queen's first thought appears to have been the young widow at desolate Claremont, and she controlled her own grief in order to be of use by her presence and sympathy there. The remains were brought to England for burial in the crypt of St. George's Chapel, Windsor; and on the day of the funeral Her Majesty was present in the Chapel during the greater part of the service. She rose when the coffin was brought in, and again when the choir sang the anthem, "Blest are the Departed;" and when the Dean of Windsor had recited, "Earth to earth, ashes to ashes, dust to dust," she quietly withdrew with the Princesses.

At Balmoral there is a favourite forest walk of the Queen round the east side of Craig Gowan, and near this walk is a memorial chair to Prince Leopold. It is of Peterhead granite, and stands in a hollow, wooded with drooping birches. The date of the Prince's death is inscribed on the stone, and also the following quaint lines:—

> "Whoe'er is distant,
> He is always near;
> Never so ever near
> As now he's gone."

In the early part of the ensuing year (1885) the news of the fall of Khartoum and the death of its heroic defender, General Gordon, came as a severe blow to Her Majesty. Her sympathy for the family of the brave General was expressed in an autograph letter to Gordon's sister, from which we quote. It was dated from Osborne, the 17th of February, 1885. "*How* shall I write to you, or how shall I attempt to express *what I feel!* To think of your dear, noble, heroic brother, who served his country and his Queen so truly, so heroically, with a self-sacrifice so edifying to the world, not having been rescued—that the promises of support were not fulfilled, which I so frequently and constantly pressed on those who asked him to go—is to me *grief inexpressible!*—indeed, it has made me ill. My heart bleeds for you, his sister, who have gone through so many anxieties on his account, and who loved the dear brother as he deserved to be. . . . My daughter Beatrice, who has felt quite as I do, wishes me to express her deepest sympathy with you. I hear so many expressions of sorrow and sympathy from *abroad;* from my eldest daughter, the Crown Princess, and my cousin, the King of the Belgians, the very warmest. Would you express to your other sisters, and your elder brother, my true sympathy, and—what I do so keenly feel—the *stain* left upon England for your dear brother's cruel though heroic fate." * Miss Gordon gave the Queen a well-worn Bible which had belonged to the General, and which he had had in use many years—a souvenir which was much prized by Her Majesty. The volume now lies on a white satin cushion, in an enamel and crystal case, beside a marble bust of the General in the south corridor of Windsor Castle.

Sorrow and joy, we say again—shade and shine! The same year that witnessed the death of General Gordon witnessed also the marriage of Princess Beatrice, the Queen's youngest child. The Prince who had won her affections was (alas, that we should have to speak of him as no longer among us!) the third son of Prince Alexander of Hesse, and he first became acquainted with the English Royal Family in 1884 on the marriage of his brother, Prince Louis of Battenberg, to Victoria of Hesse, the eldest daughter of Princess Alice. His attachment for Princess Beatrice soon became apparent, and on the 23rd of July, 1885, their hands were joined by the Archbishop of Canterbury in the little village church at Whippingham. Princess Beatrice was now Princess Henry of Battenberg, and the Queen had seen the last of her children united in the bonds of matrimony.

Early in the following year (1886) Her Majesty again opened Parliament in person, going to the House of Lords in the famous State carriage, which was drawn, as on former occasions, by eight cream-coloured ponies. The enthusiasm which marked her progress thither was hardly less hearty than when she had opened her first Parliament, nearly half-a-century before.

Nearly half-a-century before! Yes—for the year of Jubilee was drawing near, and already that interesting event was engaging the thoughts of loyal and patriotic Englishmen the wide world over. On the 4th of May, 1886, the Colonial and Indian Exhibition was opened by the Queen at South Kensington; and

* *The Letters of General C. G. Gordon to his Sister, M. A. Gordon.*

this was the last great public function in which she was engaged before the eventful year began. The actual promoter of the Exhibition was the Prince of Wales, who received Her Majesty in the great hall of the building, amid a flourish of trumpets and the acclamations of a vast number of spectators. A very distinguished company were present, among them being the

HIS ROYAL HIGHNESS THE PRINCE OF WALES.
Photo. by T. C. TURNER.

Duke of Connaught and several Royal ladies. The two Princes kissed the Queen's hand at the beginning of the ceremony, and she kissed them both on the cheek, after which the Prince of Wales conducted Her Majesty to the Royal dais, where she took her seat on the throne. Two verses of the National Anthem having been sung—the first verse in English and the second in

Sanskrit—Madame Albani, supported by a picked choir, sang an Ode, which had been specially written for the occasion by the Poet-Laureate (Tennyson) and set to music by Sir Arthur Sullivan.

> "Welcome, welcome with one voice!
> In your welfare we rejoice,
> Sons and brothers that have sent,
> From isle and cape and continent,
> Produce of your field and flood,
> Mount and mine and primal wood;
> Works of subtle brain and hand,
> And splendours of the morning land,
> Gifts from every British zone;
> Britons, hold your own!"

These were the opening lines of the Ode, and it was noticed that after every verse the Queen smiled her thanks to the singer and clapped her hands.

When the Prince had read an address, in which the nature and purpose of the Exhibition was set forth, Her Majesty rose, and made the following reply:—"I receive with the greatest satisfaction the address which you have presented to me on the opening of this Exhibition. I have observed with a warm and increasing interest the progress of your proceedings in the execution of the duties intrusted to you by the Royal Commission, and it affords me sincere gratification to witness the successful results of your judicious and unremitting exertions in the magnificent exhibition which has been gathered together here to-day. I am deeply moved by your reference to the circumstances in which the ceremony of 1851 took place, and I heartily concur in the belief you have expressed that the Prince Consort, my beloved husband, had he been spared, would have witnessed with intense interest the development of his ideas, and would, I may add, have seen with pleasure our son taking the lead in the movement of which he was the originator. I cordially concur with you in the prayer that this undertaking may be the means of imparting a stimulus to the commercial interests and intercourse of all parts of my dominions, by encouraging the arts of peace and industry, and by strengthening the bonds of union which now exist in every portion of my Empire."

Another flourish of trumpets followed the Lord Chamberlain's declaration that the Exhibition was open; and after prayer by the Archbishop of Canterbury, and the Hallelujah Chorus, Madame Albani sang "Home, Sweet Home," with thrilling effect. The Queen then bowed to the company, and stepping down from the dais, traversed the whole length of the Exhibition building, amid loud and long-sustained applause. That concluded the ceremony, which had been planned and carried through with equal success.

The opening of this truly interesting Exhibition was, as we have said, the last great public function in which Her Majesty took part before the celebration of her Jubilee. Some weeks later—on the 21st of June, 1886—the eventful year opened; and, at this point, our chapter may fitly close.

CHAPTER XIII.

THE JUBILEE AND AFTERWARDS.
(1887-1896.)

STRICTLY speaking the Queen's Jubilee year began on the 21st of June, 1886, but by the Sovereign's desire it was not formally celebrated until the year had run its course. In the meantime, the Queen's popularity suffered no diminishment by her visit to the East End of London in May, 1887, to open the People's Palace. The poor of the neighbourhood turned out in their thousands from slums and lodging-houses to see the Royal procession pass, and Her Majesty and the Prince of Wales were loudly cheered. Nor did Her Majesty lose prestige in India, when, on the 16th of February, 25,000 prisoners were released from Indian gaols in honour of the coming event. Other events of lesser importance, but connected in one way or another with the Jubilee, preceded the grand celebration in June — notably, the opening of two Jubilee Exhibitions — one at Manchester on the 4th of May by the Prince and Princess of Wales, and the other at Saltaire by the Princess Beatrice two days later. Then there was a reception by the Queen at Windsor of the Colonial Delegates early in the same month; and on the 9th the Lord Mayor and a deputation from the Corporation of London presented Her Majesty with an address of congratulation.

Jubilee Day, the 21st of June, 1887, was kept as a general holiday throughout the kingdom. Long before morning dawned the crowds had begun to assemble along the route of the procession from Buckingham Palace to Westminster Abbey; and a

THE JUBILEE AND AFTERWARDS.

clear starlit sky and strong easterly wind gave cheerful promise of Queen's weather on the coming day. These early arrivals beguiled the tedium by watching the carpenters and upholsterers, who were industriously at work throughout the night adding finishing touches to balconies and triumphal arches, erecting Venetian masts, fixing up flags and scrolls and pennons, hanging festoons of evergreens and loyally-worded banners across the streets—in short, making such decorative preparations as London had not seen the like of since the Queen had passed through it on the day of her Coronation, nearly fifty years before. One of the lettered decorations ran thus:

"Piccadilly rings with cheers,
Telling the love of fifty years."

Another:

"O Lord, stretch forth Thy mighty hand,
And bless our Queen and fatherland."

"Give you good greeting," ran a third; while Piccadilly Hall exhibited the loyal device: "*Dieu protège la Reine.*"

Cheering began even before the procession set out from the Palace. It happened that the crowds gathered on the westward side of the Mall and in the Green Park espied Her Majesty at one of the windows, gazing upon them, and this evident token of her interest in her people loosened their tongues, and a tremendous shout of welcome went up. Sharp on the stroke of eleven a fanfare of trumpets and the stirring strains of the National Anthem announced that the first procession had begun to move. This procession included the foreign Sovereigns and their representatives, as well as most of the Ambassadors, and as one after another was recognised—the King and Queen of the Belgians, the Kings of Saxony, Denmark, Greece, etc.—hearty cheers were given. It was fully half-an-hour later before the chief procession set out, and the anxiously waiting multitudes were apprised of that event by a sudden call to the soldiers, who were keeping the way of the procession, to stand to attention. Was it then that the poet got his inspiration for those stirring lines:—

> " Now the winter of sorrow is over,
>   And the season of waiting is done,
> 'Mid acclaim of the people who love her
>   Our Lady steps forth in the sun ;
> The green earth beneath and the blue sky above her,
> She walks in the sight of the millions who cover
>   The realms she hath welded to one !
> 'Tis Jubilee here, and 'tis Jubilee yonder,
> As far as the sun round her empire doth wander,
> From the east to the west wakes the world in her honour,
> The sunrise and sunset flash splendours upon her,
>   Now winter is over and done !"*

After the officers had given the word of command, there was another fanfare of trumpets and, with that, a rattle of kettle-drums, and then several of the bands started playing simultaneously. All the carriages in the procession of foreign Sovereigns and Ambassadors had been closed; but with the exception of the State carriage itself, there were only open carriages in the procession of which the Queen formed a part. A detachment of Life Guards led the way, and then came sundry aides-de-camp and equerries and the brilliant staff of the Commander-in-Chief. The first carriages to appear were those of the ladies-in-waiting: then the Prince of Wales's daughters drove by, and the Princesses Beatrice and Louise, who were cordially received. At last, the famous cream-coloured horses came in sight, and a whisper thrilled through the thronging multitudes : " The Queen is coming !" The hush of expectancy at this point was almost painful, but it was only momentary. On the first glimpse of their Sovereign, the long-controlled enthusiasm of the people burst forth, and the strains of the combined bands were completely drowned in the spontaneous shouts of welcome that arose. Hats and handkerchiefs were waved excitedly, and as Her Majesty again and again bowed her acknowledgments, it was evident that she was deeply touched. Seated with her in the carriage were her eldest daughters, the Crown Princess of Germany, and the Princess of Wales, who, we need scarcely add, were not without their meed

---

* *Buchanan Ballads*, quoted from memory.

of welcome. The cheering, thus begun, was carried on along the miles of eager spectators until the Abbey was reached. The Queen's carriage was followed by a brilliant cavalcade of horsemen, composed of the Queen's sons, sons-in-law, grandsons, and grandsons-in-law, some Indian cavalry, and the field officer's escort of the 1st Life Guards. The Prince of Wales and his brothers, the Dukes of Edinburgh and Connaught, rode in a line, and were also loudly cheered.

Inside the venerable Abbey the scene was indescribably grand, and not a few who were present afterwards confessed that they found it difficult to restrain their emotion. The nave and Royal dais were carpeted with crimson, the stalls and benches of the canons and prebendaries were draped in cloth of indigo blue, while the sun's rays, shining through the stained-glass windows, threw prismatic tints upon a variety of objects. Needless to say, the Abbey was thronged with spectators. Nobles and Ministers; Members of Parliament and provincial mayors; barristers, literary men and learned professors; officers of the Army, the Navy, and the Volunteers; and last (perhaps chiefest from a pictorial point of view) fair ladies of high and gentle birth—the flower of the land—in dresses of all colours, from white to deepest purple, from saffron to the most delicate mauves. In the sacrarium was quite a unique gathering of Princes and Highnesses of Oriental fame, whose names and titles would fill a closely-printed page. These were the Maharajah and Maharanee of Kuch Bahar, the Rao of Kutch, and the magnificent Holkar in his diamonds and imposing turban: there were three Thakur Sahibs and His Highness Abu'n Nasr Mirza Hissam us Sultaneh of Persia, and deputies from a Rajah, two Maharajahs and a Nizam; Siam was represented by Prince Devawongse Varoprakar, Japan by Prince Komatsu, and far-off Hawaii by its dusky Queen, the wife of Kalakaua.

As the Queen's procession entered the Abbey, the corps of Royal trumpeters, stationed in the organ loft, sounded a stirring fanfare, and at once the organ pealed forth. Every eye was now strained to catch a glimpse of the Royal Lady who formed the central object of that magnificent pageant—the only Queen in history who had celebrated her jubilee! Presently, amid another flourish of the silver trumpets, Her Majesty entered, preceded by Garter King-at-Arms and escorted by the Lord Chamberlain and the Lord Steward, and immediately the vast assemblage rose, in token of respectful homage. She advanced to the dais, and the other Royalties present—nearly seventy in number—arranged themselves about her in natural order of precedence. In every sense the scene was "a worthy memorial of the golden wedding of the Queen and the nation." Then the service commenced. The officiating clergy were the Archbishop of Canterbury, the Dean of Westminster, and the Bishop of London; while Dr. Bridges presided at the organ, and a choir of 300 voices did justice to the solemn music, a portion of which had been selected by the Queen herself from the compositions of the Prince Consort. Ah! if he had only been there to share her welcome!

The service over, the prescribed ceremonial was at an end, but the family character of the gathering around the Queen gave rise "to a display of affection, loyalty, and devotion between the Sovereign and the assembled Princes and Princesses of her own House, undreamt of in the Lord Chamberlain's philosophy. First, the Prince of Wales saluted Her Majesty on the hand, and received in return a kiss on the cheek. The Crown Prince and the Grand Duke of Hesse paid their homage likewise, but retired without the gracious salute of the Royal lips. Then, carried away by the impulse of the moment, Her Majesty embraced all the Princes and Princesses of her family with manifest emotion, and to complete the tenderness and pathos of the scene, called back the Crown Prince and the Grand Duke of Hesse with a winning smile, to confer upon them the privilege they had failed to receive or to claim."* With that, the organ pealed forth again, and amid the stirring strains of the priests' march in *Athalie*, the brilliant assemblage melted away; and in a little while the processions re-formed, and returned to the Palace.

The presents made to the Queen in commemoration of her

* *The Times*, 22nd June, 1887.

Jubilee considerably exceeded 700, and they were afterwards exhibited at St. James's Palace and the Bethnal Green Museum, where people came in their thousands to see them. Of caskets alone, containing addresses from the provinces of India, there were nearly 100, some of which were of silver, beautifully chased, and others of exquisitely carved ivory or sandal-wood. The Emperor of China sent a number of costly gifts, including a sceptre, a pair of ancient vases, and some curious needlework; while an enterprising firm of English florists sent a bouquet of rare orchids, valued at several hundred pounds. The bouquet stood nearly five feet high without its pedestal, and was about twenty feet in circumference! This gift made almost literal the figurative language of the poet:—

> " Empress and Queen, the *flowers* and fruits of nations
> Are heaped upon the footstool of thy throne,
> Amid the thronging hosts, the acclamations,
> And music out of silver trumpets blown." *

But the most interesting of all the gifts was the Women's Jubilee Offering, which, though intended to be only a *penny* subscription, reached the enormous sum of £75,000. Many singular instances of loyalty—in some cases humorous, in others pathetic—came under the notice of the collectors for this Offering. Thus, one old woman, so poor that she was often glad to make a meal out of the leavings of others, reproached a lady-collector in her district for not calling upon her, and protested that she would rather go without food for a day than miss the opportunity of contributing. An Irish woman, with a young family and a husband earning only eleven shillings a-week, insisted on giving a shilling, in spite of the assurance that a penny would be amply sufficient; while another observed: " I haven't got a penny, black or white, to-day, but I'll have it on Monday, be sure, for she's worthy of it." A fourth, also an inhabitant of the Green Isle, somewhat mistook the purpose of the subscription, and on parting with her contribution said:

* *Buchanan Ballads*—quoted from memory.

"Well, there's a penny, and I'm sorry to hear the dear Queen's in such need; but sure, that'll help to pay her passage to Ireland!" We must not omit to add that the bulk of the money thus collected was invested in a fund which had for its worthy object the benefit of nurses ministering among the sick poor.

Her Majesty's Scotch servants and tenantry presented her with a statue of herself in bronze by the late Sir Edgar Boehm, which was unveiled by the Prince of Wales, but the ceremony was not of a public character. The statue stands in the eastern part of the park, facing the life-size bronze of the Prince Consort, of which we have elsewhere spoken. Though the presentation and unveiling of this statue were strictly private, the ceremony may be classed as among the most interesting of the ceremonies of the Jubilee year. It opened with the Hundredth Psalm and prayer by Mr. Campbell, of Crathie, after which the Prince unveiled the statue, and made the presentation in an appropriate speech. Then Dr. Profeit read an address of congratulation; and the Queen replied in the following words:—"I thank you all most heartily for your loyal and kind address, and for the statue so beautifully designed, which you have presented to me on the occasion of my completing the fiftieth year of my reign, and which will be a lasting memorial of the affection I shall always have for my Highland home. I am deeply touched at the grateful terms in which you have alluded to my long residence among you. The great devotion shown to me and mine, and the sympathy I have met with while here, have ever added to the joys and lightened the sorrows of my life, but I miss many kind faces of old friends, now no longer with us—friends who would have rejoiced so much at the proceedings of this day, if they had been present. I heartily reciprocate your good wishes, and trust that we may all still look forward to many happy days together." It is rarely that Her Majesty's self-command fails, but on this occasion she is said to have been much affected, especially in that part of the speech wherein she alluded to the great changes that had taken place on the estate. Do we wonder?*

We may remark that the Queen *gave* as well as received gifts during her year of Jubilee. Medals struck to commemorate the occasion were sent as marks of special distinction to noblemen and others whom she honoured with her friendship; and not a few old servants and cottars, both at Balmoral and Osborne, became the envied recipients of the pretty Jubilee brooch, a tiny gold sceptre topped with a pearl, to the centre of which is affixed a crown of gold filigree set with tiny pearls.†

During the rest of June and the first fortnight in July, there was plenty to remind one that the Jubilee year was still running. The very day after the grand celebration at the Abbey a monster Jubilee treat was given to 27,000 children of the metropolitan schools in Hyde Park, and Her Majesty graciously drove thither to watch the little ones enjoying themselves. Then, on the same day, she unveiled a statue of herself at Windsor, and afterwards accepted the "Women's Jubilee Offering," of which we have already spoken. On the 23rd there was a Jubilee Thanksgiving at St. Paul's Cathedral, and on the 28th a great Jubilee ball at the Mansion House, at which several thousand distinguished persons were present, including four Kings and a bewildering number of English and foreign Princes. On the 2nd of July, 25,000 Volunteers marched past Her Majesty at Buckingham Palace, and on the 9th she held a grand review of 60,000 Regulars, Militia, and Volunteers at Aldershot. Between these two dates a State ball was given at the Palace, and the Queen went in person to South Kensington to lay the first stone of the Imperial Institute.

On the latter occasion an enormous pavilion, with accommodation for nearly 12,000 spectators, was erected, and, needless to say, this huge tent was packed to overflowing. Gazing upon the vast concourse, "the mind," says a *Times'* writer, "unconsciously reverted to the Jubilee Thanksgiving in

* *The Queen at Balmoral*, 62, 63.   † *Ibid.* 100.

Westminster Abbey. The scene was felt by all who witnessed it to be a happy sequel and a fitting complement to that historic scene." It was a day of hopeful anticipation, for the fact was being emphasised, as perhaps it had never been emphasised before, that "the triumphs of peace have contributed more than those of war to the greatness of our empire."*

As we conclude our references to this memorable year, we feel that our biography, too, is drawing to a close. There is not much left to tell.

Towards the end of August, 1888, the Queen went to Glasgow, and opened the new Municipal Buildings, erected at a cost of £500,000. The weather was superb, and the reception of Her Majesty was all that the most loyal-hearted could have wished. After driving through the principal streets of the city, she paid a visit to the International Exhibition, which had been opened by the Prince and Princess of Wales in the previous May.

On May-day of this year (the 12th of May) a little incident occurred, which illustrates the Queen's love of rural customs, and which will possibly interest the reader quite as much as accounts of State balls and processions, and the like. "As Her Majesty was driving in the neighbourhood of Windsor, she met some village children marching with their May-pole and singing their songs. She stopped her carriage, and asked them to sing to her, which they readily and gladly did, of course; and she gave them ten shillings for the feast, which is an indispensable part of the May-day village fête."†

Here is another Windsor story. In February, 1889, the Queen was driving along Thames Street, Windsor, accompanied by one of the Princesses, when her attention was attracted by a blind man, who was playing "Abide with me" on an accordion. On passing Windsor Bridge Her Majesty instructed the gate-keeper to give the old musician a florin in her name, a command which was instantly obeyed. The old man's pleasure on hearing from whom the gift had come may be imagined.

* *The Times*, 5th July, 1887. † *Life at Balmoral*, 161, 162.

But we have not yet done with the year 1888. Early in March the Emperor William I. of Germany passed away at the age of ninety-one. He had been a true friend of the Queen, and his name was greatly respected on both sides of the Channel. Alas! the equally-respected Crown Prince of Germany, the husband of our Princess Royal, and son and successor of the Emperor William, was destined to survive his father only a few months. In the interval, the Queen crossed to Germany, and paid a visit of condolence to the late Emperor's widow, the Empress Augusta. She also called upon her son-in-law, the new Emperor, who at that time was still hopeful of recovery; and Her Majesty was deeply struck with the patience and unselfish heroism which the Imperial sufferer displayed. What the Queen by her loving sympathy could do, she did; but alas! it was not in her power to avert the awful stroke that was soon to make her eldest child a widow! The Emperor Frederick died in June, and a grandson of Her Majesty — the present Emperor — ascended the Imperial Throne.

During the Queen's stay abroad this year she visited the Emperor Francis Joseph at Innsbrück, and for the first time set foot on Austrian territory. The visit was quite informal, but the railway station at which she alighted was prettily decorated with Alpine flowers and hothouse plants. The correspondent of a London daily newspaper wrote: "All along the line for miles the peasants in their picturesque holiday attire collected in crowds on the bare chance of seeing the great Empress of India sweep past their Alpine hamlets. I heard one honest Tyrolean burgher exclaim: 'I am resolved to see the most powerful of potentates;' and on being driven off the line, he, resolute in his determination, actually scaled the station building, and was discovered perched on the chimney-pot."

In the spring of the following year Her Majesty visited Biarritz in company with the Princess Beatrice, and occupied the picturesque and finely-situated villa of the Count de Rochefoucauld. The Count spared neither trouble nor expense in fitting up the place as became a Royal residence, and the Queen freely expressed her delight in the splendid results achieved. Not only was his library thrown open to Her Majesty and the Princess, but those things which virtuosos are usually so chary of trusting from their sight—his fine-art books and folios of choice French water-colour drawings—were placed at the disposal of the visitors. When out driving on one occasion, the Queen is said to have alighted near the breakwater, where an old man was fishing with a rod and line. Her Majesty approached him, and inquired: "What are you hoping to catch?" "Louvines, your Majesty," replied the angler. Surprised at being recognised in what was quite an out-of-the-way place, the Queen inquired: "How do you know who I am?" "No one could take you for anything but a Queen," returned the man—a compliment which was as neatly spoken as it was unexpected.

Wales was re-visited by her Majesty in August of this year (1889)—the first time since 1852, when Prince Albert was with her—and the Queen gave much pleasure in the Principality by addressing remarks to the people in their native dialect. Thus at Pale, where she was presented with a walking-stick, she said in Welsh: "I am very much obliged indeed to you;" and at Bala, in acknowledging the gift of a painting of Bala Lake, she said in the same tongue: "It is extremely beautiful. How kind of you!"

The visit to Wales was preceded by a visit to the Prince of Wales at Sandringham, where the tenants presented the Queen with an address of welcome. Her Majesty replied as follows: "It has given me great pleasure to receive your loyal address, and I thank you sincerely for the terms in which you welcome me to Sandringham, and for the kind expressions which you have used towards the Prince and Princess of Wales. After the anxious time I spent here seventeen years ago, when, by the blessing of God, my dear son was spared to me and to the nation, it is indeed a pleasure to find myself here again, among cheerful homes and cheerful faces, and to see the kind feeling which exists between a good landlord and a good tenant; and I trust that this mutual attachment and esteem may long continue to make you happy and prosperous, and to strengthen, if possible, the affection of the Prince and Princess of Wales for the tenants of Sandringham."

Anon, came a wedding in the family of the Prince and Princess. Their own silver-wedding had been celebrated at a grand banquet the year before, at which the Queen was present; and now, on the last Saturday of July, 1889, their eldest daughter, Princess Louise of Wales, was married to the Duke of Fife. The Queen is said to have risen early on the marriage morning, and to have sent a letter of congratulation to the bride by special messenger before the ceremony took place. The Princess was married in the private chapel of Buckingham Palace, Her Majesty's presence on the occasion and her evident good humour testifying her hearty approval of the union.

Other events which must not be passed over were the birth of a little Prince of the House of Battenberg at Balmoral, in October, 1891, and his baptism in the drawing-room of the Castle on the 29th of the month. Four years previously, a little Princess (Victoria Eugénie of Battenberg) had been born at Balmoral—a circumstance to be noted, as she was the first Royal child born in Scotland since 1600. At the birth of her little brother in 1891, "a bonfire was kindled on Craig Gowan, gillies, keepers, cottars — men, women, and childen, marched up, preceded by the music of the bagpipes, carrying their flaming torches of pine. After the bonfire was kindled, they fell to dancing on the flat, rocky space reserved for that purpose."* Then as to the christening. The last Royal christening in Scotland had taken place in 1594, when the hero of the ceremony was Prince Henry, a son of James VI. The ceremony of 1891 was performed by Dr. Cameron Lees, of St. Giles', Edinburgh, and the gold font which had been used at the christening of the Queen's children was brought into requisition. Her Majesty held the baby, who wore the historic white christening robe, which had served for so many little princes and princesses before him; while, to sustain the

* *Life at Balmoral,* 166.

Scottish character of the picture, the happy father stood by, wearing the Royal Stuart tartan.

Those are halcyon days for the Queen's grandchildren when they are staying with their Grandmother at Windsor, Osborne, or Balmoral. No one understands children better than Her Majesty, and no one better loves to see them happy. She never wearies of their shouts and laughter, and many are the Royal "treats" with which she takes pleasure in surprising them. So recently as June, 1892, Pinder's Circus came to Balmoral by Her Majesty's command, to the no small delight of the little Battenberg Princes and Princess, who were staying at the Castle. "Pinder's was formerly a successful circus, but somehow it had run down, apparently through no fault of Pinder, unless it were inability to cope with business, an inability he shares with many excellent men. At any rate, whatever the cause, the circus had steadily declined till it was reduced to a few shabby caravans, with gilt much tarnished, and hopelessly dirty—dirt seeming to have an affinity with fallen fortunes. In this plight, it arrived and camped on the moor at Ballater. While moving to and from Braemar, it had been met by the Queen . . . and Pinder's Circus was summoned to perform at Balmoral. . . . A field outside the gate and close by the Dee had been chosen for the performance. The Queen had dispatched messengers to summon her tenantry from her three estates. The little Battenberg children came from the Castle, together with all the children from manse, farmhouse, and cottage. The Queen drove down in her carriage and sat through the two hours' performance, apparently with as much enjoyment as the children. The horses, though few, were good, and there was a delightful performing donkey; and donkey, horses, and Pinder, all did their very best, warmed and cheered by the rays of Royalty. After it was over, Pinder was summoned to Her Majesty's carriage, and in the course of the conversation that ensued, she intimated her desire to buy the delightful performing donkey. But it was not his to sell, he regretfully said, 'but I'll be very happy, your Majesty, to buy and train one for you.' She made him a personal gift of money, besides that paid in the way of business by her commissioner, together with a jewelled scarf-pin, and he departed rejoicing."*

The year at which we have arrived (1892), had opened very sadly with the death of the Duke of Clarence, eldest son of the Prince of Wales, an event which must be yet fresh in the minds of the majority of our readers. He caught a chill while standing in the bitter cold by the grave of the Prince Victor of Hohenlohe—influenza and pneumonia supervened, and on the 14th of January he lay dead. A touching feature in this sad case was the young Prince's engagement to the amiable and beautiful Princess May, to whom he was to have been married in the following month. The outburst of sympathy with the Royal Family and the Princess was universal and sincere. The coffin lay for some time in the church of St. Mary Magdalene, at Sandringham, where the villagers and others flocked to see it; and it was then removed to St. George's Chapel, Windsor, where the funeral service took place. The Duke of Clarence was an amiable and modest Prince, of an earnest, affectionate nature, and though possessed of no striking abilities, he had what was infinitely more precious, a heart that sympathised with suffering in whatever form and whatever condition of life.

In March and April, Her Majesty spent over a month at Costebelle, a charming spot in the south of France, and prior to leaving, she endowed four beds in the Hyères Infant Asylum in commemoration of the visit. The remainder of the spring and the whole of the autumn was spent at Balmoral, and the summer months at Osborne, where her grandson, the young Emperor of Germany, was her guest. At Windsor, in the same year, she had two interesting visitors—one from Siberia, in the person of Miss Kate Marsden, the lepers' friend, and the other from Liberia, in the shape of an old negress, named Mrs. Martha Ricks. The latter, who had travelled over 3500 miles to see the Queen, was a little woman, seventy-six years of age, who had formerly been a slave. The good old lady had been saving up for this visit for nearly fifty years, and directly she

---

* *Life at Balmoral*, 85–88.

had accumulated sufficient for her purpose, she had taken her passage over to this country. Moreover, she had made a quilt for presentation to Her Majesty—a beautiful piece of needlework, representing on a white satin ground the coffee trees of Liberia, with the berries in all stages of fruition. "Our only friend was England," she told a reporter, "and our mother the Queen. Once we put our foot down in England we were free. We all loved England much, and we wanted to see her noble people and her Queen. We called her our mother, and call her mother now. I want to go to London to see the Queen. I know I cannot speak to her, but I hope to see her pass along, and then I will return to my farm in Liberia, and die contented. The Lord told me I should see the Queen, and I know I will." Her Majesty received the stout-hearted little woman very graciously, shaking her by the hand, and conversing with her; and Mrs. Martha Ricks went back to her farm in Liberia amazed and delighted.

In the succeeding year the two great State events were the opening of the Imperial Institute by the Queen, and the marriage of the Duke of York (Prince George of Wales) to the Princess May. Both events are still too fresh in people's minds to call for any detailed description. The Institute was opened on the 12th of May, and once more the heavens were propitious, for the weather throughout the day was simply faultless. There were three distinct processions, each interesting in its way, though the Queen's, of course, took the palm. In the first were the Dukes of Connaught and Edinburgh with their wives and children; in the second (which started from Marlborough House, not Buckingham Palace) were the Prince of Wales, Prince George of Wales, and his betrothed, the Princess May; and last of all came the great procession—the Queen's—upon which the interest of the public naturally centred. The inevitable outrider in scarlet gave earliest warning of Her Majesty's approach; then a detachment of Household Cavalry came in sight, proceeding at a walking pace; then a lumbering succession of garishly decorated State-coaches, containing the Maids of Honour, the Officers of the Royal household, etc.; then more cavalry, and some Colonial and Indian troops; then a Royal carriage containing Prince Christian and Prince Henry of Battenberg, closely followed by another detachment of troops; last of all the "cream" ponies came in sight, with their gold and crimson trappings, and eyes were strained and necks craned eagerly forward to catch a sight of the Empress-Queen. We have exhausted our adjectives when describing previous processions of Her Majesty, so how shall we speak of the outbursts of welcome with which her presence was greeted on this occasion? Enough to say that there was no falling off in the popular enthusiasm—that the cheers were as hearty, spontaneous, and well-sustained as ever—not at one point in the procession merely, but all along the route from Buckingham Palace to the Institute.

Inside the great building the ceremony was regal in the extreme. Her Majesty looked rather tired, but abating none of her customary dignity, she was helped on to the dais, and at once seated herself with an expression of relief in the chair prepared for her. Without much delay the Prince of Wales read his short address, expressing the hope that the Institute would promote the technical, scientific, and commercial progress of Her Majesty's Empire; to which address the Queen, still seated, read a reply; after which Madame Albani sang, with a sweetness all her own, the National Anthem; the Archbishop of Canterbury pronounced the benediction, and the Prince of Wales declared the Institute open. A golden key, exquisitely bejewelled, was then handed to the Queen, who fitted it to the ward of a sort of automatic slot-machine hard by—turned it—and immediately some bells high up in the Queen's Tower rang out a responsive peal. Then the Park guns boomed forth, and every one knew that the ceremony was complete.

In the following June the Queen went to Kensington Gardens to unveil a statue of herself by her gifted daughter, the Princess Louise. There was a brilliant assemblage to receive her, including quite a surprising progeny of sons, daughters, and grandchildren, but unfortunately the proceedings were a little marred by the rain. The sculptor-Princess herself placed in Her Majesty's hand the cord which drew the covering from the statue; whereupon the Queen handed the cord to the Prince of Wales, and the Prince, on his part, deputed the actual performance of the ceremony to two artillery-men. Her Majesty said: "I thank you very heartily for your loyal address, and for the kind wish to commemorate my jubilee by the erection of a statue of myself on the spot where I was born and lived till my accession. It gives me great pleasure to be here on this occasion, in my dear old home, and to witness the unveiling of this fine statue, so admirably designed and executed by my daughter." For the benefit of those who have not seen the statue, we may say that it is in marble, and represents the Queen at the time of her accession. The Portland-stone pedestal contains the following inscription:—

VICTORIA R.
1837.

In front of the Palace where she was born and where she lived till her Accession, her loyal subjects of Kensington place this statue, the work of her Daughter, to commemorate fifty years of her reign.

The great pageant of the year was, of course, the bridal procession of the Duke of York and the Princess May, when once more the Queen came forward and showed herself in public to her subjects.

The marriage took place on the 6th of July, and—need we say it?—the weather was again superb. The streets of the metropolis once more put on their holiday attire, and all London turned out to bid God-speed to the young bridegroom and his bride. The Sailor-Prince had already won golden opinions in the Navy, and the Princess had endeared herself to all by her beauty, gentleness, and worth—in fact, they both had everything to recommend them, and the greatest city in the world received them with a fervour of enthusiasm which will not soon be forgotten. The ceremony took place in the Chapel Royal, St. James's, in the presence of a brilliant company—including, besides English Royalties, the King and Queen of the Belgians, the King and Queen of Denmark, the Czarewitch, Prince Henry of Prussia, and the Grand Duke of Hesse.

From photo, by] [*Messrs. W. & D. Downey.*
FOUR GENERATIONS:
THE QUEEN, PRINCE OF WALES, DUKE OF YORK, AND INFANT.

Every one stood up as the Queen's procession entered, and as it moved slowly down the aisle, Her Majesty halted once or twice and bowed graciously—now to the left and now to the right—in response to the respectful homage of the company. During the marriage-service proper, the entire audience rose again and remained standing, with the exception of the Queen. A breathless silence is said to have fallen when the Archbishop pronounced the words : " If any one knows any just cause of impediment why this man and this woman should not be joined together in holy matrimony"—for here he came to a dead stop, as though waiting for a voice to answer. It was a relief to all when he resumed the argument of the service, which, we are happy to add, was marked by no more such awkward pauses.

About a year later Her Majesty received a telegram from White Lodge, Richmond, the residence of the young couple, announcing that the Duchess had given birth to a son; and on the 16th of July, the bells of Richmond pealed merrily in honour of the christening of the little Prince. His great-grandmother, the Queen, drove over from Windsor to take part in the ceremony, and was warmly received all along the route, though the day was miserably wet. The Prince and Princess of Wales, all the members of the Royal Family in England, the Czarewitch, and the Princess Alix assembled in the drawing-room of the White Lodge, where the famous golden font was placed before a floral screen. Her Majesty sat in front of the font, with the Royal Family grouped round her—a remarkable gathering, representing four generations of British Royalty. The Queen herself " handed the baby to the Archbishop of Canterbury, and the Duke of York pronounced his names — Edward Albert Christian George Andrew Patrick David. Twelve Royal sponsors answered for the baby, and after the ceremony the names were signed in the baptismal register and in the Queen's private record book."*
A photograph was afterwards taken of the four generations, the Queen holding her great-grandchild. Our picture on the previous page is a reproduction of this.

* *Events of the Year* (1894).

Earlier in the year the Queen was again abroad — at Florence and Coburg. At the former place she was visited by the King and Queen of Italy; and at Coburg Her Majesty attended the wedding of the Grand Duke of Hesse, who married a Princess of Saxe-Coburg-Gotha. It was eighteen years since the Queen had been in "dear Coburg," the birthplace of her husband, and the people received her with unbounded enthusiasm. When she left for England she sent an autograph letter to the Burgomaster of the town, expressing her thanks for the "happy days" spent there—a letter that was, of course, made public, and increased (if that were possible) the Queen's popularity among the good Coburgers.

Towards the close of the year—namely, the 14th of November, 1894—there were floods at Windsor, where the Court was then staying, and Her Majesty, with her wonted kindness, exerted herself in behalf of her poorer neighbours, who suffered greatly by the inundation. Many hundred gallons of soup were made in the Royal kitchen, and distributed to the flooded-out families; and in various other ways the wants of the sufferers were ministered to by the Sovereign. For a time the Royal borough was deprived of gas, and at the Castle itself they had to make shift with lamps and candles.*

In the spring of 1895 the Queen crossed over to Cherbourg in the *Victoria and Albert,* on a visit to Cimiez (Nice) and Darmstadt. At Darmstadt she stayed with the Grand Duke and Duchess of Hesse, and received visits from another of her grandsons, the German Emperor, and from her eldest daughter, the widowed Empress Frederick. She returned to Windsor early in May, and on the 24th of that month, her seventy-sixth birthday was celebrated at the Castle with unwonted jubilations. The Shahzada, Nasrullah Khan, son of the Ameer of Afghanistan, was received in audience by the Queen on the 25th; and three days later the Court went to Balmoral. During the month spent here, there was but one noteworthy event—the burning of Mar Lodge, the Duke of Fife's House, on the 14th of June. Her Majesty drove over to the fire and watched it for some

* *Events of the Year* (1894).

time. She saw but few visitors while in Scotland, but on her return to Windsor, her time was much taken up with receiving and entertaining guests. Then, about the middle of July Her Majesty went to Osborne, where the Court remained till the last week in August. The German Emperor came over for the Cowes Regatta, and the Queen gave a grand banquet in the Indian Room of Osborne House in his honour. On returning to Balmoral for the autumn, she took a great interest in the re-building of Mar Lodge, the foundation-stone of which she laid on the 15th of October. Her Majesty went out almost every day, her favourite drive being the beautiful old road leading through the forest of the Balloch Buie to Dantzig Shiel, among heather, birches and Scotch firs. Occasionally she drove over to Abergeldie and took tea with the Empress Eugénie.

Christmas was spent at Osborne, where the Queen was surrounded by her children and grandchildren, and where the Christmas-trees were lighted up as of old, and little hearts were made merry with the gifts which kindly Santa Claus, through the medium of loving parents and indulgent relations, supplied each tiny stocking. As in former days, the Royal table groaned beneath the mighty baron of beef, the boar's head, and the huge game-pie; and when the great Christmas pudding was brought in, the little Battenberg children clapped their hands and shouted just as their mother and the rest of the Queen's children may have done in the dear, dear times of long ago. Happy children! They knew not what heaviness of sorrow the coming year had in store for them. Alas! they know it now —and we all know it. The sad death of their father, from the effects of West African fever contracted in the Ashanti Expedition, is an event of yesterday. The news came to this country like a shock, for the lamented Prince had made his home with us ever since his marriage to the Princess Beatrice, and Englishmen had learnt to esteem him like one of their own princes. His body was embalmed and brought to England, and on the 5th of February, all that was mortal of Prince Henry of Battenberg was borne, with soldiers' honours, to its last resting-place. He had been married to our English Princess in

Whippingham Church, and in Whippingham Church he now lies, awaiting, we trust, a glorious resurrection.

About a week later the *Gazette* contained the following letter from the Queen, gratefully acknowledging the sympathy of her subjects in her fresh bereavement:—

"OSBORNE, 14*th Feb.*, 1896.

"I have, alas! once more to thank my loyal subjects for their warm sympathy in a fresh grievous affliction which has befallen me and my beloved daughter, Princess Beatrice, Princess Henry of Battenberg.

"This new sorrow is overwhelming, and to me is a double one, for I lose a dearly loved and helpful son, whose presence was like a bright sunbeam in my Home, and my dear daughter loses a noble devoted husband to whom she was united by the closest affection.

"To witness the blighted happiness of the daughter who has never left me, and has comforted and helped me, is hard to bear. But the feeling of universal sympathy, so touchingly shown by all classes of my subjects, has deeply moved my child and myself, and has helped and soothed us greatly. I wish from my heart to thank my people for this, as well as for the appreciation manifested of the dear and gallant Prince who laid down his life in the service of his adopted country.

"My beloved child is an example to all in her courage, resignation, and submission to the will of God.

"VICTORIA, R.I."

As soon after the funeral as was practicable, the widowed Princess, with her four children, went abroad, their destination being Cimiez (Nice)—the same spot where the Queen had stayed the previous spring. Here, on the 11th of March, they were joined by Her Majesty, who, as we write these words (29th April), is still staying there. The Hôtel de Cimiez has been fitted up for her temporary residence, and in this place she receives almost daily visits from the Princess, who resides at the adjacent Villa Liserb. They may be seen driving about in the neighbourhood, the scenery of which is charming—a paradise of terraced gardens, and steep hillsides with luxurious vegetation, with glimpses of blue sea and still bluer sky. Among the many distinguished persons who have called upon the Queen at Cimiez may be mentioned the Emperor and Empress of Austria, the King of the Belgians, the Prince of Wales, the Dowager-Empresses of Germany and Russia, and the ex-Empress Eugénie. The Queen visits but little herself; but on the 12th of April she called upon the Marquis and Marchioness of Salisbury at their villa at Beaulieu, near Nice, and took tea with them. On the 28th of April a deputation of eight fish-wives, attired in the picturesque costume of their class, visited the Hôtel de Cimiez and presented a basket of splendid roses to Her Majesty.*

* * * * *

Our task is now done. We have followed the Queen from her cradle to the present time—a period of seventy-seven years. Her Majesty has now filled the throne for a longer period than any British Sovereign with but one exception—her grandfather, George the Third. George reigned fifty-nine years and ninety-five days, and on the 24th of September of the present year (1896)—should the Queen be spared to see that not distant day—she will have beaten the record. During her long reign Her Majesty has seen much of sorrow and much of joy, but in every vicissitude the same queenly dignity, the same gentle womanliness, and the same Christian sobriety, have distinguished her. She has, indeed, approved herself in all things a *pattern* Queen.

That Her Majesty may continue, for many years, to occupy the throne which she has filled with such distinction for so long, is the wish of the writer of these pages, as it is the prayer of her loyal subjects throughout her vast Empire.

* *The Echo,* 29th April, 1896.

THE END.

CATALOGUE
OF
S. W. PARTRIDGE & CO.'S
POPULAR ILLUSTRATED BOOKS,
CLASSIFIED ACCORDING TO PRICES.

NEW BOOKS ARE MARKED WITH AN ASTERISK.

5s. each.
By G. MANVILLE FENN.
Illustrated by W. RAINEY, R.I., and F. W. BURTON.

*Cormorant Crag: A Tale of the Smuggling Days. Large Crown 8vo. Illustrated. Cloth extra, gilt top.

First in the Field: A Story of New South Wales. Large Crown 8vo. Illustrated. Cloth extra, gilt top.

Steve Young; or, The Voyage of the "Hvalross" to the Icy Seas. Large crown 8vo. Fully Illustrated. Cloth extra, gilt.

Grand Chaco (The): A Boy's Adventures in an Unknown Land. Crown 8vo. Fully Illustrated. Cloth extra, gilt edges.

Crystal Hunters (The): A Boy's Adventures in the Higher Alps. Crown 8vo. Fully Illustrated. Cloth extra, bevelled boards, gilt edges.

3s. 6d. each.

*In Battle and Breeze. Sea Stories by Geo. A. Henty, G. M. Fenn, and W. Clark Russell. Illustrated. Large Crown 8vo. Cloth extra.

Ailsa's Reaping; or, Grape-Vines and Thorns. By Jennie Chappell, Author of "For Honour's Sake," "Her Saddest Blessing," etc. Illustrated. Crown 8vo. Cloth extra, gilt edges.

Gathered Grain: Consisting of Select Extracts from the Best Authors. Edited by E. A. H. Fourth Edition. Crown 8vo. Cloth. (Not illustrated.)

Hymn Writers and their Hymns. By Rev. S. W. Christophers. 390 pages. Crown 8vo. Cloth extra. (Not illustrated.)

More Precious than Gold. By Jennie Chappell, Author of "Her Saddest Blessing," etc. With Illustrations. Crown 8vo. Cloth extra, gilt edges.

The Adventures of Don Lavington. By George Manville Fenn, Author of "Cormorant Craig," etc. Illustrated by W. Rainey, R.I. Large Crown 8vo. Cloth extra, gilt top.

'Neath April Skies; or, Hope Amid the Shadows. By Jennie Chappell, Author of "Ailsa's Reaping," "Wild Byronie," "Her Saddest Blessing," etc. Illustrated. Crown 8vo. Cloth extra, gilt edges.

Romance of Lincoln's Inn (A). By Sarah Doudney, Author of "Through Pain to Peace," "Louie's Married Life," "When We Two Parted," etc. Crown 8vo. Illustrated. Cloth boards.

3s. 6d. each (continued).

Robert Aske: A Story of the Reformation. By E. F. Pollard. Illustrated by C. J. Staniland, R.I. Crown 8vo. Cloth extra, gilt edges.

Six Stories by "Pansy." Imperial 8vo. 390 pages. Fully Illustrated and well bound in cloth, with attractive coloured design on cover, and Six complete Stories in each Vol. Vols. 1, 2, 3, and 4, 3s. 6d. each.

Pilgrim's Progress (The). By John Bunyan. Illustrated with 55 full-page and other Engravings, drawn by Frederick Barnard, J. D. Linton, W. Small, and engraved by Dalziel Brothers. Crown 4to. Cloth extra, 3s. 6d. (Gilt edges, 5s.)

Story of the Bible (The). Arranged in Simple Style for Young People. One Hundred Illustrations. Demy 8vo. Cloth extra, 3s. 6d. (Gilt edges, bevelled boards, 4s. 6d.)

Vashti Savage. By Sarah Tytler. Illustrated by Robert Barnes. Crown 8vo. Cloth extra, gilt edges.

Wild Bryonie; or, Bonds of Steel and Bands of Love. By Jennie Chappell, Author of "Her Saddest Blessing," etc. Illustrated. Crown 8vo. Cloth extra, gilt edges.

2s. 6d. each.

*Brought to Jesus: A Bible Picture Book for Little Readers Containing Twelve large New Testament Scenes, printed in colours, with appropriate letterpress by Mrs. G. E. Morton, Author of "Story of Jesus." Size, 13½ by 10 inches. Handsome coloured boards with cloth back.

Bible Pictures and Stories. Old and New Testament. In one Volume. Bound in handsome cloth, with eighty-nine full-page Illustrations by Eminent Artists.

Light for Little Footsteps; or, Bible Stories Illustrated. By the Author of "Sunshine for Showery Days," "A Ride to Picture Land," etc. With beautiful coloured Cover and Frontispiece. Full of Pictures.

Ride to Picture Land (A): A Book of Joys for Girls and Boys. By R. V., Author of "Sunshine for Showery Days." With charming coloured Frontispiece, and full of beautiful Pictures for Children. Paper boards, with coloured Design on cover.

Story of Jesus. For Little Children. By Mrs. G. E. Morton, Author of "Wee Donald," etc. Many Illustrations. Imperial 16mo.

Sunshine for Showery Days: A Children's Picture-Book. By the Author of "A Ride to Picture Land," "Light for Little Footsteps," etc. Size, 15½ by 11 inches. Coloured Frontispiece, and 114 full-page and other Engravings. Coloured paper boards, with cloth back.

Spiritual Grasp of the Epistles (The); or, an Epistle a-Sunday. By Rev. Charles A. Fox, Author of "Lyrics from the Hills," "Ankle Deep; or, The River of Pentecostal Power," etc. Small Crown 8vo. Cloth boards. (Not illustrated.)

2s. 6d. each (continued).

THE "RED MOUNTAIN" SERIES.

Crown 8vo. 320 Pages. Illustrated. Handsomely bound in cloth boards. 2s. 6d. each.

- **Green Mountain Boys (The)**: A Story of the American War of Independence. By Eliza F. Pollard, Author of "True unto Death," "Roger the Ranger," "Not Wanted," "Florence Nightingale," etc., etc.
- **Spanish Maiden (The)**: A Story of Brazil. By Emma E. Hornibrook, Author of "Borne Back," "Worth the Winning," etc. Illustrated by E. J. Walker.
- **Great Works by Great Men**: The Story of Famous Engineers and their Triumphs. By F. M. Holmes, Author of "Chemists and Their Wonders," "Four Heroes of India," etc.
- **By Sea-Shore, Wood, and Moorland**: Peeps at Nature. By Edward Step, Author of "Plant Life," "Dick's Holidays," etc. Upwards of Two Hundred Illustrations.
- **Eaglehurst Towers.** By Emma Marshall, Author of "Fine Gold," etc.
- **Eagle Cliff (The)**: A Tale of the Western Isles. By R. M. Ballantyne, Author of "Fighting the Flames," "The Lifeboat," etc. New Edition. Illustrated by W. H. Groome.
- **Edwin, The Boy Outlaw**; or, The Dawn of Freedom in England. A Story of the Days of Robin Hood. By J. Frederick Hodgetts, Author of "Older England," etc.
- **Grace Ashleigh**; or, His Ways are Best. By Mary D. R. Boyd. With Eight full-page Engravings by Robert Barnes.
- **Lady of the Forest (The).** By L. T. Meade, Author of "Scamp and I," "Sweet Nancy," etc.
- **Leaders Into Unknown Lands**: Being Chapters of Recent Travel. By A. Montefiore, F.G.S., F.R.G.S. Maps, etc.
- **Lion City of Africa (The)**: A Story of Adventure. By Willis Boyd Allen, Author of "The Red Mountain of Alaska," etc.
- **"Not Wanted"**; or, The Wreck of the "Providence." By Eliza F. Pollard, Author of "Robert Aske," etc.
- **Olive Chauncey's Trust.** By Mrs. E. R. Pitman, Author of "Lady Missionaries in Foreign Lands."
- **Roger the Ranger**: A Story of Border Life among the Indians. By Eliza F. Pollard, Author of "Not Wanted," etc.
- **Red Mountain of Alaska (The).** By Willis Boyd Allen, Author of "Pine Cones," "The Northern Cross," etc.
- **True unto Death**: A Story of Russian Life and the Crimean War. By Eliza F. Pollard, Author of "Roger the Ranger."
- **Whither Bound?** A Story of Two Lost Boys. By Owen Landor. With Twenty Illustrations by W. Rainey, R.I.
- **Young Moose Hunters (The)**: A Backwoods-Boy's Story. By C. A. Stephens. Profusely Illustrated.

1s. 6d. each.

NEW SERIES OF MISSIONARY BIOGRAPHIES.

Crown 8vo. 160 pages. Cloth extra. Fully Illustrated.

***Missionary Heroines in Eastern Lands.** By Mrs. E. R. Pitman, Author of " Lady Missionaries in Foreign Lands."

***Congo for Christ (The)**: The Story of the Congo Mission. By Rev. J. B. Myers (Association Secretary of the Baptist Missionary Society), Author of " William Carey," etc.

***Japan: Its People and Missions.**

Amid Greenland Snows; or, The Early History of Arctic Missions.

Among the Maoris; or, Daybreak in New Zealand. A Record of the Labours of Samuel Marsden, Bishop Selwyn, and others.

Bishop Patteson, the Martyr of Melanesia.

David Brainerd, the Apostle to the North American Indians.

By Jesse Page.

Griffith John, Founder of the Hankow Mission, Central China. By William Robson, of the London Missionary Society.

Henry Martyn: His Life and Labours—Cambridge, India, Persia. By Jesse Page, Author of " Samuel Crowther," etc.

John Williams, the Martyr Missionary of Polynesia. By Rev. James J. Ellis.

James Calvert; or, From Dark to Dawn in Fiji. By R. Vernon. Fully Illustrated.

James Chalmers, Missionary and Explorer of Rarotonga and New Guinea. By William Robson.

Lady Missionaries in Foreign Lands. By Mrs. E. R. Pitman, Author of " Vestina's Martyrdom," etc.

Madagascar: Its Missionaries and Martyrs. By William J. Townsend, Author of " Robert Morrison," etc.

Robert Morrison, the Pioneer of Chinese Missions. By William John Townsend.

Reginald Heber, Bishop of Calcutta, Author of " From Greenland's Icy Mountains." By A. Montefiore, F.R.G.S.

Robert Moffat, the Missionary Hero of Kuruman. By David J. Deane.

Samuel Crowther, the Slave Boy who became Bishop of the Niger. By Jesse Page.

CATALOGUE OF NEW & POPULAR WORKS. 7

1s. 6d. each.

MISSIONARY BIOGRAPHIES (*continued*).

Thomas Birch Freeman, Missionary Pioneer to Ashanti, Dahomey, and Egba. By Rev. John Milum, F.R.G.S.

Thomas J. Comber, Missionary Pioneer to the Congo. By Rev. J. B. Myers, Association Secretary, Baptist Missionary Society.

William Carey, the Shoemaker who became the Father and Founder of Modern Missions. By Rev. J. B. Myers.

NEW POPULAR BIOGRAPHIES.

Crown 8vo. 160 pages. Maps and Illustrations. Cloth extra.

***General Gordon, the Christian Soldier and** Hero. By G. Barnett Smith.

***William Tyndale, the Translator of the** English Bible. By G. Barnett Smith.

***Sir John Franklin and the Romance of the** North-West Passage. By G. Barnett Smith.

***John Knox and the Scottish Reformation.** By G. Barnett Smith.

Canal Boy who became President (The). By Frederic T. Gammon. Twelfth Edition. Thirty-fourth Thousand.

David Livingstone: His Labours and His Legacy. By Arthur Montefiore, F.G.S., F.R.G.S.

Four Heroes of India: Clive, Warren Hastings, Havelock, Lawrence. By F. M. Holmes.

Florence Nightingale, the Wounded Soldier's Friend. By Eliza F. Pollard.

Gladstone (W. E.): England's Great Commoner. By Walter Jerrold. With Portrait and thirty-eight other Illustrations.

Michael Faraday, Man of Science. By Walter Jerrold.

"One and All." An Autobiography of Richard Tangye, of the Cornwall Works, Birmingham. With Twenty-one Original Illustrations by Frank Hewett. (192 pages.)

Slave and His Champions (The): Sketches of Granville Sharp, Thomas Clarkson, William Wilberforce, and Sir T. F. Buxton. By C. D. Michael.

Henry M. Stanley, the African Explorer. By Arthur Montefiore, F.G.S., F.R.G.S.

Spurgeon (C. H.): His Life and Ministry. By Jesse Page.

Two Noble Lives: JOHN WICLIFFE, the Morning Star of the Reformation; and MARTIN LUTHER, the Reformer. By David J. Deane. (208 pages.)

Through Prison Bars: The Lives and Labours of John Howard and Elizabeth Fry, the Prisoner's Friends. By William H. Render.

Over 325,000 of these popular volumes have already been sold.

1s. 6d. each.

ILLUSTRATED REWARD BOOKS.

Crown 8vo. 160 pages. Cloth extra. Fully Illustrated.

*Duff Darlington; or, An Unsuspected Genius. By Evelyn Everett-Green. With six Illustrations by Harold Copping.

*Aileen; or, "The Love of Christ Constraineth Us." By Laura A. Barter, Author of "Harold; or, Two Died for Me," "Marjory; or, What Would Jesus Do?" etc.

*Ted's Trust; or, Aunt Elmerley's Umbrella. By Jennie Chappell, Author of "Who was the Culprit?" "Losing and Finding."

*Sisters-in-Love. By Jessie M. E. Saxby, Author of "Dora Coyne," "Sallie's Boy," etc. Illustrated by W. Rainey, R.I.

*Thomas Howard Gill: His Life and Work. By Eliza F. Pollard, Author of "Florence Nightingale," etc.

Best Things (The). By Dr. Newton. New Edition. Handsomely bound in cloth boards, and beautifully illustrated.

Clovie and Madge. By Mrs. G. S. Reaney, Author of "Our Daughters," "Found at Last," etc.

Dairyman's Daughter (The). By the Rev. Legh Richmond, M.A.

Everybody's Friend; or, Hilda Danvers' Influence. By Evelyn Everett-Green, Author of "Barbara's Brother," "Little Lady Clare," etc.

Fine Gold; or, Ravenswood Courtenay. By Emma Marshall, Author of "Eaglehurst Towers," "A Flight with the Swallows," etc.

Good Servants, Good Wives, and Happy Homes. By Rev. T. H. Walker.

Her Two Sons. A Story for Young Men and Maidens. By Mrs. Charles Garnett, Author of "Mad John Burleigh," etc.

Hilda; or, Life's Discipline. By Edith C. Kenyon.

Jack's Heroism. A Story of Schoolboy Life. By Edith C. Kenyon.

Little Princess of Tower Hill (The). By L. T. Meade, Author of "Sweet Nancy," etc.

Lads of Kingston (The). By James Capes Story.

Like a Little Candle; or, Bertrand's Influence. By Mrs. Haycraft, Author of "Little Mother," etc.

Marigold. By L. T. Meade, Author of "Lady of the Forest," etc.

Mrs. Lupton's Lodgings. By Laura M. Lane, Author of "Living it Down," "Heroes of Every-Day Life," etc.

Martin Redfern's Oath. By Ethel F. Heddle.

CATALOGUE OF NEW & POPULAR WORKS. 9

1s. 6d. each.

ILLUSTRATED REWARD BOOKS (*continued*).

Nature's Mighty Wonders. By Rev. Dr. Newton. New Series. Handsomely bound in cloth boards and beautifully Illustrated.

Nella; or, Not My Own. By Jessie Goldsmith Cooper.

Our Duty to Animals. By Mrs. C. Bray, Author of "Physiology for Schools," etc. Intended to teach the young kindness to animals. Cloth, 1s. 6d.; School Edition, 1s. 3d.

Prue's Father; or, Miss Prothisa's Promise. By Ethel F. Heddle, Author of "Martin Redfern's Oath," etc.

Raymond and Bertha: A Story of True Nobility. By L. Phillips, Author of "Frank Burleigh; or, Chosen to be a Soldier."

Rag and Tag. A Plea for the Waifs and Strays of Old England. By Mrs. E. J. Whittaker.

Rose Capel's Sacrifice; or, A Mother's Love. By Mrs. Haycraft, Author of "Like a Little Candle," "Chine Cabin," etc.

Rays from the Sun of Righteousness. By Dr. Newton. New Edition. Handsomely bound in cloth boards, and beautifully Illustrated.

Safe Compass, and How it Points (The). By Rev. Dr. Newton. New Series.

Satisfied. By Catherine M. Trowbridge.

Tamsin Rosewarne and Her Burdens: A Tale of Cornish Life. By Nellie Cornwall.

Through Life's Shadows. By Eliza F. Pollard, Author of "Not Wanted," etc.

Violet Maitland; or, By Thorny Ways. By Laura M. Lane, Author of "Living it Down," "Mrs. Lupton's Lodgings," etc.

1s. each.

COLOURED TOY BOOKS.

Animals, Tame and Wild. Fourteen Coloured Pages of Animals drawn from Life, with appropriate foot-lines. Beautiful Coloured Cover, Varnished.

Our Playtime. A Series of Full-page and Coloured Vignettes, illustrating Children at Play, with descriptive Letterpress. Beautiful Coloured Cover, Varnished. (Mounted on cloth, 2s.)

Our Lifeboats: Pictures of Peril and Rescue. A Series of Full-page and Vignetted Pictures of Lifeboats, Rocket Apparatus, Saving Life at Sea, and Heroic Exploits, with descriptive Letterpress. (Mounted on cloth, 2s.)

Off to the Fire; or, The Fire Brigade and its Work. A Series of Full-page and Vignetted Pictures of Fire Scenes, Escapes Saving Life at Fires, Steamers and Manuals in Action, etc., with descriptive Letterpress.

1s. each.

PICTURE BOOKS FOR THE YOUNG.

Fcap. 4to. With Coloured Covers, and Full of Illustrations.

***Bright Beams and Happy Scenes:** A Picture Book for Little Folk. By J. D., Author of "Mirth and Joy," "Happy Times," etc. Four full-page coloured and numerous other Illustrations. Coloured paper cover, 1s. ; cloth, 1s. 6d.

***Merry Moments.** A Picture Book for Lads and Lasses. By C. D. M., Author of "Brightness and Beauty," "Sunny Days," etc. Four full-page coloured and many other Illustrations. Coloured paper cover, 1s.; cloth, 1s. 6d.

***Holiday Hours in Animal Land.** (New Series.) By Uncle Harry. Four full-page coloured and numerous other Illustrations. Coloured paper cover, 1s. ; cloth, 1s. 6d.

Brightness and Beauty: A Picture Story Book for the Young. By C. D. M. Four full-page coloured and many other Illustrations. Coloured paper cover, 1s. ; cloth, 1s. 6d.

Mirth and Joy: A Picture Story Book for Little Readers. By J. D. Four full-page coloured and numerous other Illustrations. Coloured paper cover, 1s. ; cloth, 1s. 6d.

Bible Pictures and Stories. Old Testament. By D. J. D., Author of "Pets Abroad," etc. With Forty-four full-page Illustrations. Coloured paper boards, 1s. ; cloth gilt, 1s. 6d.

Bible Pictures and Stories. New Testament. By James Weston and D. J. D. With Forty-five beautiful full-page Illustrations by W. J. Webb, Sir John Gilbert, and others. New Edition. Fcap. 4to. Illustrated boards, 1s. ; cloth, extra, 1s. 6d.

ONE SHILLING REWARD BOOKS.

Fully Illustrated. 96 pages. Crown 8vo. Cloth extra.

***Brave Bertie.** By Edith Kenyon, Author of "Jack's Heroism," "Hilda ; or, Life's Discipline," etc.

***Three Runaways.** By F. Scarlett Potter, Author of "Phil's Frolic," "Hazelbrake Hollow," etc.

***Jim's Discovery;** or, On the Edge of a Desert. By T. M. Browne, Author of "Dawson's Madge," etc.

***Under the Blossom.** By Margaret Haycraft, Author of "Like a Little Candle ; or, Bertrand's Influence," etc.

***Always Happy;** or, The Story of Helen Keller. By Jennie Chappell, Author of "Ted's Trust ; or, Aunt Elmerley's Umbrella," "Without a Thought," etc.

Arthur Egerton's Ordeal ; or, God's Ways not Our Ways. By the Author of "Ellerslie House," etc.

Birdie and her Dog, and other Stories of Canine Sagacity. By Miss Phillips.

Bolingbroke's Folly. By Emma Leslie, Author of "A Sailor's Lass," etc.

CATALOGUE OF NEW & POPULAR WORKS.

1s. each.

REWARD BOOKS (continued).

Birdie's Benefits; or, A Little Child Shall Lead Them. By Ethel Ruth Boddy, Author of "Two Girls; or, Seed Sown Through the Post."

Babes in the Basket (The); or, Daph and Her Charge. With Ten Illustrations.

Band of Hope Companion (The). A Hand-book for Band of Hope Members: Biographical, Historical, Scientific, and Anecdotal. By Alf. G. Glasspool.

Children of Cherryholme (The). By M. S. Haycraft, Author of "Like a Little Candle," "Chine Cabin," etc.

Cared For; or, The Orphan Wanderers. By Mrs. C. E. Bowen, Author of "Dick and his Donkey," etc.

Chine Cabin. By Mrs. Haycraft, Author of "Red Dave," "Little Mother," etc.

Dulcie Delight. By Jennie Chappell, Author of "Her Saddest Blessing," "For Honour's Sake," etc.

Frank Burleigh; or, Chosen to be a Soldier. By L. Phillips.

Frank Spencer's Rule of Life. By J. W. Kirton, Author of "Buy Your Own Cherries."

Grannie's Treasures, and How They Helped Her. By L. E. Tiddeman.

Hazelbrake Hollow. By F. Scarlett Potter, Author of "Phil's Frolic," etc. Illustrated by Harold Copping.

Harold; or, Two Died for Me. By Laura A. Barter.

How a Farthing Made a Fortune; or, "Honesty is the Best Policy." By Mrs. C. E. Bowen.

How Paul's Penny became a Pound. By Mrs. Bowen, Author of "Dick and his Donkey."

Jack the Conqueror; or, Difficulties Overcome. By the Author of "Dick and his Donkey."

Jemmy Lawson; or, Beware of Crooked Ways. By E. C. Kenyon, Author of "Jack's Heroism."

Jenny's Geranium; or, The Prize Flower of a London Court.

Little Bunch's Charge; or, True to Trust. By Nellie Cornwall, Author of "Tamsin Rosewarne," etc.

Losing and Finding; or, The Moonstone Ring. By Jennie Chappell, Author of "Who was the Culprit?" etc.

Little Woodman and his Dog Cæsar (The). By Mrs. Sherwood.

Last of the Abbots (The). By Rev. A. Brown. New Edition.

Little Bugler (The): A Tale of the American Civil War. By George Munroe Royce. New Edition.

1s. each.

REWARD BOOKS (*continued*).

Mind Whom You Marry; or, The Gardener's Daughter. By the Rev. C. G. Rowe.

Mother's Chain (The); or, The Broken Link. By Emma Marshall, Author of "Fine Gold; or, Ravenswood Courtenay," etc.

Marjory; or, What Would Jesus do? By Laura A. Barter, Author of "Harold; or, Two Died for Me."

Marion and Augusta; or, Love and Selfishness. By Emma Leslie, Author of "Ellerslie House," "The Five Cousins," etc.

Nan; or, The Power of Love. By Eliza F. Pollard, Author of "Avice," "Hope Deferred," etc.

No Gains without Pains. A True Story. By H. C. Knight.

Old Goggles; or, The Brackenhurst Bairns' Mistake. By M. S. Haycraft, Author of "The Children of Cherryholme," etc.

Only a Little Fault. By Emma Leslie, Author of "Water Waifs," etc.

Our Den. By E. M. Waterworth, Author of "Master Lionel, that Tiresome Child."

Phil's Frolic. By F. Scarlett Potter, Author of "Faith's Father," etc. Illustrated by W. Rainey, R.I.

Ronald Kennedy; or, A Domestic Difficulty. By Evelyn Everett-Green, Author of "Everybody's Friend," etc.

Recitations and Concerted Pieces for Bands of Hope, Sunday Schools, etc. Compiled by James Weston, Author of "Bible Pictures and Stories," "Sunny Hours," etc.

Sweet Nancy. By L. T. Meade, Author of "Scamp and I," "A Band of Three," etc.

Twice Saved; or, Somebody's Pet and Nobody's Darling. By E. M. Waterworth, Author of "Our Den," "Master Lionel," etc.

Temperance Stories for the Young. By T. S. Arthur, Author of "Ten Nights in a Bar Room."

Una Bruce's Troubles. By Alice Price, Author of "Hamilton of King's," etc. Illustrated by Harold Copping.

Wait till it Blooms. By Jennie Chappell, Author of "Her Saddest Blessing," etc.

Who was the Culprit? By Jennie Chappell, Author of "Her Saddest Blessing," "The Man of the Family," etc.

BOOKS BY REV. DR. NEWTON.

New and Cheap Edition. 160 pages. Crown 8vo. Prettily bound in cloth boards, 1s. *each.*

Bible Jewels. | Bible Wonders.
Rills from the Fountain of Life.
The Giants, and How to Fight Them.

Specially suitable for Sunday School Libraries and Rewards.

CATALOGUE OF NEW & POPULAR WORKS. 13

1s. each.
POPULAR SHILLING SERIES.

Crown 8vo, well-printed on good paper, and bound in attractive and tasteful coloured paper covers. Fully Illustrated.

*Louie's Married Life. By Sarah Doudney.
*Living it Down. By Laura M. Lane.
The Strait Gate. ⎫
The Better Part. ⎬ By Annie S. Swan.
Mark Desborough's Vow.
Grandmother's Child, and For Lucy's Sake. ⎭

A Way in the Wilderness. By Maggie Swan.
Cousin Mary. By Mrs. Oliphant.
Eaglehurst Towers. By Mrs. Emma Marshall.
Without a Thought. ⎫ By Jennie Chappell.
Her Saddest Blessing. ⎭
Fine Gold; or, Ravenswood Courtenay. By Emma Marshall.

The above can also be had in fancy cloth, price 1s. 6d.

9d. each.
NINEPENNY SERIES OF ILLUSTRATED BOOKS.

96 pages. Small Crown 8vo. Illustrated. Handsome Cloth Covers.

*Love's Golden Key; or, The Witch of Berryton. By Mary E. Lester.
*Letty; or, The Father of the Fatherless. By H. Clement, Author of "Elsie's Fairy Bells."
Boy's Friendship (A). By Jesse Page.
Bel's Baby. By Mary E. Ropes, Author of "Talkative Friends," etc.
Benjamin Holt's Boys, and What They Did for Him. By the Author of "A Candle Lighted by the Lord."
Ben's Boyhood. By the Author of "Jack the Conqueror," etc.
Ben Owen: A Lancashire Story. By Jennie Perrett.
Cousin Bessie: A Story of Youthful Earnestness. By Clara Lucas Balfour.
Dawson's Madge; or, The Poacher's Daughter. By T. M. Browne, Author of "The Musgrove Ranch," etc.
Five Cousins (The). By Emma Leslie.
Foolish Chrissy; or, Discontent and its Consequences. By Meta, Author of "Noel's Lesson," etc.
For Lucy's Sake. By Annie S. Swan.
Giddie Garland; or, The Three Mirrors. By Jennie Chappell.
Grandmother's Child. By Annie S. Swan.
Into the Light. By Jennie Perrett.
Jean Jacques: A Story of the Franco-Prussian War. By Isabel Lawford.
John Oriel's Start in Life. By Mary Howitt.
Little Mother. By Margaret Haycraft.
Left with a Trust. By Nellie Hellis.
Master Lionel, that Tiresome Child. By E. M. Waterworth.
Man of the Family (The). By Jennie Chappell.

9d. each (continued).

Mattie's Home; or, The Little Match-girl and her Friends.
Rosa; or, The Two Castles. By Eliza Weaver Bradburn.
Sailor's Lass (A). By Emma Leslie.

6d. each.
NEW SERIES OF SIXPENNY PICTURE-BOOKS.

Crown quarto. Fully Illustrated. Handsomely bound in paper boards, with design printed in Eight colours.

Under the Umbrella, Pictures and Stories for Rainy Days.
Rosie Dimple's Pictures and Stories for Tiny Folk.
Playful Pussies' Book of Pictures and Stories.
Little Snowdrop's Bible Picture-Book.

This New Series of Picture Books surpasses, in excellence of illustration and careful printing, all others at the price.

COLOURED TOY BOOKS.

Beautifully printed in Seven Colours and Monotint in the best style of Lithography. Size 10¾ by 8½ inches. Price 6d. each; Mounted on Linen, One Shilling.

*The Bible A, B, C. A Scripture Alphabet of Bible Scenes and Characters.

*A, B, C of Birds, Beasts, and Fishes.

*Tiny Tot's Book of Fables. Contains a selection of favourite fables for childhood's days.

*The Ugly Duckling, and other Fairy Tales. By Hans Andersen, etc.

Bible Pictures for Little Folk. A beautifully-coloured picture book of Bible scenes and characters.

Book of Toys for Girls and Boys. In the shape of a toy stable, with horses standing. Contains Children at play with toys and games.

Our Pet's Animal A, B, C. A shaped book in the form of a cow. Full of well-executed animal pictures and appropriate couplets. (On linen out of print.)

Our Holiday A, B, C. Not shaped. A book of children enjoying their holidays in the country and at the seaside. (On linen out of print.)

THE "RED DAVE" SERIES.

New and Enlarged Edition, with Coloured Frontispieces. Handsomely bound in cloth boards.

*Mother's Boy. By M.B. Manwell.
*A Great Mistake. By Jennie Chappell.
*From Hand to Hand. By C. J. Hamilton.
*That Boy Bob. By Jesse Page.
*Buy Your Own Cherries. By J. W. Kirton.
*Owen's Fortune. By Mrs. F. West.
Only Milly; or, A Child's Kingdom.
Shad's Christmas Gift.
Greycliffe Abbey.
Red Dave; or, What Wilt Thou have Me to do?
Harry's Monkey: How it Helped the Missionaries.

Dick and his Donkey; or, How to Pay the Rent.
Herbert's First Year at Bramford.
Lost in the Snow; or, The Kentish Fisherman.
The Pearly Gates.
Jessie Dyson.
Maude's Visit to Sandybeach.
Friendless Bob, and other Stories.
Come Home, Mother.
Snowdrops; or, Life from the Dead.
Sybil and her Live Snowball.
Only a Bunch of Cherries.
Daybreak.
Bright Ben: The Story of a Mother's Boy.

THE MARIGOLD SERIES.

An entirely new and unequalled series of standard stories, printed on good laid paper. Imperial 8vo. 128 pages. Illustrated covers with vignetted design printed in EIGHT COLOURS. Price 6D. each, NETT.

Pride and Prejudice. By JANE AUSTEN.
From Jest to Earnest. By E. P. ROE.

The Wide, Wide World. By SUSAN WARNER.

4d. each.

NEW FOURPENNY SERIES

of Cloth-bound Books for the Young. With Coloured Frontispieces. 64 pages. Well Illustrated. Handsome Cloth Covers.

*Poppy; or, School Days at Saint Bride's.
*Carrie and the Cobbler.
*Dandy Jim.
*A Troublesome Trio.
*Perry's Pilgrimage.
*Nita; or, Among the Brigands.

The Crab's Umbrella.
Sunnyside Cottage.
Those Barrington Boys.
Two Lilies.
The Little Woodman and His Dog Cæsar.
Robert's Trust.

THE TINY LIBRARY.

Books printed in large type. Cloth.

Little Chrissie, and other Stories.
Harry Carlton's Holiday.
A Little Loss and a Big Find.
What a Little Cripple Did.
Bobby.
Matty and Tom.

The Broken Window.
John Madge's Cure for Selfishness.
The Pedlar's Loan.
Letty Young's Trials.
Brave Boys.
Little Jem, the Rag Merchant.

CHEAP "PANSY" SERIES.

Imperial 8vo. 64 pages. Many Illustrations. Cover printed in Five Colours.

*Spun From Fact. By PANSY.
*A Sevenfold Trouble. By PANSY.
*A Young Girl's Wooing. By E. P. ROE.

*From Different Standpoints.
*Those Boys.
*Echoing and Re-echoing.

Also 24 others uniform in style and price. Full list on application.

3d. each.

THE PRETTY "GIFT-BOOK" SERIES.

With Coloured Frontispiece, and Illustrations on every page. Paper boards, Covers printed in Five Colours and Varnished, 3d.; cloth boards, 4d. each.

My Pretty Picture Book.
Birdie's Picture Book.
Baby's Delight.
Mamma's Pretty Stories.
Tiny Tot's Treasures.
Papa's Present.

Pretty Bible Stories.
Baby's Bible Picture Book.
Ethel's Keepsake.
Out of School.
Pictures for Laughing Eyes.
Cheerful and Happy.

ILLUSTRATED MONTHLY PERIODICALS.

ONE PENNY MONTHLY.
THE BRITISH WORKMAN.
An Illustrated Paper containing brightly-written Articles and Stories on Religion, Temperance, and Thrift, short Biographical Sketches of Self-made Men, etc.
The Yearly Volume, with Coloured paper boards, cloth back, and full of Engravings, 1s. 6d. each; cloth, 2s. 6d.

ONE HALFPENNY MONTHLY.
THE BAND OF HOPE REVIEW.
The Leading Temperance Periodical for the Young, containing Serial and Short Stories, Concerted Recitations, Prize Competitions, etc.
The Yearly Volume, with Coloured Cover and full of Engravings, cloth back, 1s.; cloth gilt, 2s. each.

ONE PENNY MONTHLY.
THE CHILDREN'S FRIEND.
The Oldest and Best Magazine for Children. Excellent Serial and Short Stories, Prize Competitions, Puzzles, Music, etc. A charming Presentation Plate, in colours, is given away with the January number.
The Yearly Volume, Coloured paper boards, cloth back, 1s. 6d.; cloth, 2s.; gilt edges, 2s. 6d.

ONE PENNY MONTHLY.
THE INFANTS' MAGAZINE.
Full of charming Pictures and pleasant Rhymes to delight the little ones. Printed in large type. A splendid Coloured Presentation Plate given away with the January number.
The Yearly Volume, in Coloured paper boards, cloth back, 1s. 6d.; cloth, 2s.; gilt edges, 2s. 6d.

ONE PENNY MONTHLY.
THE FAMILY FRIEND.
A beautifully Illustrated Magazine for the Home Circle, containing Serial and Short Stories by the leading writers of the day. Also crisply-written Articles on popular subjects, Notes on Dressmaking, etc.
The Yearly Volume, with numerous Engravings, Coloured paper boards, cloth back, 1s. 6d.; cloth, 2s.; gilt edges, 2s. 6d.

ONE PENNY MONTHLY.
THE MOTHERS' COMPANION.
THE BEST MAGAZINE FOR MOTHERS.
Serial and Short Tales by popular authors, Helpful Papers on Health and the Management of the Home, Home Dressmaking, etc.
The Yearly Volume, with Coloured paper boards, cloth back, 1s. 6d.; cloth, 2s.; gilt edges, 2s. 6d. each.

ONE PENNY MONTHLY.
THE FRIENDLY VISITOR.
AN ILLUSTRATED GOSPEL MAGAZINE FOR THE PEOPLE.
Contains striking Gospel Stories and Articles, in large type, beautifully Illustrated. An invaluable help to District Visitors, Mission Workers, etc.
The Yearly Volume, Coloured Cover, cloth back, 1s. 6d.; cloth, 2s.; gilt edges, 2s. 6d.

8 & 9, PATERNOSTER ROW, E.C.

www.ingramcontent.com/pod-product-compliance
Lightning Source LLC
Chambersburg PA
CBHW021159230426
43667CB00006B/475